Ethnicity, Nationalism and the European Cold War

Ethnicity, Nationalism and the European Cold War

Edited by
Robert Knight

continuum

Continuum International Publishing Group

The Tower Building	80 Maiden Lane
11 York Road	Suite 704
London SE1 7NX	New York NY 10038

www.continuumbooks.com

British Library Cataloguing-in-Publication Data
A catalogue record for this book is available from the British Library.

ISBN: 978-1-4411-5027-1

Typeset by Deanta Global Publishing Services, Chennai, India
Printed by Great Britain

In memory of Mark Pittaway 1971–2010

Contents

Acknowledgements

Special thanks are owed to the British Academy, which kindly supported the three workshops (at Loughborough, Ljubljana and Oldenburg) in which early versions of these chapters were presented, as well as to Richard Evans and Alice Teichova for supporting the project from the start. We are also most grateful to Loughborough University, the Slovene Academy of Science and the Karl-Ossietsky University, Oldenburg for their hospitality. Last but not least, thanks to everyone who made these meetings so successful and enjoyable; in particular Hans Hennig Hahn, Eva Hahn, Oto Luthar, Boris Gombač, Dagmar Kusa, Jose Pirjevec, and the late and much lamented Karl Stuhlpfarrer.

Abbreviations

AdR	Archiv der Republik (Vienna)
BA	Bundesarchiv (Berlin)
BCP	Bulgarian Communist Party
BgLA	Burgenländisches Landesarchiv (Burgenland Provincial Archives, Eisenstadt)
BND	Bundesnachrichtendienst
BKP	Bulgarska Kommunisticheska Partiya (Bulgarian Communist Party)
BstU	Bundesbeauftragte für Stasi-Unterlagen (Federal Commissioner for State Security Files)
CASBI	Decree on the Control and Monitoring of Enemy Property
CFM	Council of Foreign Ministers
DC	Democrazia Cristiana (Christian Democratic Party)
FCO	Foreign and Commonwealth Office
FGKP	Fűggetlen Kisgasda Párt (Independent Smallholders' Party)
FTT	Free Territory of Trieste
FUEV	Föderalistische Union Europäischer Volksgruppen (Federal Union of European Nationalities)
GyMSMSL	Győr-Moson-Sopron Megye Soproni Levéltára (Sopron Archive of Győr-Moson-Sopron County)
KMP	Kommunisták Magyarországi Pártja (Communist Party of Hungary)
MfS	Ministerium für Staatssicherheit
MKP	Magyar Kommunista Párt (Hungarian Communist Party)
MNSz	Magyar Népi Szövetség (Hungarian Popular Alliance)

MOL	Magyar Oszágos Levéltár (Hungarian National Archive)
OSA	Open Society Archives (Budapest)
ÖVP	Österreichische Volkspartei
PCR	Partidul Comunist Roman (Romanian Communist Party)
PIL	Politika Történeti Intézet Levaltani (Archive of the Institute for Political History, Budapest)
SED	Sozialistische Einheitspartei (Socialist Unity Party)
Sifor	Servizio Informazione Forze Armate (Armed Forces Intelligence Service)
SKA	Sorbisches Kulturarchiv
SPÖ	Sozialistische Partei Österreichs (Socialist Party of Austria)
SVP	Südtiroler Volkspartei South Tyrol People's Party

About the Authors

Robert Knight is senior lecturer in International History at Loughborough University. He completed his PhD at the London School of Economics on 'British policy towards occupied Austria, 1945–1950'. He has written on modern Austrian history, including anti-semitism, restitution and the Carinthian Slovenes. His publications include 'After the Taborstrasse. Austrian restitution revisited,' in the *Leo Baeck Institute Yearbook* (2006) and 'Denazification and Integration in the Austrian Province of Carinthia,' *Journal of Modern History* (2007). From 1998 to 2003 he was a member of the Austrian Historians' Commission, which investigated Nazi expropriation and post-war restitution and compensation issues. He is currently completing a monograph on the politics of assimilation in post-war Austria.

Mark Pittaway was senior lecturer in History at the Open University from 1999 until his death in November 2010. He completed his PhD at Liverpool University on 'Industrial workers, socialist industrialisation and the state in Hungary, 1948–1958.' He quickly established a reputation as a leading scholar of central European history, especially Hungary, through a series of innovative articles and book chapters, written in both English and Hungarian. His overview *Eastern Europe 1939–2000*: States and Societies (Hoddor Arnold, 2004) was widely praised, displaying what the *Guardian* called his trademark - 'the deft combination of high politics with social history'. His monograph, *Industrial Workers and the Socialist State in Hungary* is to be published by Pittsburgh University Press.

Sabina Mihelj is senior lecturer in Media and Communication at Loughborough University. Before coming to England, she worked as a researcher at the Ljubljana Graduate School of the Humanities and taught in the Sociology Department of University of Ljubljana. She has published a wide range of journal articles and book chapters on media and nationalism, Cold War culture, television history, religion and the new media, and cosmopolitanism, European communication and comparative media research. She is the author of *Media Nations: Communicating Belonging and Exclusion in the Modern World* (Palgrave, 2011).

Martin Mevius is assistant professor in Modern History at University College Utrecht, with a particular research interest in the national legitimacy of communist parties. He studied modern history at the University of Amsterdam and completed his doctorate at St Antony's College, Oxford. His *Agents of Moscow: the Hungarian Communist Party and the Origins of Social Patriotism 1941–1953* was published in 2005 (Oxford University Press) to high praise. He was a post-doctoral researcher at the University of Amsterdam, supported by a Veni grant from the Netherlands Organisation for Scientific Research. Recent publications include an edited collection, *The Communist Quest for National Legitimacy in Europe, 1918–1989* (Routledge, 2010).

Vasil Paraskevov is assistant professor of Modern Bulgarian history at Konstantin Preslavsky University, Shumen. His completed his PhD thesis on *The Bulgarian Agrarian National Union: Nikola Petkov, 1945–1947* in 2006. He was a visiting Leverhulme Fellow at Loughborough University in 2009. His monograph on British–Bulgarian relations, *Bulgaria and Great Britain before and at the beginning of the Cold War: Politics, Economy and Propaganda, 1944–1953* was published by Konstantin Preslavsky University Press (2011).

Günther Pallaver is professor of Political Science at the University of Innsbruck. He was born in Bozen/Bolzano (Italy) and gained doctorates in History and Law at Innsbruck University. His main research interests are comparative political systems, especially the political system of Italy; regional political systems, especially South Tyrol; ethnic minorities, ethnic conflicts and ethno-regional parties, political communication, federalism and international relations between Italy and Austria. His recent publications include a chapter on the South Tyrol People's Party in *From Protest to Power. Autonomist parties and the challenges of representation* (Braumüller, 2011) and 'Reconciliation following terrorism in South Tyrol', in *Reconciliation after Terrorism: Strategy, Possibility or Absurdity?* (Routledge, 2011). He is President of the South Tyrol Political Science Association.

Peter Barker was senior research fellow and director of the Centre for East German Studies at the University of Reading (2002–08). His main areas of research are in the political history of the GDR and the Sorbian ethnic minority in Lusatia. Among his publications are *Slavs in Germany: The Sorbian Minority and the German State since 1945* (Edwin Mellen Press, 2000), the co-edited collection, *Views from Abroad - Die DDR aus britischer Perspektive*, (Bertelsmann, 2007) and 'Kirchenpolitik und ethnische Identität: Das Beispiel des Sorbischen Evangelischen Superintendenten in Sachsen' in *Lětopis* (2006).

Introduction

Robert Knight

1 The Return of the Tribes

The abruptness with which the Cold War ended was reinforced by a sense that an unexpected switch had taken place: the familiar ideological players had been taken off the pitch and substituted by ethnic or national ones. The political philosopher Michael Walzer encapsulated this in his dramatic announcement, three years after the fall of the Berlin Wall, that 'the tribes have returned'.[1] The tribes brought with them a host of thorny, even insoluble problems: those discussed by Walzer included the reconciliation of collective rights with individual freedom and the establishment of criteria for the right of secession. 'Ethnic politics' can be understood as the political mobilization around this kind of issue. It may be instigated or encouraged by a range of actors: states, lobbies or 'ethnic entrepreneurs'.[2] What they have in common is the expression of grievances and entitlements – real, imagined or exaggerated – which assume the central importance of a collective identity based on common descent and shared culture. The remedy for the perceived injustice may be sought in a change in the internal constitution of a country or, in the extreme case the revision of state boundaries. It may be aggressive and expansionist but it often sees itself as a purely defensive resistance to the threat of assimilation, whether from ethnic competitors or the state.[3]

This collection seeks to illuminate the relationship between this kind of politics at a time when it appeared to have been consigned to the dustbin of history by the confrontation between capitalism (or liberal democracy) and Soviet communism (or Marxist-Leninism). Its aim is to contribute to the debate stimulated by its unpredicted end. As Gordon Johnson has written, this 'rendered provisional all previous accounts of its dynamics, significance and scope; interim judgments were subject to confirmation and revision as well as new questions, new evidence and new approaches.'[4]

A first step towards this debate is to note that post-Cold War discussions have implied rather diverse, even contradictory, understandings of the relationship between ethnic politics and the Cold War. Sometimes, ethnic nationalism appears as an irresistible, elemental force which rose from the deep to destroy the multi-national polities of the Soviet Union and Yugoslavia (and perhaps the bi-national Czechoslovakia); elsewhere it was the ineptness of communist regimes in managing ethnic conflict which was high-lighted as the root of the problem: in the case of Yugoslavia (Slobodan Milošović in Serbia, and Fran Tudjman in Croatia) and Ceauşecu's Rumania, it had been used by failing communist despots as a last ploy to shore up their position and survive the transition to post-communist rule.[5] Some saw the issue as a Balkan or Yugoslav pathology reflecting the region's 'ancient hatreds' (as in Robert Kaplan much criticized book).[6] John Mearsheimer, the leading proponent of the International Relations 'defensive realist' school, gave a passing nod to this interpretation when he predicted that the 'return to the future' which now beckoned would mean that 'the longstanding blood feuds among the nationalities in Eastern Europe are likely to re-emerge in a multi-polar Europe'. His wider argument was that the end of communism meant the replacement by the stable bipolarity of the Cold War with a dangerously unpredictable multi-polar Europe.[7] Some historians saw the acute danger of a return to the vulnerable fragmented diplomatic system of pre-war Europe.[8] Michael Ignatieff argued no less pessimistically that in East and West constraints on ethnic hatred had been removed in both West (USA and Northern Ireland) and Eastern Europe. The departure of 'the imperial police' and a collapse of nation state structures had left 'hundreds of ethnic groups at the mercy of each other.'[9] Last but not, least Norman Naimark interpreted twentieth century history as a spreading bush fires of ethnic hatred, which a feeble international community had failed to extinguish.[10]

On the other hand some sociologists saw the arrival of ethnic politics and conflict in central Europe and the former Soviet Union as a reversion to normality, compared to which the Cold War – if it featured at all – seemed little more than an anomalous blip on the radar screen. Milton Esman, for example, saw the end of the Cold War as confirming that ethnic politics was 'today's most pervasive and dangerous expression of organised conflict.'[11] For Anthony Smith ethnic nationalism in Eastern Europe was part of a wider revolt against state intervention and cultural homogenization, 'a new phase of the whole process of demotic vernacular mobilisation that has been sweeping various parts of the world since the eighteenth century and possibly earlier.' Unlike most observers he found nothing particularly surprising about the recent turn of events.[12]

Two decades later some of the gloom of the 1990s has lifted. The direst of the early predictions have not materialized; Europe has not descended into a free-for-all of ethnic hatred[13] and even the bloody collapse of Yugoslavia can now, at the risk of complacency, be seen less as a portent than as the terrible exception that proves the rule of stabilization. In this, the intervention of international actors (OSCE, EU) have clearly played a major – albeit contested – role.[14] But the destructive potential of ethnic politics is clearly far from exhausted; extreme right-wing or populist parties throughout Europe continue to mobilize resentment against minorities, refugees and asylum seekers. In doing so, they frequently appeal to and foster emotions of ethnic vulnerability.

Equally important here, the centrality of ethnic nationalism in the collapse of communism has been revised. While it is clear that separatist movements in the Baltic States, Ukraine, Georgia and elsewhere played an important role at several points in the collapse of the Soviet Union and in weakening the legitimacy of communist regimes throughout Eastern Europe it is widely accepted that they formed only one link – and not necessarily the strongest – in a complex causal chain of economic breakdown, loss of legitimacy and ebbing elite self-confidence. Furthermore, the understanding of contingent factors such as the diffusion of unrest from Eastern Europe to the Soviet Union (and back) and human agency, and above all the role of Michael Gorbachev, have undermined the portrayal of ethnic nationalism as an irresistible force.[15]

At the same time, moving to the historical questions that are behind this book, the way ethnicity and ethnic politics functioned and was experienced during the Cold War itself remains open to debate. The current consensus is that it was a peripheral phenomenon, subordinated to the dictates of 'high politics' but many questions still remain about how ethnic loyalties, resentments and hatreds were actually controlled or 'managed'.[16]

A considerable body of literature suggests that ethno-nationalist appeals never ceased to be important for Eastern Europe regimes. As long ago as 1973, Robert King pointed out that behind the rhetoric of unity and internationalism long-standing points of friction at the borders continued between communist states. Since Stalin's death it had increased as regimes sought to shore up their popularity by appeals to '*Staatsvolk* nationalism'.[17] Katherine Verdery has shown how economic failure in Romania brought a 'scarcity regime' which forced the ruling Communist Party to shift its legitimation to the traditional nationalist terrain of the interwar period.[18] This was often accompanied by a weakening of the control from the centre as regional identities, which had previously been 'ignored or battered' were mobilized, often by local communists.[19] In the multi-national Soviet Union the practices of Leninist nationality policy meant that while central party orthodoxy was rigidly enforced the 'indigenisation' (*korenisatziya*) also allowed ethno national identities to be fostered.[20]

Reflecting this, Andre Gerrits has criticized one of the images most frequently deployed to describe the arrival of ethno-national conflict and the fall of communism – the melting glacier. In this metaphor 'traditional nationalist emotions, resentments and conflicts were supposedly covered by a layer of ice (the *Pax Sovietica*) and only revived when the ice began to melt, when (international) political conformity and harmony enforced by the Soviet Union collapsed.' In fact, Gerrits argues

> nationalism and the minority issue were never put in a freezer. Indeed, they were frequently used and manipulated by communist regimes. They were a constituent part of the communist experiment from the very beginning, and they served as one of the most powerful, albeit ultimately ineffective, instruments for acquiring legitimacy.[21]

This collection pursues this sceptical line but seeks to broaden it by looking not just at communist regimes but at both sides of the Iron

Curtain and the interaction between East and West. It seeks to understand how ethnic politics, which was usually rooted in the local or the regional milieu, was related to, or interacted with, the international struggle.

2 Misperceptions and Myopia?

Some have broadened Gerrits' point into a criticism of western perceptions, arguing that the failure of (western) outsiders to register the importance of ethnic politics during the Cold War stemmed from a systematic misapprehension. George Schöpflin, for example, saw 'the sudden re-emergence of nationalism' as an 'an optical illusion' since 'in reality, under the surface of events and indeed not merely under the surface, ethnicity and nationhood not only remained in being, but they contributed significantly to the pattern of politics, though it was seldom understood in this way.'[22] Similarly, in the pessimistically titled *Pandaemonium* Daniel Moynihan referred to a 'fog descending over Europe' which concealed the salience of ethnicity. In his introduction to the same book, Adam Roberts described Western observers as having been 'mesmerised' into missing the importance of ethnic conflict.[23] Walker Connor, the prominent sociologist of ethnicity, even diagnosed a fundamental 'divorce between intellectual theory and the real world.'[24]

These kinds of criticism are not new. Connor himself made a very similar point twenty years before in the course of the 'rediscovery' of ethnic politics in Western Europe, of which he was a pioneer. Around the same time, Joseph Rothschild listed no fewer than fifteen explanations for the 'prolonged myopia' which the social sciences had displayed towards 'politicized ethnicity' (but which he thought was now coming to an end). At least three of them are worth noting here: the assumption that the 'so-called nation state' was normative; the propensity of 'the development-and-modernization theorists to exaggerate the capacity of elites to plan and mould public values, identities, and allegiances in an integrationist direction'; and the discrediting of ethnic ideas as a result of the Nazi experience.[25]

Cold War historiography for its part concentrated for a long time on diplomacy and 'high politics'.[26] That meant above all the rationality and morality of the strategies of leaders and policy-makers – particularly of the two superpowers – at moments of crisis. This preference should certainly not be dismissed and can be seen as an appropriate response to the unprecedented dangers of the nuclear age; similarly the concerns of historians in a second phase of historiography in the 1960s and 1970s reflected the substantial issues raised by US involvement in Vietnam. But in any case, well before the Cold War ended the historiographical focus was shifting, becoming less dominated by contemporary controversies and deploying a wider range of archival resources. This 'historicisation' meant that greater weight was given to the role of European governments, and societies, which were increasingly studied not just as constraints on policy-makers but in their own right. Since the end of the Cold War, as the threat of conflict between the superpowers has receded the Cold War has also increasingly been seen as cultural history. In some work culture was discovered as an additional, previously, neglected battle-site, alongside politics and the military ('the cultural Cold War') but more recently 'Cold War culture' has moved into the centre of attention. In Gordon Johnston's words this 'poses a broader set of questions about patterns of behaviour, attitudes and structures of thought and meaning associated with the Cold War.'[27]

The contributors to this collection have been influenced by these shifts in the sense that they see the Cold War as involving more than geopolitical and military confrontation. They also understand that power did not always flow in one direction only, downwards from the super-power to the client state (or ally) or from the national centre to the region.[28] They see ethnic identities as fluid and deep-rooted, less as the defined characteristics of clearly bounded groups than as 'perspectives on the world', in Rogers Brubaker's phrase.[29] In short, these identities are too complex and dynamic to be reduced to malleable resources or tools in the hands of national and international policy makers.

This point was (almost) conceded by the doyen of US Cold War diplomatic historians, John Lewis Gaddis when wrote (in the hubristically entitled *Now We Know*) that the end of the Cold War had

> revealed how durable national, cultural, ethnic, religious, and linguistic particularities really are; but that is only to acknowledge *that*

they must have been present throughout the Cold War itself as they had been for decades, even centuries, preceding it. They ensured that the 'third world' would find its own way whatever cold warriors in Washington or Moscow did.'[30]

Unlike other revelations in Gaddis's book these 'particularities' had not needed the opening of Soviet or East European archives to be discovered. But they did perhaps require a greater readiness to understand them than was shown by Gaddis who tended, both during and after the Cold War to view nationalism as a disruptive force opposed to the orderly functioning of diplomacy and closely related to 'revolution, religious fundamentalism, racism and . . . authoritarianism.'[31]

The contributions which follow elucidate ethnic particularities by examining their contribution to Schöpflin's 'pattern of politics' at six specific sites of ethnic interaction. Three of them are at the East-West border (Italy/Yugoslavia, Austria/Hungary and Bulgaria/Turkey): two of them involve minority disputes between states on the same side of the Iron Curtain and in the case of the Sorb minority there was no neighbouring 'kin-state' to counteract the policies of the dominant German (GDR) society.

The very diversity of ethnicity makes generalizations unwise and it would clearly be foolish to construct an overarching 'grand theory' of ethnic politics in the Cold War on the basis of these cases. Nor is it suggested here that a neglected 'ethnic Cold War' is awaiting discovery. Nevertheless three common themes may be worth noting here:

First, if the Cold War is seen, as it has in recent years, as a competition between two 'modernising cousins'[32] ethnic identities (like religious beliefs) could easily appear as an obstacle on the onward march of progress on either side of the Iron Curtain. Where the traditional leadership was religious (Catholic leaders of the Sorbs, the imams of the Bulgarian Turks) the fear was that they could provide alternative values. In the case of the Sorbs modernization arrived in the form of the gigomanic open-cast mining which destroyed the traditional Sorbian milieu. For the Bulgarian Turks, having first been given a relatively far-reaching autonomy, it meant coercive secularization, and an invasion of the private sphere including the de-islamization of personal names.

Second, the Cold War shifted the calculus of ethnic politics. That does not mean that minorities always became the helpless pawns of the superpowers (a favourite topos of minority leaders). In the case of South Tyrol at least at the start of the Cold War Günther Pallaver argues that the minority gained by the West's fear of communism. Like the mobilization in 'defence' of *Deutschtum* in the Austrian province of Carinthia, it provided a chance to reinvent what might have otherwise have been a discredited cause by adopting the language of anti-communism. Similarly Sabina Mihelj argues that in Triest, the Cold War could encouraged a discursive readjustment, which allowed the perpetuation of deeply rooted anti-Slav stereotypes. In the 1950s on the other hand Catholic anti-communism provided common ground across the ethnic divide in Tyrol the conservative South Tyrol People's Party (SVP) supported the Christian Democrats in Rome even when this meant soft-pedalling on the autonomy provisions supposedly agreed in 1946. Minorities might also benefit from the propaganda dimensions to ethnic disputes. Communist regimes claimed that their Leninist nationalities policies were a demonstration of progressive credentials. Racism and segrega-tion in the US South was constantly cited as their mirror image and the Civil Rights struggle was extensively covered in the press. However (as Martin Mevius shows for the Hungarian–Rumanian relations) this propaganda could rebound by directing attention to unresolved issues closer to home.

Third, if ethnicity involves, in line with one Frederik Barth's well-known definition, 'boundary maintenance' it is worth asking how it was involved in the construction of the Cold War boundary, which also linked a sense of community with a perception of an external threatening 'other'.[33] Clearly there was no simple mapping of ethnic boundaries onto geo-strategic or military borders. In some cases as in Western stereotypes of Slavs the Cold War did seem to clothe racialized images in a more universal language.[34] Elsewhere, for example Hungarian attitudes towards Rumania, ethnic stereotypes were in tension with the demands of ideologically-sanctioned solidarity.

Notes

[1] Michael Walzer, 'The New Tribalism: Notes on a Difficult Problem', *Dissent*, 39 (1992), 164–71.

[2] Joseph Rothschild, *Ethnopolitics: A conceptual framework*, New York: Columbia University Press, 1981.

[3] Many of the definitional problems revolves round two 'demarcation issues'; the distinction between ethnicity and nationalism on the one hand and between ethnic nationalism and civic (or political) nationalism on the other. For discussions see i.a. James Kellas, *The Politics of Nationalism and Ethnicity* (2nd ed), Basingstoke: Macmillan, 1998, 2–9: Marcus Banks, *Ethnicity: Anthropological Constructions*, London and New York: Routledge, 1996.

[4] Gordon Johnston, 'Revisiting the Cultural Cold War', *Social History*, 35 (3), (2010), 295. 290–307.

[5] Jaques Rupnik, *The Other Europe* (revised edn.), London: Weidenfeld and Nicolson, 1989, 144.

[6] Robert Kaplan, *Balkan Ghosts: A Journey through History*, New York: St.Martin's, 1993; for criticism see i.a. John Mueller, 'The Banality of "Ethnic War"', in Michael Brown, Owen Cote, Sean Lynn-Jones and Steven Miller (eds), *Nationalism and Ethnic conflict* (revised edn), London: MIT Press, 2001, 97–125; Riikka Kuusisto, 'Savage Tribes and Mystic Feuds: Western Foreign Policy Statement on Bosnia in the Early 1990s', in Andrew Hammond (ed), *The Balkans and the West: Constructing the European Other, 1945–2003*, Aldershot: Ashgate, 2004, 169–83.

[7] John Mearsheimer, 'Back to the Future: Instability in Europe after the Cold War,' *International Security*, 15 (1), (1990), 6, (note 2).

[8] Michael Burns, 'Disturbed Spirits: Minority Rights and New World Orders, 1919 and the 1990s', in Samuel Wells and Paula Bailey Smith, *New European Orders, 1919 and 1991*, Washington: Woodrow Wilson Centre Press, 1996, 41–61.

[9] Michael Ignatieff, *Blood and Belonging: Journeys into the New Nationalism*, London: Vintage 1994, 6–8.

[10] Norman Naimark, *Fires of Hatred: Ethnic Cleansing in Twentieth-Century Europe*, Cambridge, MA: Harvard University Press, 2001.

[11] Milton Esman, *Ethnic Politics*, Cornell: Cornell University Press, 1994, 17, 25.

[12] Anthony Smith, *National Identity*, London: Penguin, 1991, 141.

[13] David Lake and Donald Rothchild, *The International Spread of Ethnic conflict: Fear, Diffusion and escalation*, Princeton, NJ: Princeton University Press, 1998.

[14] Jan Zielonka, *Europe as Empire: the Nature of the Enlarged European Union*, Oxford: Oxford University Press, 2006, 34–5.

[15] Max Beissinger, *Nationalist Mobilization and the Collapse of Soviet State*, Cambridge: Cambridge University Press, 2002; Mark Kramer, 'The Collapse of East European Communism and the Repercussions within the Soviet Union (part 3)', *Journal of Cold War Studies*, 7, (2005), 3–96; Astrid Tuminez, 'Nationalism, Ethnic Pressures, and the Breakup of the Soviet Union', *Journal of Cold War Studies*, 5 (4), (2003), 81–136.

[16] Kellas, *Politics of Nationalism.*

[17] Robert King, *Minorities under Communism. Nationalities as a source of Tension among Balkan Communist States*, Cambridge: Cambridge University Press, 1973, 256.

[18] Katherine Verdery, *National Ideology under Socialism: Identity and Cultural Politics in Ceauşescu's Romania*, Berkeley: University of California Press, 1991; see also Mark Pittaway, *Eastern Europe 1939–2000*, London: Hodder Arnold 2004.

[19] Judy Batt and Kataryna Wolczuk (eds) *Region, State and Identity in Central and Eastern Europe*, London: Frank Cass, 2002, 8.

[20] Rogers Brubaker, *Nationalism reframed: Nationhood and the national question in the New Europe*, Cambridge: Cambridge University Press, 17.

[21] Andre Gerrits and Dirk Jan Wolffram, (eds.), *Political Democracy and Ethnic Diversity in Modern European History*, Stanford: Stanford University Press, 2005, 13.

[22] George Schöpflin, 'Nationalism and Ethnicity in Europe, East and West in Charles A. Kupchan (ed), *Nationalism and Nationalities in the New Europe*, Ithaca: Cornell University Press, 1995, 38.

[23] Daniel Moyniham, *Pandemonium: Ethnicity in International Politics*, Oxford: Oxford University Press, 1993, 9; Adam Roberts, Introduction, *ibid*, x.

[24] Walker Connor, *Ethnonationalism: the Quest for Understanding*, Princeton: Princeton University Press, 1994, 28.

[25] Joseph Rothschild, *Ethnopolitics*, A conceptual Framework, New York: Columbia University Press, 1981, 20–5.

[26] See Patrick Major and Rana Mitter, 'Culture,' in Saki Dockrill and Geraint Hughes (eds), *Palgrave advances in Cold War history*, Basingstoke: Palgrave 2006, 215–6, 241. Tony Shaw, 'The Politics of Cold War Culture,' *Journal of Cold War Studies*, 3 (3), (2001), 59–76; David Crowley, and Susan Reid (eds), *Style and Socialism: Modernity and Material Culture in Postwar Eastern Europe*, Oxford: Berg, 2000.

[27] Johnston, Revisting the Cultural Cold War, 307.

[28] See i.a. Eleonore, Breuning, Jill Lewis Gareth Pritchard (eds), *Power and the People: A Social History of Central European Politics, 1945–56*, Manchester: Manchester University Press, 2005; Odd Arne Westad, 'The Cold War and the international history of the twentieth century,' in Westad and Melvyn Leffler (eds), *Cambridge History of the Cold War*, vol 1, Cambridge: Cambridge University Press, 2010, 1–19.

[29] Rogers Brubaker, *Ethnicity without Groups*, Cambridge, MA: Harvard: 2004, 17.

[30] John Lewis Gaddis, *We now know. Rethinking Cold War History*, Oxford: Oxford University Press 1997, 190 (emphasis added).

[31] John Lewis Gaddis, *The Long Peace: Inquiries into the History of the Cold War*, New York Oxford: Oxford University Press, 1987, 235–6; John Lewis Gaddis, 'The Cold War, the Long Peace, and the Future', in Michael J. Hogan (ed), *The End of the Cold War. Its Meaning and Implications*, Cambridge: Cambridge University Press 1992, 21–38, here 33.

[32] Nils Gilman, *Mandarins of the Future. Modernization theory in Cold War America*, Baltimore-London, 2003, 14; Odd Arne Westad, *The Global Cold War: Third World Interventions and the Making of Our Times*, Cambridge: Cambridge University Press, 2007. Odd Arne Westad, 'The Cold War and the international history of the twentieth century,' *Cambridge History of the Cold War*, (vol 1), 16.

[33] Frederik Barth, *Ethnic Groups and Boundaries: The Social Organisation of Culture Difference*, London: Allen and Unwin, 1969, 15.

[34] Hans Henning Hahn and Eva Hahn, 'Nationale Stereotypen. Plädoyer für eine historische Stereotypenforschung', in Hans Hennig Hahn (ed), *Stereotypen, Identität und Geschichte. Die Funktion von Stereotypen in gesellschaftlichen Diskursen*, Frankfurt am Main: Peter Lang, 2002, 17–56.

Bibliography

Banks, Marcus (1996), *Ethnicity: Anthropological Constructions*. London and New York: Routledge.

Barth, Frederik (1969), *Ethnic Groups and boundaries: the social organization of cultural difference*. London: Allen and Unwin.

Batt Judy and Kataryna Wolczuk (eds) (2002), *Region, State and Identity in Central and Eastern Europe*. London: Frank Cass.

Beissinger, Mark J (2002), *Nationalist Mobilisation and the Collapse of the Soviet Union*. Cambridge: Cambridge University Press.

Breuning, Eleonore, Jill Lewis, Gareth Pritchard (eds) (2005), *Power and the People: A Social History of Central European Politics, 1945–56*. Manchester: Manchester University Press,

Brubaker, Rogers (1996), *Nationalism reframed: Nationhood and the national question in the New Europe*. Cambridge: Cambridge University Press.

Brubaker Rogers (2004), *Ethnicity without Groups*. Cambridge, MA: Harvard University Press.

Burns, Michael (1996), 'Disturbed Spirits: Minority Rights and New World Orders, 1919 and the 1990s', in Samuel Wells and Paula Bailey Smith (eds), *New European Orders, 1919 and 1991*, Washington: Woodrow Wilson Centre Press, 41–61.

Connor, Walker (1994), *Ethnonationalism: the quest for Understanding*. Princeton: Princeton University Press.

Crowley, David and Susan Reid (eds) (2000), *Style and Socialism: Modernity and Material Culture in Postwar Eastern Europe*. Oxford: Berg.

Esman, Milton (1977), *Ethnic Conflict in the Western World*. Cornell: Cornell University Press.

Gaddis, John Lewis (1987), *The Long Peace: Inquiries into the History of the Cold War*, New York Oxford: Oxford University Press.

Gaddis, John Lewis (1997), *We now Know. Rethinking Cold War History*, Oxford: Oxford University Press.

Gaddis, John Lewis (1992), 'The Cold War, the Long Peace, and the Future', in Michael J. Hogan, (ed) (1992), *The End of the Cold War. Its Meaning and Implications*. Cambridge: Cambridge University Press, 21–38.

Gerrits, Andre and Dirk Jan Wolffram, (eds) (2005), *Political Democracy and Ethnic Diversity in Modern European History*. Stanford: Stanford University Press.

Gilman, Nils (2004), *Mandarins of the Future: Modernisation Theory in Cold War America*. Baltimore: Johns Hopkins University Press.

Hahn, Hans Hennig and Eva Hahn (2002), 'Nationale Stereotypen. Plädoyer für eine historische Stereotypenforschung', in Hans Hennig Hahn (ed), *Stereotypen, Identität und Geschichte. Die Funktion von Stereotypen in gesellschaftlichen Diskursen.* Frankfurt am Main: Peter Lang.

Ignatieff, Michael (1994), *Blood and Belonging: Journeys into the New Nationalism.* London: Vintage.

Johnston, Gordon (2010), 'Revisiting the cultural Cold War', *Social History*, 35 (3), 2010, 290–307.

Kaplan, Robert (1993), *Balkan Ghosts: A Journey through History.* New York: St. Martin's Press.

Kellas, James (1998), *The Politics of Nationalism and Ethnicity* (2nd edn.), Basingstoke: Macmillan.

King, Robert (1973), *Minorities under Communism. Nationalities as a source of Tension among Balkan Communist States,* Cambridge: Cambridge University Press.

Kramer, Mark (2005), 'The Collapse of East European Communism and the Repercussions within the Soviet Union' (part 3), *Journal of Cold War Studies* 7 (1), 3–96.

Kuusisto, Riikka (2004), 'Savage Tribes and Mystic Feuds: Western Foreign Policy Statement on Bosnia in the Early 1990s', in Andrew Hammond (ed), *The Balkans and the West: Constructing the European Other, 1945–2003,* Aldershot: Ashgate, 169–183.

Lake, David and Donald Rothchild (1998), *The International Spread of Ethnic conflict: Fear, Diffusion and escalation.* Princeton, NJ: Princeton University Press.

Major, Patrick and Rana Mitter (2006), 'Culture,' in Saki Dockrill and Geraint Hughes (eds), *Palgrave Advances in Cold War history,* Basingstoke: Palgrave.

Mearsheimer, John (1990), 'Back to the Future: Instability in Europe after the Cold War', *International Security*, 15 (1), 5–56.

Schöpflin, George (1995), 'Nationalism and Ethnicity in Europe, East and West in Charles A. Kupchan (ed), *Nationalism and Nationalities in the New Europe.* Ithaca: Cornell University Press, 37–65.

Shaw, Tony (2001), 'The Politics of Cold War Culture,' *Journal of Cold War Studies,* 3 (3), 59–76.

Smith, Anthony (1991), *National Identity.* London: Penguin.

Tuminez, Astrid (2003), Nationalism, Ethnic Pressures, and the Breakup of the Soviet Union', *Journal of Cold War Studies,* 5 (4), 81–136.

Verdery, Katherine (1991), *National Ideology under Socialism: Identity and Cultural Politics in Ceaucescu's Romania.* Berkeley: University of California Press.

Walzer, Michael (1992), 'The New Tribalism: Notes on a Difficult Problem', *Dissent*, 39, 164–71.

Westad, Odd Arne (2007), *The Global Cold War: Third World Interventions and the Making of Our Times.* Cambridge: Cambridge University Press.

Zielonka, Jan (2006), *Europe as Empire: the Nature of the Enlarged European Union.* Oxford: Oxford University Press.

Chapter 1

Western Perspectives on Ethnic Politics

Robert Knight

1 Ethnic Politics in the Cold War

Despite some federalist hopes and dreams, the post-war international order was rebuilt on the basis of nation states and their mistrust of minority rights.[1] Ethnic ties and ethnic claims were viewed with particular suspicion because they seemed to threaten national sovereignty and cohesion. Ethnic homogeneity, as Inis Claude wrote in 1955, 'frequently appeared as a value in itself'.[2] The founding fathers of the United Nations certainly had no interest in strengthening the ability of ethnic minorities to resist assimilation.[3] Indifference or hostility towards collective minority rights – the obverse of the 'strange triumph of Human Rights'[4] – can also be seen in the peace settlement. In contrast to the treaties signed after World War I Western governments followed what one British official called 'the general policy to avoid laying down any minority rights in *this* peace settlement'.[5] There was no restoration of the (limited) possibilities of appeal which had been enjoyed under the League of Nations.[6] For example the provisions for autonomy to the South Tyrol German-speaking population agreed in 1946 and incorporated into the 1947 Italian Peace Treaty were extensive on paper but there was little international interest in ensuring that Italy implemented them. Similarly, the protection for Austria's Slovenes and Croats laid down in the 1955 Austrian State Treaty was not followed up with any energy by the four signatory powers.

This attitude is not hard to understand. Even in the World War I treaties, Britain and France, as *status quo* powers, had seen minority rights as a dangerous Pandora's box.[7] The experience of Hitler hardened this view so that at the end of the war, in Claude's words, 'statesmen, generally backed by a public opinion which was deeply impressed by the perfidy of irredentist and disloyal minorities, were disposed to curtail rather than to expand, the rights of minorities'.[8] The failure of appeasement and the Munich agreement were taken as conclusive proof that the only way to 'deal with dictators' was to stand up to them.[9] This perspective, though understandable, was selective in that it focused exclusively on Chamberlain's diplomatic miscalculations and their exploitation by the predatory Nazi 'kin-state'. That obscured the underlying, 'transferable' element of the 'Munich problem' – the reconciliation of minority rights and state cohesion in an ethnically diverse society. Thanks to Hitler and the Sudeten German Party, most post-war claims to minority rights risked being dismissed as pretexts for subverting the state: the perspective was summed up by the belief that 'every protected minority will ultimately find its Henlein'.[10]

Of course, the turn against minority rights and ethnic claims went deeper than this shamefaced memory of Munich. The very idea of basing collective claims on a putative community of descent was now indelibly marked by Nazi racism and genocide. Even if racism was hardly absent in post-war Europe, the overt use of the language of racial superiority and anti-Semitism was thoroughly discredited.[11] That made any hint that ethnic categories were being rehabilitated deeply suspect. Even non-dominant minorities who made no claims to racial superiority were open to the accusation that they were reopening 'the race question'. Proponents of ethnic group rights lost most of the influence and standing they had enjoyed before the war. Individuals rather than groups were seen as the prime bearers of rights.[12] For example, the Universal Declaration of Human Rights (1948) laid down Educational rights in Article 26 in relation to educational opportunities and parental choice. It had nothing to say about the possibility that education might help minorities redress structural disadvantages in the cultivation of its language or culture.[13] On this point, the Soviet Union, for all its theoretical adherence to Leninist principles of national autonomy and its advocacy of collective 'social rights', did not seem to disagree much.

The norm of the nation-state was also embedded in Western perceptions of communist take-overs in Eastern Europe. Soviet domination came to be seen as a dual-linked oppression; both the rights of national self-determination and democratic rights were being trampled underfoot. As this view solidified, the exclusionary implications of ethnic nationalism seemed a secondary issue. In echoes of nineteenth-century liberal views of the Ottoman and Tsarist empires, Eastern European nations were seen as captive nations awaiting their moment of liberation.

The marginalization of ethnic explanations can be seen in the aftermath of the Yalta conference (February 1945). Attacks on the agreements portrayed it as a gross act of national betrayal and, like Munich before it, the betrayed nation was generally assumed to be a nation-state. Admittedly, Poland's pre-war ethnic plurality, which provided the rationale for the revision of its Eastern borders, was used by Churchill in his House of Commons defence of Yalta on his return. But this kind of argument was soon displaced by the extinction of Polish democracy and the alleged connivance of Western leaders in it.[14] The continuing violence among Poles, Ukrainian and Lithuanians on Poland's eastern borders received little attention, while the expulsion of the German population was reinterpreted as an ideologically motivated act. When Churchill returned to the subject in his 'Iron Curtain' speech of March 1946, he fitted it into his warning message of the Soviet menace. Unlike a year before, he now made no mention of German racial persecution of Jews and Slavs as the context for the expulsion of the Germans. Neither did he discuss his own ambiguous role in the West's acceptance of the necessity of the expulsions.[15] Instead, he accused 'the Russian-dominated Polish Government' of making 'enormous and wrongful inroads upon Germany', and instigating mass expulsions 'on a scale grievous and undreamed of';[16] the city of Stettin (Szczecin) was not a site of ethnic interaction but the end point of the perimeter which marked the extent of Soviet encroachment. Behind the line lay Eastern Europe's nations, referred to by Churchill as 'ancient states' with 'their famous capitals and the populations around them'. Trieste, at the other end of the curtain, was also reframed. Here too Churchill had been instrumental in the process the previous summer when he

had successfully urged the US government to draw a line against any
further advance of Yugoslav troops. As a result, the city became an
early Cold War hot spot rather than just another 'ethnic squabble'.[17]
In Pamela Ballinger's words, the 'Anglo-American interpretation of
the Italo–Yugoslav border dispute as a thinly veiled act of communist
expansion prevailed over . . . competing interpretations emphasizing
a complex history of nationalist contestation'.[18]

This 'de-ethnicisation' can also be seen in another classic text of
the early Cold War, the 'Truman doctrine' (March 1947). Truman's
speech was of course a decisive step in the globalization of US policy
towards Soviet policy, and contained suitably Manichean rhetoric.[19]
Less often noted is the way Truman's simplification downplayed the
ethnic dimensions of the crisis. By implication, the Greek nation he
portrayed was ethnically homogeneous.[20] Greek territorial claims
(against Albania and 'Yugoslav Macedonia') or Greek proposals 'to
rid themselves of disloyal Slavophone elements' (estimated at half
the population of 60,000) in exchange for around 20,000 Greeks
(now in Bulgaria) were not mentioned and the ethnic grievances
raised by the Yugoslav government were seen as mere pretexts.[21] The
State Department corrected its envoy (Mark Ethridge) in order to
make 'a clear-cut distinction between general conditions . . . which
make possible or serve as pretexts for frontier violation and actual
direct causes and responsibility for such violation'. Using internal
conditions in one country to justify territorial violations would be
'clearly contrary' to the UN Charta.[22] Officials were also concerned
that the 'occurrence of a large number of typical Balkan border
incidents should not be allowed to divert attention from the systematic
aggressive policies' of Greece's three communist neighbours.[23] Of
course, in Greece, as with Trieste, ethnic (and other) grievances were
indeed being used by Yugoslavia. But the point here is that in the
simple Cold War narrative, the exploitation was the main story, the
grievances themselves were secondary issues.

This process also reinforced a straightforward 'majoritarian'
understanding of democracy, in which a militant communist minority
(supported by an international communist movement) was pitted
against a unitary Greek nation. In this view, the party or parties with
the most votes in election won the legitimate right to speak for the

nation. If they proved fallible or became unpopular they could always be voted out of office. As Truman put it (conceding that 'the Greek Government is not perfect'), one of the chief virtues of democracy was that 'its defects are always visible and, under democratic processes, can be pointed out and corrected'. But this was precisely what was not possible in ethnically divided societies, where majority-minority relationship were structurally embedded so that ethnic competition became a 'zero-sum conflict'.[24]

Truman's scenario of a world divided between despotism and democracy was sustained over the following decade by the prevailing totalitarianism model of communism. In the schematic presentation of the 'syndrome' by Carl Friedrich and Zbigniew Brzezinski, the repression exercised by communist regimes was so overwhelming that it allowed almost no space for resistance.[25] That applied in the first case to the supposedly helpless and atomized individual but it also meant that the mobilization of collective identities, like nationalism or ethnicity, was also given little chance (although Friedrich and Brezinski did give consideration to the possibility of communist regimes using it to strengthen their hold on power).[26] This lack of interest in nationalism even extended to Nazi Germany, the supposed comparator of the communist totalitarian state.[27] The Nazi utopia of 'the folk community' was seen as the functional equivalent of the communist 'world brotherhood of the proletariat' both of them being means of mass mobilization, but the actual target was on the left – 'the classless society of the socialist tradition'.[28]

On this analysis it was hard to see how communist rule might ever change, let alone collapse.[29] It is therefore perhaps not surprising that little consideration was given to what a post-communist world might look like. Friedrich and Brzezinski gave merely a hint that they anticipated, on classical liberal lines, that liberated states would wish 'to further understanding between nations'. This would mean the 'possibility for peaceful coexistence of the nations peopling this world'.[30]

Of course, neither the ethnic diversity of Eastern Europe and the Soviet Empire nor the resulting tensions were a secret, even if reliable information was not easy to get hold of. And the politics of the anticommunist refugees who had fled to the West suggested that these tensions went too deep to be suppressed in the interests of anti-communist unity.[31] In the case of the future of the territory to the east of the Oder–Neisse line, ethnic conflict also involved the large Polish community in the United States, on the one hand, and West German governments, on the other, which included the representatives of the expellee parties. US officials could hardly gloss over this difference altogether although the unresolved legal status of the border meant they could allow German expellee politicians to believe that a restoration the 1937 borders was still possible. West German governments for their part practised what Pertti Ahonen has called a 'juggling act' between 'the promotion of forward-looking, democratic values and structures' on the one hand and 'the pacification of compromised, discontented elements' on the other.[32] Other equally toxic ethnic differences continued to simmer in the diaspora: between Slovak separatists and Czechoslovak exile politicians over the future of Czechoslovakia; between Ukrainians and refugees from the Baltic states, who anticipated the 'dismemberment' of Russia, and former Vlassovite Russian nationalists on the other; last not least conflicts – sometimes violent – between Serb and Croat exile groups over the future existence of Yugoslavia or continuation of war time conflicts. US policymakers sought to defer any decisions on these differences until future liberation, in the meantime including Czechoslovakia, Russia and Yugoslavia in the list of captive nations.[33]

The suppression of the 1956 Hungarian revolution made it clear that any direct or military 'liberation' was highly unlikely. At the same time, there was growing evidence that East European regimes were ready to diverge from Soviet instruction. Some Western observers began to wonder how much longer Soviet domination could last. In 1965, Ghita Ionescu argued that Stalin's empire had already broken up since his successors were 'incapable of imposing the kind of ideological uniformity and economic dominance he had'.[34] He also discussed nationalist grievances as 'the most virulent motive of dissent' against communist rule; there were two aspects to this: the resistance of a people which sees national sovereignty being curbed by 'suzerain power' and also the claims by 'ethnic or regional groups ... that the central administration oppresses or neglects them'.[35] Brzezinski, moving away from the schematism of the totalitarian interpretation, now concluded that Eastern European states were moving from being satellites into the position of junior allies, while communist totalitarian rule was mutating into 'domesticism'. He referred to Tito and Ceauşescu, whose leadership was supported by a new generation of technocrats and managers, who were less ideologically purist than their predecessors. Brzezinski saw a danger in Western encouragement of anti-Soviet nationalist dictatorships unleashing xenophobia and ethnic conflict. For this reason he thought it would be shortsighted for the West to try to 'ride the tiger' of nationalism in the hope that it would threaten the Soviet-dominated world only.[36] Other Western observers began to see the Soviet Union less as an implacable totalitarian enemy than as a manageable, if unpredictable competitor. One advantage of a *Pax Sovietica* was its ability to keep the tiger within bounds. Mark Kramer has referred to 'the stabilizing effect of the Soviet military presence in Eastern and Central Europe [which] was widely taken for granted and even appreciated, at least tacitly'.[37]

2 The 'Ethnic Revival' in Western Europe

Downplaying ethnic claims and ethnic explanations was an (understandable) response to Nazi rule and reflected the polarizing logic of the Cold War. It was also in line with the prevailing theoretical assumptions of social sciences, which tended to see ethnicity as a vestigial phenomenon, or limited to traditional societies. To the 'mandarins of the future' its political importance in the Third World was as a potential obstacle in the 'nation-building', which was meant both to strengthen resistance to communism and to create the basis for economic growth, perhaps even the 'take-off' envisaged in Walt Rostow's well-known model of development.[38] In some versions of modernization theory, 'integration' played a key role, acting as a glue which could achieve social cohesion in very different contexts.[39] For advocates and students of European unity, integration involved the closer coordination of trade policy, the avoidance of any return to pre-war economic nationalism and, at the federalist end of the scale, the creation of supranational institutions or even a United States of Europe. Carl Friedrich, for example, wondered if those who were 'unifying (and integrating) Europe' could not be seen as 'nation-builders' no less than 'Nehru or those who try to weld tribes into nations'.[40] In the case of the influential political scientist Karl Deutsch, integration meant the process of ever intenser and denser communication, ultimately leading to a higher level of 'community'.[41] \Deutsch's scientific agenda had a political dimension, in which there was a progressivist teleology as well as a concern about the robustness of western values in the face of the communist challenge. Though Deutsch certainly acknowledged the existence of inertial forces slowing down integration, he was generally confident that they would be overcome. The key question in relation to national-building was how nations 'triumph over smaller units, such as tribes, castes, or local states, and more or less integrate them into the political body of the nation?'[42] At least before the revival of Gaullism in the 1960s, Deutsch considered the possibility that 'a North Atlantic Community might develop between democracies on both sides of the Atlantic'.[43] In this process there was in principle 'no upper limit on the number of ethnic and linguistic groups that could be integrated'.[44] Andrei Markovits, himself a student of Deutsch, has aptly described him as an 'eternal optimist'.[45] That optimism has been viewed critically by Michael Latham as the delusion that 'the "traditional" world was plastic and malleable', which led many social scientists 'to overestimate their ability to redirect and channel nationalist forces'.[46]

In the course of the 1960s, modernizing confidence began to ebb and expectations were lowered. Outside Europe the unity of anti-colonial nationalist movements began to fracture after independence and, as in the case of Nigeria, state boundaries came under attack from secessionist movements.[47] The view that ethnicity was only salient in traditional societies was also undermined by its mobilization in industrial society, in combination with forms of ethnic unrest. In the United States, the reality and the desirability of the 'melting pot' was questioned by African–Americans in the civil rights movement as well as immigrant groups resisting integration, at least on the terms that seemed to be on offer. The subject of ethnicity – and the word itself – spread throughout political and academic discourse.[48] As it did, some of its students sought to decontaminate it, that is remove the taint of racism and right-wing extremism. For example, the sociologist Joshua Fishman argued that 'while there is a racist potential in modern ethnicity that is not sufficient to dam the phenomenon'.[49] In Western Europe the unequal treatment of post-war immigration led to social and ethnic ('racial') unrest among second-generation immigrants and undermined the prevailing complacent assumptions that racial conflict was a specific problem of the United States.[50]

Perhaps most important here, there was an unexpected mobilization of ethnicity in Western Europe. The diversity of these 'ethno-regionalist' or 'ethno-regionalist' movements makes it hard to generalize about them.[51] They included urban terrorists using Marxist slogans as well as neo-fascist groups; Basque militants opposed to Franco's regime, Catholics demanding civil rights in Northern Ireland, Corsican protesters against French centralization and French-language separatists in the German-speaking Canton of Bern, to name only a few.

It is also difficult to locate these new movements in relation to the Cold War. On one interpretation they became possible because the East–West battle was now muted. Fear of communism as an ideology or of nuclear attack was declining within the post-war generation. Traditional party loyalties were being undermined by an unprecedented economic growth and the extension of welfare provision.[52]

The emergence of 'ethno-regionalist' mobilization also directly contradicted Deutsch's observation that Western European nationalism had 'settled down'.[53] Critics of modernization theory like Walker Connor concluded that 'ethnic consciousness, far from disappearing was "definitely on the ascendancy as a political force"'.[54] He saw this as a refutation of the 'American scholarship' which had analyzed and dismissed ethnicity as a force in advanced industrial societies. On the contrary, he argued it was an inevitable part of the processes of homogenization, urbanization and centralism. Increased communication had not destroyed ethnic difference but heightened consciousness of it and facilitated the mobilization against the unequal treatment of different ethnic groups.

The new ethnic mobilization also meant a challenge to Truman's simple contrast between totalitarianism and democracy. To some of its critics this amounted to a rejection of liberal values and a covert attempt to reintroduce outlawed racialist categories into European politics. Samuel Salzborn has recently argued along these lines, claiming that ever since the end of the Third Reich a determined intellectual lobbying campaign had been waged by a network of activists, including several who had been complicit in National Socialism. Their aim was nothing less than the rehabilitation of an ethnicized political theory, which would eventually allow Europe to be reorganized along 'organic' ethnic lines. Ethnic groups rather than individuals would be the bearers of rights. By the 1960s, Salzborn argues, this lobbying activity had successfully permeated mainstream structures in Western Europe (in particular, the European federalist movement) and begun to undermine the civic, republican values which had underpinned Europe's post-war territorial settlement.[55]

Though Salzborn is convincing in his *exposé* of the lineage of a part of the ethnic revival, he probably overstates its coherence and level of organization. But his identification of the post-war territorial and political territorial settlement as a target of the 'ethnic revival' points to the way 'Yalta' was now recoded, partly as an extension of de Gaulle's (abortive) attempt to break through the supposed superpower *Diktat* and establish a '*Europe of des patries*'. One leading figure in the ethnic revival, Guy Héraud, looked forward to a *Europe des ethnies*. In this perspective Yalta symbolized not just Soviet imprisonment of nations (and western connivance in it) but the imprisonment of Europe's diverse ethnic groups.[56] Héraud, like Fishman, thought it was time for ethnic movements to lose the stigma of Munich.

In elaborating this point others argued that the basic message of the new movements was emancipatory; their anti-statism was not an attempt to destabilize the post-war order but to supply the basic need for warmth and *Gemeinschaft*, which had been ignored by centralization and homogeneity. For this reason, Fishman aligned them with the libertarian politics, which was emerging from the ferment of the 1960s, including the hippies.[57] Similarly, Anthony Smith sought to counter those who were 'aghast at what appeared to be a revival of "tribalism"... only ten or fifteen years after its apparent destruction in the bunker of Berlin'.[58] He argued that the ethnic revival was part of a wider radical rejection of 'the prevailing statist framework' and a quest for more 'natural' and 'spiritual' forms of existence. He traced its pedigree back to the enlightenment and a 'critical discourse, appealing to general principles like popular sovereignty, inalienable rights and cultural diversity'. Since the war many movements had undergone a 'radical ideological metamorphosis', which meant they were more likely to be on the left than on the right. In short, for Smith, this was a welcome grass-roots revolt against the straightjacket imposed at Yalta.[59]

Whether viewed critically or positively the ethnic mobilization of the 1970s had important implications for Eastern Europe, and the Soviet Union, especially if it was indeed a global phenomenon, as relevant for industrialized as for agrarian societies. But overall, most analysts stuck to Western Europe (apart from the occasional passing reference to the 'Croatian Spring'). On the other hand, scholars of Eastern Europe or Soviet policy, although well aware of signs of disaffection or unrest, including some which would erupt 20 years later, were cautious about drawing wider conclusions, or seeing it as part of a systemic crisis. In fact, in the decade after the crushing of the Prague Spring, Soviet control of Eastern Europe stabilized and the cohesion of the Soviet Union was rarely questioned. Joseph Rothschild, for all his deep knowledge of Eastern Europe, saw a 'historically ironic reversal' of the inter-war situation. The challenge to state legitimacy in the West was now 'potentially more serious than it was and at least as serious . . . as in the East European countries' where ('with the possible exception of East Germany, the Soviet Union and Yugoslavia') . . . the state did 'not appear to be targets of domestic ethnopolitical repudiations and delegitimations'.[60] Several experts on Soviet society accepted the official estimate that, as Brezhnev proclaimed in 1972, the 'nationality question' had been 'fully, definitively, and irreversibly resolved'.[61] This perception was probably further reinforced by the dominant 'neo-realist' theories in International Relations, which privileged the international 'system' over the unit and saw the tendency towards an equilibrium between the two superpowers. In a notable hostage to fortune, its leading figure, Kenneth Waltz, made the production of 'reliable and explanations or predictions' a central criteria for the validity of a theory.[62]

The Helsinki Final Act (1975) came close to the *de facto* recognition of the Soviet dominance of Eastern Europe, including the absorption of the Baltic States, even if it did not amount to the complete Western legitimation Soviet leaders were looking for. It kept open the possibility of peaceful reunification of Germany. In West Germany the Oder–Neisse border was now widely accepted as permanent and the increasing contacts between West Germany and Poland helped defuse the issue. According to Levy and Dierkes West German national identity gradually evolved from an 'ethno-national idiom' to an 'economic identity'.[63] Some even saw West Germany as the first 'post-national' society. The unexpected resurrection of human rights in the aftermath of Helsinki was driven by dissident groups in Eastern Europe rather than Western governments. The Ford administration, in the aftermath of the Vietnam debacle, was not looking for reasons to intervene in Eastern Europe.[64] In any case, Article VIII of Helsinki Final Act did not tread any new ground in terms of minority protection; it was a fairly conventional reiteration of the right of self-determination as well as the national sovereignty. The alignment of human rights and minority rights came after the fall of communism, thanks to the interventionist policies of the OCSE and its High Commissioner on National Minorities.[65]

A decade before the fall of the Berlin wall, minority protection, affirmative action, the right of secession, the validity and limits of liberalism and a host of other public policy and philosophical issues were being debated in the West.[66] The academic study of nations and nationalism, which had been in the doldrums, moved up the academic agenda. Yet in the two most influential discussions, there was little indication of the developing crisis in Central and Eastern Europe. Benedict Anderson's influential *Imagined Communities* (1983) took most of its contemporary examples from South America and South-East Asia although there was a tangential reference to the difficulties facing Yugoslavia since Tito's death (1980). Starting from a recognition of the greater durability and power of nationalism compared with Marxism, Anderson warned of the possibility of conflict in Eastern Europe between nationalistically-minded Marxist regimes, giving Yugoslavia and Albania as examples. In contrast to Smith, Anderson also endorsed the stabilization achieved in Eastern Europe by the Red Army's 'overwhelming presence', which had 'ruled out armed conflict between the region's Marxist regimes'. Ernest Gellner's *Nations and Nationalism* (1985) was also only obliquely concerned with contemporary Central Europe even though one of his targets was clearly a kind of national mythmaking, which was recognizably central European.[67] His stress on the constructed or synthetic nature of nations, arising from the need of modern industrial organization for a codified homogeneous culture, was in principle equally relevant for civic nationalism as for ethnic: it could be achieved either by assimilation or by exclusion. But the debunking thrust of Gellner's argument, for example, his dig at the peasant dress code of Budapest urban opera goers, was more relevant to ethnic-based claim to authenticity.[68] Perhaps more striking is Gellner's lack of concern about the destructive danger of ethnic nationalism. He refers dismissively to the 'Dark Gods' theory, which holds that nationalism is 'the re-emergence of the atavistic forces of blood or territory'. Against this theory (the third of four 'false theories' of nationalism) he argues that

> man of the age of nationalism is neither nicer nor nastier than men of other ages . . . His crimes . . . are more conspicuous only because, precisely, they have become more shocking, and because they are executed with more powerful technological means.[69]

Five years later Gellner's tone had changed. Addressing a (still) Soviet academic audience, he concluded that with the benefit of hindsight both Marxism and liberal social thought had 'underestimated the political vigour of nationalism'.[70] Whereas in 1985 Marxism had been one of his four false theories, now he explained that it shared the mistake of liberalism of assuming that ethnicity-like cultural differences 'will go down the drain' under the conditions of work in industrial society. Gellner concluded that, contrary to both, 'Modern industrial High Culture is not colourless, it has an "ethnic" colouring, which is of its essence'.[71] Though Gellner was clearly greatly affected by the outbreak of violence in Yugoslavia and elsewhere in Eastern Europe he was far from the rather apocalyptic interpretations offered by Michael Ignatieff and others.[72]

Anthony Smith (Gellner's former student) also recognized the relevance of the worsening situation for his earlier stress on the primacy and historicity of ethnic identities. Initially he had greeted the Eastern European revolutions as the continuation of the emancipatory movement in western Europe. It meant that 'the interventionist state' had 'rekindled among its ethnic minorities those aspirations for autonomy and even separation that had previously been muted or repressed'.[73] Now he noted more sombrely that violence was the inevitable accompaniment of competing ethnic claims. He predicted that there could be 'little escape from the many conflagrations that the unsatisfied yearnings of ethnic nationalism are likely to kindle'.[74]

Notes

[1] Mark Mazower, *Hitler's Empire; Nazi Rule in Occupied Europe*, London: Penguin, 2009, 563–5.

[2] Inis Claude, *National Minorities: An International Problem*, Cambridge, MA: Harvard University Press, 1955, 69.

[3] Asborn Eide, 'The Sub-Commission on Prevention of Discrimination and Protection of Minorities, in Philip Alston (ed), *The United Nations and Human Rights: A critical appraisal*, Oxford: Oxford University Press, 1992, 213, 219–21.

[4] Mark Mazower, 'The Strange Triumph of Human Rights 1933–1950', *The Historical Journal*, 47 (2), (2004) 379–98.

[5] Cited in Robert Knight, 'Ethnicity and Identity in the Cold War: The Carinthian Border Dispute, 1945–1949,' *International History Review*, 22 (2), (2000), 274–303 (emphasis in original).

[6] Antony Alcock, *A History of the Protection of Regional Cultural Minorities from the Edict of Nantes to the Present Day*, London: Palgrave-Macmillan, 2000, 100–6.

[7] See Patrick B Finney, '"An evil for all concerned." Great Britain and Minority Protection after 1919', in *Journal of Contemporary History*, 30 (3), (1995), 533–51.

[8] Inis Claude, *National Minorities*, 69: *An International Problem*, Cambridge, MA: Harvard University Press, 1955.

[9] Mike Sewell, *The Cold War* (Cambridge Perspectives in History), Cambridge: Cambridge University Press, 2002, 14; Patrick Finney, 'The Romance of Decline: The Historiography of Appeasement and British National Identity,' *Electronic Journal of International History*, 1, June 2000*http://www.history.ac.uk/ ejournal/art1.html* [accessed 10 August 2010].

[10] Inis, National Minorities, 57.

[11] Mark Mazower, *Hitler's Empire*, 593: Tom Nairn, *Faces of Nationalism: Janus Revisited*, London: Verso, 1997, 9–11.

[12] Samuel Salzborn, Ethnisierung der Politik: *Theorie und Geschichte des Volksgruppenrechts in Europa*, Frankfurt am Main-New York: Campus, 2005, 193–214.

[13] See Johannes Morsink, *The Universal Declaration of Human Rights. Origins, Drafting and Intent*, Philadelphia: University of Pennsylvania Press, 1999.

[14] Bernd Stöver, *Die Befreiung vom Kommunismus: Amerikanische Liberation Policy im Kalten Krieg*. Cologne: Böhlau, 2002, 638–42.

[15] Michael Frank, *Expelling the Germans. British Opinion and Post-1945 Population transfer in Context*, Oxford: Oxford University Press, 2007, 118–20, 141, 250.

[16] Churchill 'sinews of peace' speech, *http://www.fordham.edu/halsall/mod/churchill-iron.html* [accessed 20 December 2010].

[17] See Glenda Sluga, *The Problem of Trieste and the Italo–Yugoslav Border:. Difference, Identity and Sovereignty in Twentieth-Century Europe*, New York: State University of New York, 2001.

[18] Pamela Ballinger, 'Politics of the Past: Redefining Insecurity along the "World's Most Open Border,"' in Jutta Weldes, Mark Laffey, Hugh Gusterson and Raymond Duvall (eds), *Cultures of Insecurity: States, Communities, and the Production of Danger*, Minneapolis: University of Minnesota Press, 1999, 73. See also Melvin Leffler, *A Preponderance of Power: National Security, the Truman Administration, and the Cold War*, Stanford: Stanford University Press, 1992, 75.

[19] Truman address to Congress, 12 March 1947, *http://avalon.law.yale.edu/20th_century/trudoc.asp* [accessed 10 August 2010]

[20] George Alexander, *The Prelude to the Truman Doctrine: British Policy in Greece* Oxford: Clarendon, 1944–1947, 199–204.

[21] Secretary of State George Marshall to Mark Ethridge, 28 February 1947, *Foreign Relations of the United States 1947*, vol V (The Near East and Africa), Washington: US Government Printing Office 1971, 823–4.

[22] Marshall to Ethridge, 7 May and 10 May 1947, *ibid*, 826–7, 847–9.

[23] Marshall to Ethridge, 26 June 1947, *ibid*, 862.

[24] See John McGarry and Brendan O'Leary, *The Politics of Ethnic Conflict Regulation: Case Studies of Protracted Ethnic Conflict*, London-New York: Routledge, 1993, 25.

[25] Carl Friedrich and Zbigniew Brzezinski, *Totalitarian Dictatorship and Autocracy*, New York: Prager, 1956.

[26] Abbott Gleason, *Totalitarianism: the Inner History of the Cold War*, Oxford: Oxford University Press, 1993, 121–3.

[27] Peter Novick, *The Holocaust and Collective Memory: the American Experience*, London: Bloomsbury, 2001, 87.

[28] Friedrich and Brzezinski, *Totalitarian Dictatorship*, New York: Praeger, 1956.

[29] Dankwart A Rustow, 'Communism and change', in Chalmers Johnson (ed), *Change in Communist systems*, Stanford, CA: Stanford University Press, 1970, 348.

[30] Friedrich and Brzezinski, *Totalitarian Dictatorship*, 52, 68.

[31] Stöver, *Befreiung*, 87; see also Tony Smith, *Foreign Attachments: the power of the Ethnic in the making of American foreign Policy: The power of Ethnic Groups in the Making of American Foreign Policy*, Cambridge: Harvard University Press, 2000; Ieva Zake (ed), *Anti-communist minorities in the US: Political Activism of Ethnic Refugees*, New York: Palgrave-Macmillan, 2009.

[32] Pertti Ahonen, *After the Expulsion: West Germany and Eastern Europe 1945–1990*, Oxford: Oxford University Press, 2003, 8–9.

[33] Stöver, *Befreiung*, 285–7.

[34] Ghita Ionescu, *The Break-up of the Soviet Empire in Eastern Europe*, London: Penguin, 1965.

[35] Ghita Ionescu, *The Politics of the European Communist states*, London: Weidenfeld and Nicolson, 1967, 37.

[36] Brzezinski, *Alternative to Partition, For a broader concept of America's role in Europe*, New York: McGraw-Hill, 1965, 174–5; *Idem, The Soviet Bloc. Unity and Conflict, Ideology and Power* (revised and enlarged edn.), Cambridge, MA: Harvard University Press, 1966, 439. See also Paul Lendvai, *Eagles in Cobwebs: Nationalism and Communism in the Balkans*, London: Macdonald, 1969, 19.

[37] Mark Kramer 'Introduction' in Philipp Ther and Siljak, (eds), *Redrawing Nations: Ethnic Cleansing in East-Central Europe, 1944–1948.* Lanham: Rowman and Littlefield. (2001), 7.

[38] See Nils Gilman, *Mandarins of the Future. Modernization theory in Cold War America*, Baltimore-London: Johns Hopkins University Press, 2003.

[39] See Bo Stråth, 'The Swedish Image of Europe as the Other,' in Bo Stråth (ed), *Europe and the Other and Europe as the Other*, Brussels etc: Peter Lang, 2000, 391–401; Alan Milward and Vibeke Sørensen, 'Interdependence or integration? A national choice', in Alan Milward, Ranieri Ruggiero, Vibeke Sørensen and Frances Lynch, *The Frontier of National Sovereignty: History and theory 1945–1992*, London: Routledge 1993, 1–32.

[40] Carl Friedrich, 'Nation-building?' in Karl Deutsch and Willam Foltz, (eds), *Nation-building*, New York: Prentice-Hall, 1963.

[41] See Karl Deutsch, *Nationalism and Social communication: An Inquiry into the foundations of Nationality*, Cambridge MA: John Wiley, 1953.

[42] Karl Deutsch, 'Introduction: Some problems in Nation-Building', in Deutsch and William Foltz eds, *Nation building*, New York: Atherton, 1963, 4.

[43] Karl Deutsch et.al., *Political Community and the North Atlantic Area: International Organization in the light of historical Experience*, Princeton, NJ: Princeton University Press, 1957, 5, 20.

[44] Deutsch, *Political Community*, 158.

[45] Andrei S. Markovits, 'From Prague to America – Karl W. Deutsch between Experience and Knowledge', in Dan Diner and Moshe Zimmermann, (eds) *Disseminating German Tradition: the Thyssen Lectures*, Leipzig: Leipziger Universitätsverlag, 2009, 101–22.

[46] Michael Latham, *Modernization as Ideology. American Social Science and "Nation Building" in the Kennedy Era*, Chapel Hill: University of North Carolina Press, 2000, 211.

[47] See David L Horowitz, *Ethnic Groups in Conflict*, Berkeley: University of California Press, 1985.

[48] Steve Fenton, *Ethnicity*, Cambridge: Cambridge University Press, 2003, 91.

[49] Joshua Fishman, 'Social theory and Ethnography: neglected perspectives on language and ethnicity in Eastern Europe', in Peter Sugar (ed), *Ethnic diversity and Conflict in Eastern Europe*, Santa Barbara: CA 1980, 86.

[50] Nathan Glazer and Daniel Moynihan (eds), *Ethnicity, Theory and Experience*, Cambridge, MA: Harvard, 1975; Nathan Glazer and Ken Young eds, *Ethnic*

Pluralism and Public Policy: Achieving Equality in US and Britain, Lexington, MA: Lexington Books, 1983.

[51] See Ferdinand Müller-Rommel, 'Theoretical Considerations', in Lieven De Winter and Huri Türsan (eds), *Regionalist Parties in Western Europe*, London-New York: Routledge, 1998, 18.

[52] James Kellas, *The Politics of Nationalism and Ethnicity* (2nd edn), New York: Macmillan, 1998, 106: Arendt Lijphart, 'Political theories and the Explanation of Ethnic conflict in the Western World', in Milton Esman (ed), *Ethnic Conflict in the Western World*, Cornell: Cornell University Press, 1977, 55–62.

[53] Deutsch, *Atlantic Community*, 158–9.

[54] Walker Connor, *Ethnonationalism: the quest for Understanding*. Princeton: Princeton University Press. (1994), 35.

[55] Salzborn Samuel, *Ethnisierung der Politik: Theorie und Geschichte des Volksgruppenrechts* in Europa. Frankfurt-New York: Campus, (2005), 162–170.

[56] Guy Héraud, *L'Europe des Ethnies*, Paris: Presses d'Europe, 1963.

[57] Joshua Fishman et. al, *The Rise and Fall of the Ethnic Revival: Perspectives on Language and Ethnicity*, Berlin-New York-Amsterdam: Mouton, 1985, xii.

[58] Anthony Smith, *The Ethnic Revival in the Modern World*, Cambridge: Cambridge University Press, 1981.

[59] Smith, *Ethnic Revival*, 177, 183.

[60] Joseph Rothschild, *Ethnopolitics: A Conceptual Framework*, New York: Columbia University Press, 1981, 17.

[61] Astrid Tuminez 'Nationalism, Ethnic Pressures, and the Breakup of the Soviet Union', *Journal of Cold War Studies*, 5 (4), (2003), 88.

[62] Kenneth Waltz, *Theory of International Politics*, New York: McGraw Hill, 1979, 19; Jonathan Haslam, *No Virtue like necessity. Realist thought in international relations since Machiavelli*, New Haven, CT: Yale University Press, 2002, 224, 239–40.

[63] Daniel Levy and Julian Dierkes, 'Institutionalising the past: shifting memories of nationhood in German education and immigration policies', in Jan-Werner Müller (ed), *Memory and Power in Post-war Europe: Studies in the Presence of the Past*, Cambridge: Cambridge University Press, 2002, 244–64.

[64] Vernon van Dyke, 'Individual and Group rights', in Donald P. Kommers and Gilbert D Loescher (eds), *Human Rights and American Foreign Policy*, London: University of Notre Dame Press, 1979, 34–5.

[65] Patrice McMahon, 'Ethnic peace in the east: transnational networks and the CSCE/OSCE,' in *Ethnopolitics*, 5 (2), (2006), 101–23.

[66] Will Kymlicka (ed), *The Rights of Minority Cultures*, Oxford: Oxford University Press, 1995.

[67] See Nicholas Stargardt, 'Gellner's Nationalism: the Spirit of Modernisation?' in John Hall and Ian Jarvie (eds), *The Social Philosophy of Ernst Gellner*, Amsterdam-Atlanta, GA: Rodopi, 1996, 175.

[68] Stargardt, Gellner's Nationalism, 176–7.

[69] Gellner, Nations and Nationalism 130.

[70] Ernest Gellner, 'From Kinship to Ethnicity', *Encounters with Nationalism* Oxford: Blackwell, 1994, 38 (first published in a Soviet journal in 1989).

[71] Gellner, *Encounters*, 37, 42.

[72] John Hall, *Ernest Gellner An Intellectual Biography*, London-New York: Verso, 2010, 238–330.

[73] Smith, *National Identity*, 138.

[74] Anthony Smith, 'Causes and implications of Ethnic Conflict', in Michael Brown (ed), *Ethnic Conflict and International Security*, Princeton: Princeton University Press, 1993, 40.

Bibliography

Ahonen, Pertti (2003), *After the Expulsion: West Germany and Eastern Europe 1945–1990*. Oxford: Oxford University Press.

Alcock, Antony (2000), *A History of the Protection of Regional Cultural Minorities, from the Edict of Nantes to the Present Day*. London: Palgrave-Macmillan.

Alexander, George (1982), *The Prelude to the Truman Doctrine: British Policy in Greece 1944–1947*. Oxford: Clarendon.

Appy, Christian (2000), *Cold War constructions: The political Culture of United States imperialism 1945–1966*. Ameherst, MA: University of Massachusetts Press.

Ballinger, Pamela (1999), 'The Politics of the Past: Redefining Insecurity along the "World's Most Open Border"', in Jutta Weldes, Mark Laffey, Hugh Gusterson and Raymond Duvall (eds), *Cultures of Insecurity: States, Communities, and the Production of Danger*. Minnesota: University of Minnesota Press.

Brown, Michael, Owen Cote, Sean Lynn-Jones and Steven Miller (eds), (2001), *Nationalism and Ethnic conflict* (revised edn). London: MIT Press.

Brubaker, Rogers, Margit Feischmidt, Jon Fox and Liana Grancea (2006), *Nationalist Politics and Everyday Ethnicity in a Transylvanian Town*, Princeton: Princeton University Press.

Brzezinski, Zbigniew (ed), (1969), *Dilemmas of Change in Soviet Politics*. New York: Columbia University Press.

Brzezinski, Zbigniew (1965), *Alternatives to partition: For a broader conception of America's Role in Europe*. New York Toronto-London: McGraw-Hill.

Brzezinski, Zbigniew (1967), *The Soviet Bloc. Unity and Conflict. Ideology and Power in the Relations among the USSR, Poland, Yugoslavia, China and other Communist States* (revised and enlarged edn.), Cambridge, MA: Harvard University Press.

Caplan, Richard and John Feffer, (eds) (1996), *Europe's New Nationalism: States and Minorities in Conflict*. New York-Oxford: Oxford University Press.

Carment, David and Patrick James (eds) (1997), *Wars in the midst of Peace the international politics of ethnic conflict*. Pittsburgh: Pittsburgh University Press.

Chalmers, Johnson (ed), (1970), *Change in Communist systems*. Stanford, CA: Stanford University Press.

Cheles, Luciano, Ronnie Ferguson, and Michalina Vaughan, (1991), *The Far Right in Western and Eastern Europe*. London - New York: Longman.

Claude, Inis (1955), *National Minorities: An International Problem*. Cambridge, MA: Harvard University Press.

Colhoun, Craig (1997), *Nationalism*. Buckingham: Open University Press.

Connor, Walker (1984), *The National Question in Marxist-Leninist Theory and Strategy*. Princeton: Princeton University Press.

Deutsch, Karl (1953), *Nationalism and Social communication: An Inquiry into the foundations of Nationality*. Cambridge: MA.

Deutsch, Karl *et. al.*, (1957), *Political Community and the North Atlantic Area: International Organization in the light of Historical Experience*. Princeton, NJ: Princeton University Press.

Deutsch, Karl and Willam Foltz (eds) (1963), *Nation-building*. New York: Prentice-Hall.

Diuk, Nadia and Adrian Karatnycky (1993), *New Nations Rising: the fall of the Soviets and the Challenge of Independence*. New York: John Wiley.

Eide, Asborn (1992), 'The Sub-Commisssion on Prevention of Discrimination and Protection of Minorities', in Philip Alston (ed), *The United Nations and Human Rights: a critical appraisal*. Oxford: Oxford University Press.

Fenton, Steve (2003), *Ethnicity*. Cambridge: Polity.

Finney, Patrick B (1995), 'An evil for all concerned.' Great Britain and Minority Protection after 1919', *Journal of Contemporary History*, 30, 533–51.

Finney, Patrick (2000), 'The Romance of Decline: The Historiography of Appeasement and British National Identity', *Electronic Journal of International History*, 1 [*http://www.history.ac.uk/ejournal/art1.html*].

Fishman, Joshua (1980), 'Social theory and Ethnography: neglected perspectives on language and ethnicity in Eastern Europe, in Peter Sugar (ed), *Ethnic diversity and Conflict in Eastern Europe*. Santa Barbara: Clio.

Fishman, Joshua (1985), *The Rise and Fall of the Ethnic Revival: Perspectives on Language and Ethnicity*. Berlin–New York–Amsterdam: Mouton.

Foltz, William J (1963), 'Building the Newest Nations: short-term Strategies and Long-run Problems,' Deutsch, Karl and Willam Foltz (eds), *Nation-building*, New York: Prentice-Hall, 117–31.

Foreign Relations of the United States 1947 (1971), vol. V (*The Near East and Africa*), Washington: US Government Printing Office,

Frank, Michael (2007), *Expelling the Germans. British Opinion and Post-1945 Population transfer in Context*, Oxford, Oxford University Press.

Friedrich, Carl J and Zbigniew Brzezinski (1956), *Totalitarian Dictatorship and Autocracy*, New York: Prager.

Friedrich, Carl J (1963), 'Nation-building?', in Karl Deutsch and Willam Foltz, (eds), *Nation-building*, New York: Prentice-Hall.

Gerrits, Andre (1992), *Nationalism and Political Change in Post-Communist Europe*. The Hague.

Glazer, Nathan and Daniel Moynihan (eds), (1975), *Ethnicity: Theory and Experience*. Cambridge, MA, Harvard University Press.

Glazer, Nathan and Ken Young (eds), (1983) *Ethnic Pluralism and Public Policy, Achieving Equality in the United States and Britain*, Lexington, MA: Lexington Books.

Gleason, Abbott (1993), *Totalitarianism: the Inner History of the Cold War*, Oxford: Oxford University Press.

Gould-Davies, Nigel (1999), 'Rethinking the Role of Ideology in International Politics during the Cold War,' *Journal of Cold War Studies*, 1 90–109.

Hall, John (2010), *Ernest Gellner: An Intellectual Biography*. London-New York: Verso.

Hammond, Andrew (ed) (2004), *The Balkans and the West: Constructing the European Other, 1945–2003:* Aldershot.

Haslam, Jonathan (2002), *No Virtue like necessity. Realist thought in international relations since Machiavelli*. New Haven, CT: Yale University Press.

Héraud, Guy (1963), *L'Europe des Ethnies*. Paris: Presses d'Europe.

Hinds, Lynn Boyd, and Theodore Otto-Windt, *The Cold War as Rhetoric. The Beginnings 1945–1950*, New York: Praeger, 1991.

Hixson, Walter L (1997), *Parting the Curtain: Propaganda, Culture and the Cold War, 1945–1965*. New York: St Martin's Press.

Hogan, Michael (1998), *A Cross of Iron: Harry S Truman and the Origins of the National Security state*. New York: Cambridge University Press.

Horowitz, David L (1985), *Ethnic Groups in Conflict*. Berkeley: University of California Press.

Ionescu, Ghita (1976), *The Politics of the European communist states*. London: Wedenfeld and Nicholson.

Ionescu, Ghita (1984), *The Break-up of the Soviet Empire in Eastern Europe*. London, Penguin.

Janos, Andrew C (2000) *East Central Europe in the modern World. The Politics of the Borderlands from pre-to post-communism*, Stanford: Stanford University Press.

Jenkins, Richard, (1997), *Rethinking Ethnicity: Arguments and Explorations*, London: Sage.

Knight, Robert (2000), 'Ethnicity and Identity in the Cold War: The Carinthian Border Dispute, 1945–1949', *International History Review*, 22 (2), 274–303.

Kramer, Mark (2001), 'Introduction', in Philipp Ther and Ana Siljak (eds), *Redrawing Nations: Ethnic Cleansing in East-Central Europe, 1944–1948*. Lanham: Rowman and Littlefield.

Kürti, László and Juliet Langman (eds) (1997), *Beyond borders: Remaking cultural identities in the new East and Central Europe*. Boulder Co: Westview.

Kuznick, Peter J and James Gilbert eds (2002), *Rethinking Cold War Culture*. Washington, DC: Smithsonian Institution Press,

Kymlicka, Will (ed) (1995) *The Rights of Minority Cultures*, Oxford: Oxford University Press.

Latham, Michael (2000), *Modernization as Ideology. American Social Science and "Nation Building" in the Kennedy Era*. Chapel Hill: University of North Carolina Press.

Leffler, Melvyn (1992), *A Preponderance of Power: National Security, the Truman Administration, and the Cold War*. Stanford: Stanford University press

Leffler, Melvyn (2007), *For the Soul of Mankind: The United States, the Soviet Union, and the Cold War*. New York: Hill and Wang.

Leffler, Melvyn, and David S. Painter (eds) (2005), *The Origins of the Cold War: An International History*. London: Routledge.

Leffler, Melvyn and Odd Arne Westad (eds) (2010). *The Cambridge History of the Cold War*. (3 vols), Cambridge: Cambridge University Press.

Lendvai, Paul (1969), *Eagles in Cobwebs: Nationalism and Communism in the Balkans.* London: Macdonald.

Levy, Daniel and Julian Dierkes (2002), 'Nationhood in German legislation,' in Jan-Werner Müller (ed), *Memory and Power in Post-war Europe: Studies in the Presence of the Past,* Cambridge: Cambridge University Press.

Lewis, Jill, Gareth Pritchard and Eleanor Breuning (eds), (2005), *Power and the People: A Social History of Central European Politics.* Manchester: Manchester University Press.

Lijphart Arendt (1977), 'Political theories and the Explanation of Ethnic conflict in the Western World' in Milton Esman (ed), *Ethnic Conflict in the Western World,* Cornell: Cornell University Press.

McGarry, John and Brendan O'Leary, (1993), *The Politics of Ethnic Conflict: Case Studies of Protracted Ethnic Conflicts.* London-New York.

McMahon, Patrice (2006), 'Ethnic peace in the east: transnational networks and the CSCE/OSCE,' *Ethnopolitics,* 5 (2), 101–23.

Markovits, Andrei S. (2009), 'From Prague to America – Karl W. Deutsch between Experience and Knowledge', in Dan Diner and Moshe Zimmermann (eds), *Disseminating German Tradition: the Thyssen Lectures.* Leipzig: Leipziger Universitätsverlag, 101–22.

Mazower, Mark (1997), 'Minorities and the League of Nations in Interwar Europe,' *Daedelus,* 126 (2), 59–60.

Mazower, Mark (2004), 'The Strange Triumph of Human Rights 1933–1950', *The Historical Journal,* 47 (2), 379–89.

Mazower, Mark (2009), *Hitler's Empire; Nazi Rule in Occupied Europe,* London: Penguin.

Miller, David (1995), *On Nationality.* Oxford: Oxford University Press.

Milward, Alan, Ruggiero Ranieri, Vibeke Sørensen, Frances Lynch (1993), *The Frontier of National Sovereignty: History and Theory 1945–1992,* London: Routledge 1993.

Mitter, Rana and Major, Patrick (eds), (2004), *Across the Blocs: Cold War Cultural and Social History,* London: Taylor and Frances.

Morsink, Johannes (1999), *The Universal Declaration of Human Rights. Origins, Drafting and Intent.* Philadelphia: University of Pennsylvania Press.

Moynhihan, Daniel and Nathan Glazer, (1963), *Beyond the Melting Pot,* Cambridge, MA: MIT Press.

Moyniham, Daniel (1993), *Pandemonium: Ethnicity in International Politics,* Oxford: Oxford University Press.

Mueller, John (2001), 'The Banality of "Ethnic War"', in Michael Brown, Owen Cote, Seam Lynn-Jones and Steven Miller (eds), *Nationalism and Ethnic conflict* (revised edition), London: MIT Press, 97–125.

Müller Jan-Werner (ed) (2002), *Memory and Power in Post-war Europe: Studies in the Presence of the Past,* Cambridge: Cambridge University Press.

Müller-Rommel, Ferdinand (1998), 'Ethnoregionalist Parties in Western Europe: Theoretical Considerations and Framework of Analysis' in Lieven De Winter and Huri Türsan (eds), *Regionalist Parties in Western Europe,* London: Routledge, 17–27.

Naimark, Norman M. (2001), *Fires of Hatred: Ethnic Cleansing in Twentieth-Century Europe.* Cambridge, MA-London: Harvard University Press.

Nairn, Tom (1997), *Faces of Nationalism: Janus Revisited.* London: Verso.

Nashel, Jonathan (2000), 'Modernization Theory in Fact and Fiction', in Christian G. Appy (ed), *Cold War Constructions: The political Culture of United States Imperialism, 1945–1966.* Amehurst, MA: University of Massachusetts Press, 132–54.

Ninkovich, F (1981), *The Diplomacy of Ideas: US Foreign Policy and Cultural Relations 1938–1950.* Cambridge.

Novick, Peter (2001), *The Holocaust and Collective Memory: the American Experience,* London: Bloomsbury.

Offner, Arnold (2002), *Another Such Victory. President Truman and the Cold War 1945–1950,* Stanford.

Pittaway, Mark (2004), *Eastern Europe, 1929–2004.* London: Hodder Arnold.

Reynolds, David, *From World War to Cold War: Churchill, Roosevelt, and the International History of the 1940s.* Oxford: OUP, 2006.

Roberts, Adam (2010), 'An 'incredibly swift transition': reflections on the end of the Cold War', in Westad and Leffler, eds, *The Cambridge History of the Cold War,* (vol. 3), Cambridge: Cambridge University Press.

Robin, Ron, (2001), *The Making of the Cold War Enemy: Culture and Politics in the Military-Industrial Complex.* Princeton, NJ: Princeton University Press.

Rothschild, Joseph (1981), *Ethnopolitics: A conceptual framework.* New York: Columbia University Press.

Rothschild, Joseph and Nancy M. Wingfield (2008), *Return to Diversity: A political History of East Central Europe since World War II* (4th edn). New York-Oxford: Oxford University Press.

Rupnik, Jaques (1989), *The Other Europe* (revised edn), London: Weidenfeld and Nicolson.

Rustow, Dankwart A (1970), 'Communism and change', in Chalmers Johnson (ed), *Change in Communist systems.* Stanford, CA: Stanford University Press, 343–58.

Salzborn, Samuel (2005), *Ethnisierung der Politik: Theorie und Geschichte des Volksgruppenrechts in Europa.* Frankfurt am Main-New York: Campus.

Selverstone, Mark (2009), *Constructing the Monolith: the United States, Great Britain, and International Communism, 1945–1950.* Cambridge, MA: Harvard University Press.

Seton-Watson, Hugh, (1964), *Nationalism and Communism. Essays 1946–1965,* New York Praeger.

Sewell, Mike (2002), *The Cold War.* (Cambridge Perspectives in History), Cambridge: Cambridge University Press.

Shaw, Martin (1996), 'Global Society and Global Responsibility: the Theoretical, Historical and Political limits of "International Society', in Rick Fawn and J Larkins (eds), *International Society after the Cold War: Anarchy and Disorder reconsidered.* New York: St Martins.

Simpson, Christopher (ed) (1998), *Universities and Empire: Money and Politics in theSocial Sciences during the Cold War.* New York: New Press.

Sluga, Glenda, (2001), *The Problem of Trieste and the Italo–Yugoslav Border. Difference, Identity and Sovereignty in Twentieth Century Europe*. New York: SUNY Press.

Smith, Anthony (1981), *The Ethnic Revival in the Modern World*. Cambridge: Cambridge University Press.

Smith, Anthony (1993), 'Causes and implications of Ethnic Conflict,' in Michael Brown (ed), *Ethnic conflict and International Security*, Princeton: Princeton University Press, 3–41.

Smith, Tony (2000), *Foreign Attachments: the Power of Ethnic Groups in the Making of American Foreign Policy*, Cambridge, MA: Harvard University Press.

Smith, Tony (1994), *America's mission, the United States' struggle for democracy in the twentieth Century*. New Jersey: Princeton University Press.

Stargardt, Nicholas (1996), 'Gellner's Nationalism: the Spirit of Modernisation?', in John Hall and Ian Jarvie (eds), *The Social Philosophy of Ernst Gellner*, Amsterdam-Atlanta, GA: Rodopi.

Stöver, Bernd (2002), *Die Befreiung vom Kommunismus: Amerikanische Liberation Policy im Kalten Krieg. 1947–1991*. Cologne: Böhlau.

Stråth, Bo (ed) (2010), *Europe and the Other and Europe as the Other*. Frankfurt am Main: Peter Lang.

Sugar, Peter (ed), (1980), *Ethnic diversity and Conflict in Eastern Europe*, Santa Barbara, CA: Clio.

Ther, Philipp and Ana Siljak (eds) (2001), *Redrawing Nations: Ethnic Cleansing in East-Central Europe, 1944–1948*. Lanham, MD: Rowman and Littlefied.

van Dyke, Vernon (1979), 'The Individual, the State and Ethnic Communities in Political Theory', in Donald P Kommers and Gilbert D Loescher (eds), *Human Rights and American Foreign Policy*. London: University of Notre Dame Press, 36–62.

Waltz, Kenneth (1979), *Theory of International Politics*. New York: McGraw Hill.

Walzer, Michael Edward T. Kantowicz, John Higham and Mona Harrington, (1982) *The Politics of Ethnicity*. Cambridge, MA: Harvard University Press, 1982.

Weldes, Jutta, Mark Laffey, Hugh Gusterson and Raymond Duvall (eds) (1999), *Cultures of Insecurity: States, Communities, and the Production of Danger*. Minneapolis: University of Minnesota Press.

Westad Odd Arne (ed) (2000), *Reviewing the Cold War. Approaches, Interpretations, Theory*. London: Routledge.

Westad, Odd Arne (2010), 'The Cold War and the international history of the twentieth century,' in Westad and Leffler (eds), *Cambridge History of the Cold War* (vol 1). Cambridge: Cambridge University Press.

Wittner, Lawrence, (1982), *American Intervention in Greece 1943–1949*. New York: Columbia University Press.

Zake, Ieva, (ed) (2009) *Anti-communist minorities in the US: Political Activism of Ethnic Refugees*. New York: Palgrave-Macmillan.

Chapter 2

Re-thinking Ethnicity and the Origins of the Cold War: The Austrian–Hungarian Borderlands

Mark Pittaway

Following the deportations of ethnic German residents from the city of Sopron and its surrounding villages in April 1946, a small number of those so identified were allowed to remain. Their continued presence in village communities that often lay little more than a thirty minute walk from Hungary's border with Austria attracted the ire of the Hungarian Communist Party (*Magyar Kommunista Párt*/MKP), and the recently constituted Hungarian State Police that they effectively controlled. This ire was heightened by the paranoia prevailing within the MKP about its relative isolation from a largely hostile local society. This combined with the growing polarization between supporters of the MKP and its opponents, the centre-right Independent Smallholders' Party (*Független Kisgazda Párt/FGKP*), who had won an overwhelming victory in the parliamentary elections of November 1945. Determined to continue their project of building a political system centred around the MKP, the communists divided the population into supporters and enemies of the political system they were seeking to create.[1]

The police's treatment of ethnic Germans in the borderland around Sopron sheds important light on the way ethnic constructions became implicated in the state-led division of Hungarian society. In December 1946, the local police, supported by border guard troops, raided houses in the village of Fertőrákos searching for evidence of smuggling. The raids, which were accompanied by considerable brutality on the part of both police and border guards, were part of a calculated campaign of harassment against the ethnic German population. Those woken by the authorities in the early hours of the morning were warned 'in a humiliating fashion' that they were considered politically suspect. One resident was dragged from his bed by the border guard troops at 3.30 a.m. and taken to the village school, where a senior police officer demanded to know why he had 'a moustache like Hitler'.[2] Another faced demands to show the border guard troops where he was hiding his 'machine gun' as part of an attempt to find evidence of German preparations for an armed rebellion.[3]

Showing that they suspected that ethnic Germans harboured National Socialist sympathies, or were preparing an armed uprising against the Hungarian state, the raiders also accused them of being engaged in cross-border smuggling. Given the continuing poor living standards of Hungary's urban population, and the memories of hyper-inflation (which had continued until the currency reform of August 1946), the spectre of 'speculators' was conveniently linked by the MKP to the different political opponents of the new order in order to mobilize their limited support base within the industrial working class and rural poor. Those raiding the homes in Fertőrákos were determined to link ethnic Germans to smuggling and speculation and they confiscated almost everything not bolted to the floors of the houses to back up the charge. One family was subject to the confiscation of 'one pair of children's shoes, one pair of girl's baby shoes, two pairs of children's stockings, three metres of woven cloth, two hundred and fifty grams of salt and six hundred Schillings.' Even though they were legally owned, they could be used to label the family as 'speculators'.[4] The raids can also be interpreted as part of the process of separation of ethnic German communities from the broader Hungarian society of which they were part. In this way, they underpinned the expulsions and were central in establishing the social roots of Hungary's socialist dictatorship in ethnically mixed regions.[5] On the other side of the border, the expulsions also played a fundamental role in the reconstruction of provincial identities in the Austrian province of Burgenland. In 1949, the social logic of separation which they generated between the Austrian and Hungarian

components of the borderland culminated in the effective closure of
the international border.[6] The political legacy of this local separation
process was the background for the tension which residents on both
sides of closed border experienced until the summer of 1956, when
the physical border between the two countries was temporary
dismantled. But the brief thaw of the summer of 1956, which was
abruptly terminated by the outbreak and subsequent suppression of
the Hungarian revolution, led to a renewal of mistrust between
Budapest and Vienna.[7]

In the past decade-and-a-half, there has been an explosion of
historical research and writing about post-war expulsions. Often
inspired by the 'myth of ethnic war' that dominated interpretations
of the conflicts between Yugoslavia's successor states,[8] this literature
has equated the process of post-war expulsion with the ethnic
cleansing that characterized those conflicts, and sometimes broader,
and more serious patterns of the twentieth-century genocide. Married
to this is an interest in issues of nationalism and nation-state building,
in which post-war expulsion has been seen as part of a process of
completing the creation of 'perfectly formed' nation-states in Central
Europe.[9] While there is much to say in criticism of the misplaced
assumptions of some of this literature, here it is sufficient to note
first, that – save for a few honourable exceptions – the early post-war
and Cold War political contexts of the expulsion process and its
consequences have been neglected.[10] Second, the literature has
privileged perspectives from nationalism studies, which rarely
concede the notion that nationalism plays different and sometimes
contradictory roles within different political cultures, and that nation-
building across Europe has been an incomplete and discontinuous
process. Third and perhaps most seriously, it essentializes ethnic
identities, and fails to account for their constructed, discontinuous
and contradictory natures. As Rogers Brubaker and his colleagues
put it in their study of the attempts to mobilize ethnic identities in
the Transylvanian city of Cluj in the mid-1990s, few scholars of ethnic
conflict have asked the 'basic questions about ethnicity: where it is,
when it matters, and how it works.'[11] In relation to the politics of the
early Cold War that suggests that instead of seeing events like post-
war expulsions as ethnic conflict pure and simple, we need to examine

how ethnic identities were implicated, constructed and deployed within the scope of broader political conflicts. If we adopt this approach and take the questions that follow from it seriously, we can begin to ask how far ethnicity played a role in the Cold War.

We also need to de-centre some of our understanding of Cold War politics. In Europe, these have been largely determined by the way in which the military outcome of war meant the constraining of the juridical and practical sovereignty of European states, initially by the four victorious powers, and then increasingly by the ever more powerful superpowers. While most writing on the Cold War has concentrated on this post-war political dynamic of politics, less attention has been paid to the way in which local conflicts, both within and between states, persisted across the historical watershed of 1945, and reproduced themselves in a variety of ways, according to post-war circumstances.[12] Often our grasp of this aspect of the post-war settlement has been obscured by the hegemonic notion of the twentieth century as a century of 'two halves'.[13] Instead, we need to see that the dynamics of the Cold War politics arose from the mutual influence of the local, the national and the international.[14] This also means that when considering the early post-war period, we need to pay more attention to the ways in which ethnicity was politicized in the preceding period.

Before 1918, the border region under discussion here – consisting of northern Burgenland in Austria and the counties of Győr-Moson and Sopron in Hungary – had formed a unified region. It constituted a wealthy agricultural region within Hungary whose products went not just to Vienna, but also to industrial centres in Wiener Neustadt, Pozsony/Bratislava, and Győr. It was also ethnically diverse: on the eve of World War I, 46 per cent of the population were German, 43 per cent were Magyar, while a further 10 per cent were Croatian.[15] Political polarization after World War I was linked to ethnic polarization between Germans and Magyars, and resulted in the incorporation of the western parts of the region into Austria, as the province of Burgenland. What had been an advanced agricultural region of Hungary found itself in the inter-war years with an economically and politically peripheral status. At the same time its multiethnic population and many of its public institutions, shaped by Hungarian rule, marked it out from the rest of Austria.[16] The territories left on the Hungarian side, especially Sopron, the principal city, were severed from the markets centred on Vienna and plunged into economic crisis. They attempted to compensate – with mixed success – by emphasizing their political loyalty to Budapest.[17] Austria's incorporation into Germany in 1938 and the onset of war changed the situation. Though Burgenland disappeared as a political unit, it was treated by Berlin as a distinctive space that could serve as a bridge between the National Socialist regime and the ethnic German minority in Hungary. Radical racist measures decimated Burgenland's Jewish and Roma populations, while in Hungary, the growing prestige of radical right-wing ideas among the population led the state to respond with anti-semitic measures. It also forced national and local authorities to fight a rearguard action against a German minority, which radicalized under the influence of Berlin, as the country became increasingly entangled in the war. Throughout the war years, interaction between the German and Hungarian sides of the border remained intense and the frontier was porous. It was only the popular experiences of the end of the war which initiated the dynamic of separation.[18]

Expulsion was a fundamental part of this dynamic. The politicization of the German minority in Sopron and Moson had produced sporadic political conflict between Magyar nationalists and local members of the *Volksbund* – the pro-Berlin organization of the German minority. This culminated in 1942 in serious tensions and violence between nationalist Magyar students (supported tacitly by the authorities) and *Volksbund* students during recruitment drives by the Waffen SS.[19] However, the depth of this conflict should not be exaggerated. Ethnic identities in Hungary's western borderland were fluid. The published results of the 1941 census recorded that 719,762 or 4.9 per cent of Hungary's population identified themselves as German speakers – although it is worth mentioning that these figures were strongly contested by the political representatives of the German minority.[20] In many western border districts the proportions were higher – in Győr-Moson county, 37.2 percent of the population declared themselves German speakers, in Sopron the figure was 39.3 percent, while in the cities of Mosonmagyaróvár and Sopron, the figures were 29.9 and 12.7 per cent, respectively.[21] Many ethnic Germans had a 'dual' Magyar and German identity, with German often functioning as a local language, rarely used beyond the boundaries of home villages, while kinship and friendship ties often transcended the ambiguous ethnic divide.[22] It is also important to note that ethnic German identity did not necessarily mean sympathy for Germany's political goals; *Volksbund* organizations only ever operated in twenty-five villages in Győr-Moson and Sopron counties.[23] Furthermore, the patterns of support for Berlin in communities where ethnic German identities were strong, displayed remarkable similarities with those among Magyars for the Arrow Cross. It had increased its support and prestige during the late 1930s, in reaction to the virtual elimination of unemployment after Austria's incorporation into Germany.[24] But its support collapsed after 1942 as the costs of participation in the war became clearer.[25]

All this suggests that while there was clearly a pre-history to the political mobilization of ethnic identities at the end of the war, we should be wary of tracing an unproblematic or direct link between these earlier conflicts and the confused expulsion drives of 1945–48. Expulsion was the project of a state that was suffering from confusion about goals and facing considerable difficulties in implementing them because of the fluidity of ethnic identities and the sporadic nature of political conflict. Rather than being a successful case of the mobilization of ethnic difference in support of state-builders, and especially the MKP, it proved deeply unpopular among most of the population, and in the western borderland, it actually undermined the legitimacy of the 'new' state. In large part, the difficulty stemmed from confusion as to whether the state intended to hold all those identified as ethnic Germans collectively responsible for the tragedy of World War II, or whether it was more interested in anti-fascist retribution against those who had supported Berlin and collaborated directly with the German occupation. This confusion in turn was the legacy of the ambiguous attitude of the Hungarian state towards its national minorities. Since 1867, Hungarian governments had sought to strengthen the Magyar nature of the state – a process that intensified following the shock of the Treaty of Trianon, but it was always legally and ideologically possible to be both a loyal Hungarian citizen and to preserve one's separate language and cultural autonomy.[26] This ambiguity had been used by local representatives of the Hungarian state in the Sopron and Moson regions to beat back the challenge of the *Volksbund*. They had intimidated those who co-operated with or joined the *Volksbund* with accusations of 'political disloyalty', while still maintaining that those who demonstrated loyalty to Hungary by supporting the governing party, and state-sponsored cultural organizations, were free to use their native language and celebrate their ethnicity.[27]

This practice influenced the ways in which local authorities were asked to draw up their lists of candidates for expulsion after the arrival of Soviet troops in April and May 1945. The state asked local authorities for lists of residents who were 'German citizens', had 'lost German citizenship by virtue of taking on Hungarian citizenship,' had 'volunteered for military service in the *Waffen SS*' or had been 'members of the Volksbund'. Those who spoke German as a first language, but had remained 'loyal to Hungary' were exempt. Thus, while much propaganda proclaimed that Hungary's Germans were to be held 'collectively responsible' as an ethnic group, actual practice stressed politically 'fascist' behaviour, or perceived 'disloyalty' to the Hungarian state as the criteria for removal.[28] The confusion that resulted could be manipulated by residents and the local authorities; a strategy that was strengthened by the fluidity of ethnic identities. In Kópháza, a predominantly ethnically Croatian village south-east of Sopron, adjacent to the border with Austria, the local notary maintained that of the eleven German citizens living in the village, nine were of Croatian ethnicity, two were ethnically Magyar, and none ethnically German! He argued furthermore that none 'had fascist sympathies' and, by implication, should not have their property confiscated or be marked for expulsion.[29]

There was also arbitrariness in the criteria used to draw up the lists. One example was the way Austrian citizens were dealt with; while arguing that Austrian citizens could not be regarded automatically as German citizens, the authorities also had to 'pay attention to' Austria's 'true relationship to the German Reich, which had existed over several years', a euphemism for almost automatically classifying Austrian citizens as Germans.[30] Similar practices were deployed by local authorities to classify those minors who had formally been citizens of the 'Protectorate of Bohemia-Moravia' as Germans, even where their ethnicity was identified as Czech, and to mark them for expulsion on the lists.[31] Arbitrary practice in drawing up expulsion lists was re-inforced by the destruction of documentary evidence about political behaviour in the days before the Red Army arrived. In Ágfalva the notary admitted that his list had been drawn up on his personal view of who the 'Germans' in the village were and not on the basis any documentary evidence; it had also contained the names of some he believed to be patriotic Hungarians.[32]

The way ethnic identities were implicated in what was essentially an act of collective political retribution was often contradictory. These contradictions frustrated both the disorganized expulsion efforts in 1945 and the organized deportations of spring 1946. Frustration among the MKP and its supporters grew. Raids like that in Fertőrákos, described above, were an attempt to bridge some of the contradictions of the expulsion process. The outcomes of the raids could be manipulated in order to shape propaganda that Germans as an 'ethnic group' were the enemy, thereby supporting arguments for continuing the expulsions.[33]

Contradictions can also be seen in responses to the expulsion process just over the border in northern Burgenland. In these communities it played a crucial role in the reconstruction of Austrian national, and Burgenland provincial identities. In this way helped define the process of social separation between. the two sides of the border at the start of the Cold War. At first sight, however, this process was far from an obvious one, and revealed the complex entanglement of different identities in a fluid political situation, and the international constraints of four-power occupation. The newly restored Austrian state defined itself against Germany, in ways that went much further than mere rhetoric. In spring 1945, the provisional government in Vienna instructed districts to separate residents into 'Austrians' and those it termed 'Germans who came from the Reich' (*Reichsdeutschen*) as a prelude to their removal from Austrian soil.[34] In 1946 local authorities faced a steady stream of appeals from female Austrian partners married to German citizens, who discovered that they were denied Austrian citizenship because of their marital status, and faced deportation to Germany.[35]

Post-war constructions of 'Austrianness' did not merely demarcate Austria and Germany they also celebrated provincial identities.[36] In the case of the borderland, this meant that Austrian identity was closely tied to the identity of the province of Burgenland. The province had been carved out of Hungary at the end of the First World War, after its German minority demanded that it be ruled by Vienna, rather than Budapest. Owing its origin in part to a political project of ethnic Germans within the pre-war Kingdom of Hungary, the predominant versions of its provincial identity in the inter-war years had claimed that it had a fundamental kinship to those western Hungarian counties populated by German speakers.[37] Pan-German nationalists dreamed of the territorial extension of the province. While the province was divided after Austria's incorporation into Germany, between the *Gaue* of Lower Donau (Niederdonau) and Styria, Burgenland's own Nazis had argued - against Berlin - that their province should become a *Gau* in its own right within the expanded Reich, because of its a distinctive 'mission' as a 'borderland' (*Grenzland*) acting as a bridge between Germany, and German speakers in Hungary.[38] Berlin's only concession to this pro-Burgenland sentiment was to establish a Nationality Groups Office (*Volkstumstelle*) in the former capital of Eisenstadt. Its task was to supervise the territories' ethnic minorities, and maintain close contact with pro-Berlin, ethnic German activists in the neighbouring city of Sopron.[39]

The post-war context was less than favourable for a revival of these ideas of Burgenland identity, precisely at the time the Hungarian state was engaged in a campaign for the expulsion of the German minority. The waves which followed between 1945 and 1946 generally, and especially the deportation of 1946, played a fundamental role in the construction of Burgenland and, by extension, Austrian identities in the region and shaped perceptions of the Hungarian neighbour that strengthened the authority and legitimacy of the Austrian state. In border villages, where ties of kin often spread into villages on the Hungarian side, the expulsions provoked particular outrage. When ethnic Germans returned home to north-western Hungarian villages like Magyarkimle in late 1945 to find their homes and land had been re-distributed to settlers, they launched an armed uprising with the goal of re-claiming their property, using flight over the border, and networks of solidarity with kin on the Austrian side, to sustain their fight. Although they were beaten back by the armed police who then flooded the region, both Budapest and its local representatives remained worried at their lack of control.[40]

Public opinion, the political parties, opinion formers and even officials in the Burgenland government responded to Hungarian violence against borderland Germans by claiming them as 'Austrians' and arguing that the lands they inhabited were, in fact, eastern Burgenland. This adaptation of earlier pan-German arguments to post-war circumstances sought to differentiate Hungary's German speakers from Germans proper, and underline their kinship to 'Austrians' living on the Burgenland side of the border. In the words of one opponent of expulsion, used by Burgenland officials to make the case against Hungary, 'Hungary's German speakers refer to themselves as *n* Donau Swabians [*Donauschwaben*] and Heathland farmers [*Heidebauern*] and are so known by the Hungarians; they know nothing of Germany.' These officials of the Burgenland government also lobbied Vienna to intervene with the occupying powers – especially the Red Army – against the expulsions, on the grounds that ethnic Germans settled right on the border 'can be seen as good Austrians'.[41] Others argued for a solution that allowed for the Moson and Sopron districts closest to the border to be removed from Hungary and incorporated into Burgenland.[42]

Neither the Hungarian state nor the left-wing parties who most enthusiastically supported expulsion were prepared to make any concession to calls for the exemption of borderland German speakers on grounds of their 'Austrianness'. Aware of calls in the Burgenland press for a re-drawing of the border, the Hungarian police rounded up five ethnic Germans for spreading pro-Austrian propaganda in Sopron early in 1946. In a political trial designed to serve as a warning to authorities across the border, prosecutors accused them of conspiring with leading Burgenland politicians to launch an armed uprising in Hungary aimed at securing territorial changes. The barely concealed aim of this show trial was to warn Vienna to restrain the Burgenland administration. Vienna, worried that the Hungarian authorities might complain effectively to the Soviet military administration, complied.[43] Early in 1946 the Hungarian state prepared for the organized deportation of most of those it identified as Hungary's ethnic Germans to Germany. The MKP press in western Hungary celebrated what it believed would be the end of the tension generated by the more generalized expulsion efforts, it had organized since spring 1945: 'The time is coming fast, when we will be able to start deporting the Hungarian Swabians'.[44]

In spring 1946 the MKP-controlled Ministry of the Interior pressed ahead ever more ruthlessly with deportation with deportation. Aware of the possibility for manipulation, they attempted to scrap the local lists prepared a year earlier and draw up their own, but these were still mired in the same contradictions about who was to be expelled and why. Furthermore the implementation was heavy-handed. In Sopron, 300 policemen were imported from outside the region in order to ensure that order was kept during the process.[45] As the lists were prepared over the Easter weekend the city was sealed from the outside world, the serving of alcohol was banned in local restaurants, and a night-time curfew enforced.[46] The police hunted down those on the list who were in hiding; during one night-time raid in early May 1946 almost 80 per cent of the city's houses were searched.[47]

The 1946 deportations were a demonstration of arbitrary state power. The impression of a despotic state it left created a real fear that transcended the ethnic divide. The sight of deportees being rounded up and placed on cattle-trucks recalled popular memories of the deportation of local Jews in 1944. In Moson magyaróvár, the local organ of the left-wing Social Democratic Party, normally supportive of the MKP, reflected a commonly held opinion when it equated the removal of Germans with the events of two years earlier: Expulsion . . . . two years ago it was called deportation.[48] Reactions to expulsion therefore reflected the way it demonstrated the power and will of the state to act against the civilian population. Despotism weakened the state's legitimacy and its institutions found that as a consequence the willingness of the population to co-operate with them weakened. For example the MKP mayor of Moson magyaróvár complained in April 1946 that the deportations were having a corrosive effect on the political authority of the organs of the new state in his city.[49]

Faced with the threat of deportation from Moson or Sopron to Freilassing in southern Bavaria in 1946, many fled over the border,

with the intention of returning at a later date.[50] To pre-empt
confiscations some took their property with them.[51] When they
reached the Austrian side of the border these 'German' refugees
were met with sympathy from the population. Furthermore the
'settlers' who had taken their homes and property were unpopular,
and were blamed in border villages like Nickelsdorf and Zurndorf for
cross-border crime.[52] Minor officials showed similar sympathy for the
plight of the refugees, granting border passes (in contravention of
the regulations) so that they could return to Hungary to visit relatives
and provoking the fury of the Hungarian authorities.[53] This sympathy
and the belief that those expelled were of 'Austrian character'
provoked a relaxation of both work permit and citizenship regulations
that made it easier for them to claim Austrian citizenship.[54]

Overall the deportations created a dynamic of mutual suspicion on
both sides of the border which drove the process of separation. While
in Austria they led many to see the state beyond the border as
threatening, and generated considerable local sympathy for refugees,
in Hungary these reactions helped foster a climate of suspicion. Both
the local and national state saw the relatively open border as an active
threat to the country's security. This was reinforced by the apparent
attempts of deportees to return home. In one of several such incidents,
police were called Fertőrákos in March 1947 after five former residents
returned from Austria in order to re-settle and take back the property
that had been confiscated from them and re-distributed to new
settlers.[55] The border also played a central role in the Hungarian
left's politics of economic security. During 1947 the MKP smashed
the Small-holders Party by using the police to cement its control of
the popular front coalition and thus prepare the ground for the
construction of communist dictatorship. A vital part of this campaign
was the mobilization of industrial workers and the poor, by putting
the blame for their poor material situation, persistent high prices,
and the food shortages, on 'speculators' and 'the reaction'.[56]
'Germans' who had escaped deportation were often blamed for
'smuggling' and 'speculation' and these accusations were then used
to justify further confiscation of property and expulsion in 1948.[57]

The deterioration of cross-border relations and the politicization of
smuggling continued as the dictatorship became overt in 1948 and

1949. With opponents of the emerging regime fleeing in large numbers and Hungary gripped by Cold War paranoia, 'Germans' returning to Hungary and Austrian smugglers were labelled 'spies' and 'enemies' against whom Hungary's western border needed to be secured. One piece of propaganda of this kind in March reported that

> the cells in the Moson Magyaróvár police station were full yesterday of illegal border crossers. Horse and livestock traders, ethnic Germans [*svábo*] seeking to return, German and Austrian citizen after food and escaping fascists waited out the afternoon.[58]

Budapest implemented a scheme that involved the physical closure of the border, the creation of barbed wire fences separating the two countries, the construction of a network of watch-towers, and the clearing of all land of vegetation within five hundred metres of the border.[59] When it demanded that Austria create a similar zone on its side of the border, and Vienna refused, Hungary retaliated by closing the border to all Austrian farmers with properties on their side, causing furious reactions in Burgenland border villages.[60] The Iron Curtain was in place.

Notes

[1] For a discussion of this process in Hungary as a whole, see Mark Pittaway, 'The Politics of Legitimacy and Hungary's Postwar Transition', *Contemporary European History*, 13 (4), (2004), 453–75. For western Hungary, see Mark Pittaway, 'Making Peace in the Shadow of War: the Austrian–Hungarian Borderlands, 1945–1956', *Contemporary European History*, 17 (3), (2008), 345–64.

[2] Sopron Archive of Győr–Moson–Sopron County (Győr-Moson-Sopron Megye Soproni Levéltára/GyMSM). Papers of the Chief Notary of the Sopron District (Soproni járás főjegyzőjének iratai) (XXI/21)/15d., Jegyzőkönyv felvéve folytatólagosan 1946. évi december hó 10.-én a községi jegyzői irodában, 1.

[3] GyMSM.SL, XXI/21/15d., Jegyzőkönyv felvéve folytatólagosan 1946. évi December hó 10.-én a községi jegyzői irodában, 2.

[4] GyMSM.SL, XXI/21/15d., Jegyzőkönyv felvéve folytatólagosan 1946. évi December hó 10.-én a községi jegyzői irodában, 2.

[5] Ágnes Tóth, *Migrationen in Ungarn, 1945–1948. Vertreibung der Ungarndeutschen, Binnenwanderungen und Slowakisch-Ungarischer Bevölkerungsaustausch* (trans. Rita Fejér), Munich: Oldenbourg, 2001; András Kirsch, *A Soproni németek kitelepítése 1946*, Sopron: Escort Kiadó, 2006.

6 Pittaway, Making Peace.

7 Mark Pittaway, 'Challenging and Confirming Europe's Cold War Divide: The 1956 Revolution and the Austrian–Hungarian Borderland', *http://oro.open. ac.uk/20178/1/bordersceharticle.pdf* [accessed 3 June 2011].

8 V.P. Gagnon, Jr., *The Myth of Ethnic War. Serbia and Croatia in the 1990s*, Ithaca, NY-London: Cornell University Press, 2004.

9 Norman M. Naimark, *Fires of Hatred. Ethnic Cleansing in Twentieth-Century Europe*, Cambridge MA: Harvard University Press, 2001.

10 For an honourable exception see Pertti Ahonen, *After the Expulsion. West Germany and Eastern Europe, 1945–1990*, Oxford-New York: Oxford University Press, 2003.

11 Rogers Brubaker, Margit Feischmidt, Jon Fox and Liana Grancea, *Nationalist Politics and Everyday Ethnicity in a Transylvanian Town*, Princeton, NJ: Princeton University Press, 2006, 7.

12 Mark Pittaway, with Hans Fredrik-Dahl, 'Legitimacy and the Making of the Post-War Order', in Martin Conway and Peter Romijn (eds), *The War for Legitimacy in Politics and Culture, 1936–1946*, Oxford & New York: Berg, 2008, 177–209.

13 Ian Kershaw, 'Europe's Second Thirty Years War', *History Today*, 55 (9), (2005), 10–17.

14 Melvyn P. Leffler and David S. Painter, (eds), *The Origins of the Cold War. An International History* (2nd edn), London-New York: Routledge, 2005.

15 Mariann Nagy, 'Magyarország mezőgazdasága a 20. század elején', in Pál Beluszky, (ed), *Magyarország történeti földrajza I kötet*, Pécs, & Budapest: Dialóg Campus, 2005, 372–8; Sándor Békesi, *Verklärt und Verachtet. Wahrnehmungsgeschicte einer Landschaft: der Neusiedler See*, Frankfurt am Main: Peter Lang, 2007, 139–56.

16 August Ernst, *Geschichte des Burgenlandes*, (2nd edn), Vienna-Munich: Verlag für Geschichte und Politik, & R. Oldenbourg Verlag, 1991, 186–214; Gerald Schlag *Aus Trümmern Geboren. . . . Burgenland 1918–1921*, Eisenstadt: Amt der burgenländischen Landesregierung, 2001; Peter Haslinger, 'Building a Regional Identity: The Burgenland, 1921–1938', *Austrian History Yearbook*, 23 (2001), 105–23.

17 Imre Tóth, 'Aktuális Sopron-képek a XX. században. A hatalom és a város viszonya 1921-től 2001-ig', in Éva Turbuly (ed), *A város Térben és időben. Sopron kapcsolatrendszerének változásai. Konferencia Sopron szabad királyi város 725 évéről*, Sopron: Győr-Moson-Sopron Megye Soproni Levéltára, 2002, 203–22.

18 Mark Pittaway, 'Confronting War and Facing Defeat in the Austrian–Hungarian Borderland, 1938–1945', (unpublished paper, American Association for the Advancement of Slavic Studies, 2007).

19 Federal Archive (Bundesarchiv/BA), Berlin-Lichterfelde, hereafter, BA, NS19/1529, 126–31; István Hiller, *A soproni egyetemi hallgatók mozgalmai a két világháború között, 1919–1945*, Sopron: Soproni Szemle Kiadványai, 1975, 190–4.

20 Günter Schödl, 'Lange Abschiede: Die Südostdeutschen und ihre Vaterländer (1918–1945', in Günter Schödl, (ed), *Deutsche Geschichte im Osten Europas. Land an der Donau*, Berlin: Siedler, 1995, 520.

²¹ Az 1941 évi népszámlalás községek szerint, Budapest: Stephaneum Nyomda, 1947, 536–8, 602–3.

²² This point is made for another part of Hungary by the ethnographer Györgyi Bindorffer in *Kettős Identitás: Etnikai és nemzeti azonosságtudat Dunabogdányban* Budapest: Új Mandátum Könyvkiadó – MTA Kisebbségkutató Intézet, 2001.

²³ György Zielbauer, *Adatok és tények a magyarországi németség történetéből (1945–1949)*, Budapest: Akadémiai Kiadó, 1989, 16.

²⁴ For the *Volksbund*, see GyMSM.SL., Papers of the Chief Magistrate of the Csepreg District (Csepregi járás főszolgabírájának iratai), IV.B.417/114d., I. Csepregi járás; on the Arrow Cross, see Mark Pittaway, 'Hungary', in R.J.B. Bosworth (ed), *The Oxford Handbook of Fascism*, Oxford-New York: Oxford University Press, 2009, 380–97.

²⁵ GyMSM.SL, XXI/21/a, 1d., Ágfalvai jegyzőtől. Hiv.szám 2/1945.Eln., Ágfalva, 1945. május 28.-én.

²⁶ Sándor Balogh, 'A nemzetiségi politika másfél évszázada a jogszabályok tükrében', in Sándor Balogh and Levente Sipos (eds), *A Magyar Állam és a nemzetiségek. A magyarországi nemzetiségi kérdés történetének jogforrásai, 1848–1993*, Budapest: Napvilág Kiadó, 2002, 5–27.

²⁷ BA, R1501/3333, 110–6.

²⁸ Comprehensive lists for the Sopron district are contained in GyMSM.SL, XXI/21/a, 1d.

²⁹ GyMSM.SL, XXI/21/a, 1d., Kópháza község. Kimutatás a német állampolgárokról. Kópháza, 1945. máj. 4-én

³⁰ GyMSM.SL, XXI/21/b, 4d., 1066/1945, KEOKH. Szám: 25/162.VII.e.1945. eln., Másolat.

³¹ GyMSM.SL, XXI/21/a, 1d., Kimutatás az Ágfalván lakó német állampolgárokról.

³² GyMSM.SL, XXI/21/a, 1d., Ágfalvai jegyzőtől. Hiv.szám 2/1945.Eln., Ágfalva, 1945. május 28.-én.

³³ 'Több visszaszökött SS-legényt fogott el az államvédelmi rendőrség', *Soproni Újság* (28 March 1947), 2.

³⁴ Lower Austrian Provincial Archive (Niederösterreichisches Landesarchiv, St. Pölten/ NÖLA, St.P.), Lower Austrian Governor's Office (Landeshauptmannschaft Niederösterreich) (Ia-10) /B.nm.208/Stammzahl 29/bis ONv.74/1945, Bezirkshautmannschaft (BH) Scheibbs. Zl.XI-55/: Behandlung der Flüchtlinge und Ausländer, Scheibbs, 20 June 1945.

³⁵ BH Eisenstadt, II-1946, Bezirkshauptmannschaft Eisenstadt. Zl. II-86–46, Eisenstadt, 24 January 1946, Burgenland Provincial Archives/Burgenländisches Landesarchiv (BgLA).

³⁶ Robert Kreichbaumer, 'Einleitung', in Robert Kreichbaumer (ed), *Liebe auf den Zweiten Blick. Landes- und Österreichbewußtsein nach 1945*, Wien: Böhlau, 1998, 7–13.

³⁷ Alfons Barb, 'Der Burgenländer', in Elisabeth Bockhorn, Olaf Bockhorn, and Veronika Plöckinger (eds), *'Die Geburt des Burgenländers' Ein Lesebuch zur Historischen Volkskultur im Burgenland,* (Wissenschaftliche Arbeiten aus dem Burgenland, vol. 111), Eisenstadt: Amt der Burgendländischen Landesregierung, 2004, 83–9.

38 Dokumentationsarchiv des Österreichischen Widerstandes (DÖW) Vienna, 11498.

39 Austrian State Archive, Archive of the Republic, (Österreichisches Staatsarchiv, Archiv der Republik/ÖStA, AdR), Commissar for the Reunification of Austria with the German Empire/Reichskommissar für die Wiedervereinigung Österreichs mit dem Deutschen Reich (Bürckel Materie), Zl.2770, Kt.83, 37.

40 Győr Archive of Győr-Moson-Sopron County (Győr-Moson-Sopron Megye Győri Levéltára /GyMSMGyL), Győr-Moson megye és Győr thj. város főispánja (Papers of the Prefect of Győr-Moson County and the City of Győr, (XXIf.1) b.5d., Kedves Medei képviselő elvtárs!

41 ÖStA/AdR, Federal Ministry of Foreign Affairs, (Bundesministerium für Auswärtige Angelegenheiten/BMfAA), II-Pol, Gz.110.054-pol/46, Z.110.394-pol/46.

42 ÖStA/AdR, BMfAA, II-Pol, Gz.110.054-pol./46, Z.42.072-pol./46.

43 DÖW, 20000/j5, Vom Volksgericht in Győr. Zahl:Nb.859/1946/13; ÖStA, AdR, BMfAA, II-Pol/Ungarn 9, Gz.105.319-pol/47, Z.108.721-pol./1947.

44 'A mosoni svábok milliós értékeket lopnak ki a határon túlra', *Dunántúli Szabad Nép* (11 January 1946), 3.

45 'A hét végéig 420 kitelepítési tisztviselő és alkalmazott számára kell helyet biztositani magánlakásokban', *Soproni Újság* (12 April 1946), 3.

46 'A polgármesterhelyettes nyilatkozata a kitelepítésre kerülők névsoráról', *Soproni Újság* (25 April 1946), 3.

47 'Razzián a 'mozgási korlátozás' ideje alatt', *Soproni Újság* (5 May 1946), 3.

48 'Akiket elvittek, és akik itt maradtak', *Mosonmagyaróvári Barátság* (2 June 1946), 2.

49 GyMSMGy.L, .XXIf.1b.5.d, Mosonmagyaróvár megyei város polgármesterétől. Jelentés, 1946 április hóról.

50 GyMSMGy.L.XXIf.1b.5d.; Mosonmagyaróvár megyei város polgármesterétől. Jelentés, 1946 május hóról.

51 BgLA BH Mattersburg, XI-Situationsberichte, Grenzgendarmeriekommandos Schattendorf, April 1946.

52 Situationsbericht für März 1947, Neusiedl am See, 30 March 1947, BgLA, A/VII-II/II-1, Zahl: Präs.2/27–1947.

53 ÖStA/AdR, BMfAA, III-Wpol/Grenzen 2 Ungarn, Gz.120.025-W/Pol/47, Z.121.000-W/Pol/47.

54 BH Mattersburg, XI-Polizei, Arbeitsamt Burgenland. Eisenstadt, 15 June 1948, BgLA.

55 'Több visszaszökött SS-legényt fogott el az államvédelmi rendőrség', *Soproni Újság* (28 March 1947), 2.

56 Pittaway, Politics of Legitimacy, 468–73.

57 ÖStA, AdR, BMfAA, III-Wpol/Grenzen, 2 Ungarn, Gz.102.793-WPol/49, Z.102.793-WPol/49.

58 'Megszünt a határon való átsétálgatás', *Moson magyaróvár* (30 March 1949), 3

59 Hungarian National Archives (Magyar Országos Levéltár/MOL), Határőrség Országos Parancsnokság iratai (Papers of the Border Guard National Command (XIX-B-10), 16d., A nyugati határ megerősítésével kapcsolatos műszaki munkálatok.

60 ÖStA, AdR, BMfAA, III-Wpol/Grenzen 2 Ungarn, Gz.103.828-WPol/49, Z.103.828-WPol/49.

Bibliography

Ahonen, Pertti (2003), *After the Expulsion. West Germany and Eastern Europe, 1945–1990*, Oxford & New York: Oxford University Press.

Az 1941 évi Népszámlalás községek szerint, (1947), Budapest: Stephaneum Nyomda,

Balogh, Sándor (2002), 'A nemzetiségi politika másfél évszázada a jogszabályok tükrében', in Sándor Balogh and Levente Sipos, (eds), *A Magyar Állam és a Nemzetiségek. A magyarországi nemzetiségi kérdés történetének jogforrásai, 1848–1993*. Budapest: Napvilág Kiadó, 5–27.

Barb, Alfons (2004), 'Der Burgenländer' in Elisabeth Bockhorn, Olaf Bockhorn, and Veronika Plöckinger (eds), *'Die Geburt des Burgenländers' Ein Lesebuch zur Historischen Volkskultur im Burgenland* (Wissenschaftliche Arbeiten aus dem Burgenland, vol. 111). Eisenstadt: Amt der Burgendländischen Landesregierung, 2004.

Bindorffer, Györgyi (2001), *Kettős identitás: Etnikai és nemzeti azonosságtudat Dunabogdányban* Budapest: Új Mandátum Könyvkiadó – MTA Kisebbségkutató Intézet.

Brubaker, Rogers and Margit Feischmidt, Jon Fox and Liana Grancea, *Nationalist Politics and Everyday Ethnicity in a Transylvanian Town*. Princeton, NJ: Princeton University Press, 2006.

Ernst, August (1991), *Geschichte des Burgenlandes*, (2nd edn), Vienna-Munich: Verlag für Geschichte und Politik, & R. Oldenbourg Verlag.

Gagnon, Jr., V.P. (2004), *The Myth of Ethnic War. Serbia and Croatia in the 1990s*. Ithaca, NY & London: Cornell University Press.

Haslinger, Peter (2001), 'Building a Regional Identity: The Burgenland, 1921–1938', *Austrian History Yearbook*, 23, 105–23.

Hiller, István (1975), *A soproni egyetemi hallgatók mozgalmai a két világháború között, 1919–1945*, Sopron: Soproni Szemle Kiadványai.

Kershaw, Ian (2005), 'Europe's Second Thirty Years War', *History Today* 55 (9), 10–17.

Kirsch, András (2006), *A Soproni németek kitelepítése 1946*. Sopron: Escort Kiadó Kreichbaumer, Robert (1998), 'Einleitung', in Robert Kreichbaumer, (ed), *Liebe auf den Zweiten Blick. Landes- und Österreichbewußtsein nach 1945*, Wien, Köln, & Weimar: Böhlau.

Leffler Melvyn P. and David S. Painter, (eds) (2005), *The Origins of the Cold War. An International History* (2nd edn), London-New York: Routledge.

Naimark, Norman M. (2001), *Fires of Hatred. Ethnic Cleansing in Twentieth-Century Europe*, Cambridge, MA - London: Harvard University Press.

Pittaway, Mark (2004), 'The Politics of Legitimacy and Hungary's Postwar Transition', *Contemporary European History* 13 (4), 453–75.

Pittaway, Mark (2008), 'Making Peace in the Shadow of War: the Austrian–Hungarian Borderlands, 1945–1956', *Contemporary European History*, 17 (3), 345–64.

Pittaway, Mark (2009), 'Hungary', in Richard. J.B. Bosworth, (ed), *The Oxford Handbook of Fascism*. Oxford & New York: Oxford University Press, 380–97.

Pittaway, Mark with Hans Fredrik-Dahl (2008) 'Legitimacy and the Making of the Post-War Order', in Martin Conway and Peter Romijn (eds), *The War for Legitimacy in Politics and Culture, 1936–1946*. Oxford & New York: Berg, 177–209.

Schlag, Gerald (2001), *Aus Trümmern Geboren . . . Burgenland 1918–1921*. Eisenstadt: Amt der burgenländischen Landesregierung.

Schödl, Günter (1995), 'Lange Abschiede: Die Südostdeutschen und ihre Vaterländer (1918–1945)', in Günter Schödl, (ed), *Deutsche Geschichte im Osten Europas. Land an der Donau*. Berlin: Siedler.

Tóth, Ágnes (2001), *Migrationen in Ungarn, 1945–1948. Vertreibung der Ungarndeutschen, Binnenwanderungen und Slowakisch-Ungarischer Bevölkerungsaustausch.* (trans. Rita Fejér) Munich: Oldenbourg.

Tóth, Imre (2002), 'Aktuális Sopron-képek a XX. században. A hatalom és a város vizsonya 1921-től 2001-ig', in Éva Turbuly (ed), *A Város térben és időben. Sopron kapcsolatrendszerének változásai. Konferencia Sopron szabad királyi város 725 évéről*. Sopron: M. Soproni Lvt, 203–22.

Zielbauer, György (1989), *Adatok és tények a magyarországi németség történetéből (1945–1949)*. Budapest: Akadémiai Kiadó.

Chapter 3

Identity, Sovereignty and the Cold War at the Italo–Yugoslav Border: Between Empire, Nationhood and Class[1]

Sabina Mihelj

1 Alternatives to Homogeneity?

'The working men have no country' reads the beginning of a well-known passage from the *Communist Manifesto*, which is often quoted as evidence of communism's internationalist inclinations and hostility to nationalism.[2] At first sight, nationalism and Marxism do indeed appear to rest on mutually incompatible visions of humanity: while the former sees humanity as fundamentally divided into nations, the latter insists that the truly important divisions within the social world are aligned with class and cut across national loyalties. Given this basic divergence, it is not difficult to see why nationalist and communist leaders have often tried to discredit the others' views by portraying them as distorted or misleading representations of social reality. According to classical Marxist theory, nationalism is little more than an ideological veil, which serves to obscure underlying class conflict and prevents the proletariat from realizing its own interests. By contrast, nationalist leaders opposed to communism have often insisted that communism is itself an ideologically distorted view of society, which threatens to tear apart national unity and even endangers the survival of the nation.

Although certainly apt in many cases, this black-and-white contrast between nationalism and communism is of little help when investigating the role of nationalism in the Cold War. A closer look at the historical development of communist doctrine and political strategies reveals several points at which nationalist and communist coexist or even fuse. For a start, the rise of communism itself owes a great deal to its successful manipulation of nationalist aspirations. This was justified by both Marx and Lenin as an acceptable means of furthering the communist cause in pre-revolutionary societies.[3] The successful appropriation of nationalist sentiments also proved crucial in ensuring the long-term survival of communist regimes, once established. Though the operations of the repressive apparatus and, in Eastern Europe, the threat of the Red Army were certainly essential, they were not sufficient to keep communists in power for over four decades. To shore up popular support for their regimes, communist elites had to resort to other solutions, and nationalist narratives, folkloric traditions and symbols provided a rich and effective resource.[4] In this way, communist leaders, like their predecessors and successors, sought to capture the legitimating potential of nationalism and deploy it to their own advantage. Yet this does not mean that communist regimes simply manipulated nationalism. As will be argued here, an instrumentalist explanation cannot adequately account for the complexity of nationalist manifestations under communism.

'Classic' nationalism theory does not much help our understanding of communist nationality policies. For example, Ernest Gellner's well-known definition of nationalism as 'primarily a political principle, which holds that the political and the national unit should be congruent' requires that nationalism demands culturally homogeneous nation-states and runs counter both to the mixing of different nations under the same political roof and to the dispersal of a single nation across different states.[5] One problem with this and similar theories is the broad-brush portrayal of the link between modernization, cultural diversity and the state. It assumes that cultural homogeneity is unavoidable for modern social organizations, that nation-states have become the ubiquitous container for it and that all nationalist movements therefore must ultimately aspire to achieve the convergence of the state with the nation. As Brendan O'Leary puts it, Gellner 'appeared to assume that the range of possibilities in modern times is bifurcated to a simple choice between nationalist homogenisation through assimilation, and nationalist secession which produces another nationalist homogenisation'.[6]

Admittedly, there is plenty in the long historical record of state partition, ethnic cleansing, coercive assimilation and forced population transfers to support this account. Yet, it is surely too indiscriminate to encompass the full range of responses to cultural diversity in the modern world. While many modernizing states have indeed embraced the nation-state ideal as the only legitimate model of socio-political organization, cultural heterogeneity, fuelled by the contemporary reality of migration flows, has actually persisted to a far greater degree than Gellner's definition implies. In 1971 when the term 'nation-state' was already well entrenched in everyday language, political debate and scholarly discussion, only about a third of all the states in the world contained a nation that accounted for more than 90 per cent of the total population.[7] Four decades later little has changed. Admittedly, as a result of the breakup of multinational socialist federations, the total number of would-be nation-states has increased. But the vast majority still contains at least one significant ethnic (or national) minority. Although extreme nationalist movements may still find it undesirable, many mainstream forms of nationalism have largely accepted the legitimacy of national minorities. The overall trajectory of the nation-state into modernity has been fraught with difficulties, far from linear, and constantly entangled with other forms of socio-political organization.[8]

Communist federations such as the Soviet Union, Yugoslavia and Czechoslovakia represented one of these 'rival' types of socio-political organization. Their nationality policies often explicitly encouraged the cohabitation of different nations within the same political unit. They recognized the existence of distinct, autonomous national identities at the sub-state level while at the same time promoting a common Soviet (Czechoslovak, Yugoslav) identity. These communist nationality policies are not the only ones that seem to escape Gellner's definition.[9]

If the nation-state is indeed seen as only *one* among several modern forms of polities, then it is plausible to assume that the cultural homogeneity discussed by Gellner should also be seen as only one possible modern form of identity and legitimacy. Building on this assumption, the remainder of this chapter examines the competing forms of identity and legitimacy at the Italo–Yugoslav border in the decade following World War II. Its key proposition is that in this border region the Cold War entailed not only an ideological confrontation between two different political visions but also a confrontation between two competing forms of nationalism. Nationhood remained an important basis of collective identification and political legitimization in all parts of the region. But it was incorporated into the political system and public discourse in significantly different ways on opposite sides of the Iron Curtain.

2 Competing Forms of Legitimacy and Identity at the Italo–Yugoslav Border

Observed from afar, the history of border formation in the north-eastern Adriatic may appear to be a textbook example of the linkage of nation-state building and ethno-cultural homogenization. As part of the former imperial borderland, the region has seen many administrations come and go, including the Venetian and Austro-Hungarian empires, the Kingdom of Italy, Nazi Germany, Allied Military Government, the Italian republic and Tito's Yugoslavia. Each of them contributed to a complex patchwork of cultural legacies and left the north-eastern Adriatic with a culturally and ethnically mixed population; the region's main urban centre, the port city of Trieste, was home to Italians, Slovenians, Croats, Czechs, Germans, Hungarians, Jews, Armenians, Greeks and Serbs, as well as several smaller minorities.[10] From the late nineteenth century this multi-ethnic tapestry began to unravel. The rise of nation-states triggered conflicting visions of identity and borders, processes of cultural assimilation, inter-ethnic violence and migration, all of which gradually simplified ethno-cultural complexity and fostered homogeneity.[11] Today most of the four countries whose borders meet in the region – Italy, Austria, Slovenia and Croatia – are effectively conceived of as nation-states with an 'ethno-cultural' majority of 90 per cent of the total population or more.

While this account is not incorrect, its insight into the nature of nationalism and ethnicity in this part of the world is rather limited.

From early on, the ethnic and cultural complexities of the region inspired principles of sovereignty and border legitimation in which cultural diversity was seen less as an obstacle to be eliminated than as an asset to be preserved. For instance the Austro–Hungarian compromise of 1867 allowed Slovenes and Croats in Carniola and Istria to establish a range of cultural institutions and obtain considerable public prominence in order to accommodate their increasingly vocal nationalist demands.[12] Although these policies in turn provoked resentment among local Italian nationalists, and certainly did not bring about a harmonious multiethnic coexistence, they were repeatedly invoked by later administrations and pressure groups. Even the Nazi occupiers, who took over power after Italy's capitulation in September 1943, sought to present themselves as heirs of the Habsburg Empire, promising to restore the multiethnic harmony and commercial prosperity which the region had supposedly enjoyed before the advent of fascism. These promises were designed to appeal to the local Slav population, which had been disenfranchised by fascist assimilationist policies but now had to be mobilized in the anticommunist struggle against the partisans. They were also aimed at the Italian-speaking mercantile elites, frustrated by the dwindling volume of overseas trade, which had followed Trieste's incorporation into Italy.[13] Similar nostalgic ideas, organized around the image of Habsburg Trieste as a cosmopolitan commercial hub, were evoked by various autonomist movements, which argued that Trieste should enjoy the status of a 'free city' and as such serve the needs of the hinterland while still maintaining a measure of local autonomy.[14]

Following World War II alternative principles of identity and legitimacy like these were given a new lease of life. Poised at the southern tip of what was soon to be known as the Iron Curtain, the disputed territory assumed an unprecedented geopolitical significance, which firmly anchored its fate to the logic of the Cold War.[15] This changing geopolitical context was also reflected in the fluctuating fortunes of competing proposals for the solution to the 'Trieste problem'. The Council of Foreign Ministers (United States, the Soviet Union, France and Britain) initially put its faith in a 'scientific' solution aimed at establishing 'objective' patterns of ethnic settlement. But it soon became clear that this was a blind alley: the members of the international boundary commission could not agree on a definition and method of measuring and came back empty-handed.[16] The assumption that borders should be drawn by making ethnicity coincide with polity had to be discarded and the Council of Foreign Ministers turned to alternative solutions. This resulted in the proposal for establishing an independent, multinational and multilingual state, to be called the Free Territory of Trieste (FTT), whose administration would be entrusted to the United Nations – an arrangement modelled on the League of Nations administration of Danzig in the interwar period.[17] This solution was eventually enshrined in the Paris Peace Treaty, signed in February 1947.

However, by the time the FTT was due to be translated into political reality the global geopolitical situation had changed. In spite of growing local support for the new territorial and political arrangement[18] the intensification of the rivalry between the United States and the Soviet Union made the day-to-day functioning of the Free Territory impossible. The fact that many local supporters of the Free Territory had pronounced left-wing leanings, and favoured an autonomous Trieste under Yugoslav sovereignty aroused suspicions among pro-Italian groups (of various political colours) and western observers alike.[19] Trieste's socialists were known for their support for multinational coexistence and communist internationalism, inspired by Austro-Marxist conceptions of sovereignty and 'personal autonomy'.[20] Their views on the nationalities question also had a lot in common with those defended by South Slav social democratic groups in the Habsburg Empire[21] and appeared disconcertingly similar to solutions adopted in Tito's Yugoslavia at the time. Despite the fact that Trieste's autonomist movement also encompassed a right-wing group that eventually formed a separate party[22] the apparent overlaps with 'communist' principles – in particular, the fact that both envisaged the accommodation of ethno-national difference under the same political roof – proved disturbing. In the end this contributed to the gradual abandonment of the Free Territory as a solution to the Trieste problem. Other proposals, including those based on the requirement to make political borders coincide with ethnic ones, were allowed back onto the negotiating table.

The persistence of nationalist animosities in the region was a major factor as well. The permanent blockade against normal political and economic functions provided a breeding ground for discontent in the Free Territory and a stimulus to permanent mass mobilization. There were often violent clashes, even bloodshed, as well as mass migration. As ethnic tensions showed no sign of abating, representatives of the Anglo-American military administration became increasingly willing to listen to Italian nationalist arguments about the 'natural' antipathy between Italians and Slavs.[23] In this sense the abandonment of the Free Territory also indicated the acceptance by 'high politics' of the persistence of local nationalist antagonisms. Equally important was the electoral defeat of the Italian Communist Party in the national elections in February 1948 and Yugoslavia's expulsion from the Cominform later in the same year. These events made the threat of a Soviet take-over of Trieste seem far less likely and steadily downgraded the Italo–Yugoslav border dispute from a major Cold War front line to a more limited quarrel. In October 1953, after another round of mass demonstrations and escalating tensions between the two neighbouring states, Western allies announced the imminent withdrawal of their units from the Free Territory, providing both sides with a further incentive for reaching a compromise.[24] The following year, the FTT was finally dismembered and divided between the two neighbouring states. Although no principle was officially adopted as the basis of the division, and decisions were largely driven by pragmatic considerations, the influence of ethno-national criteria and beliefs in the inherent hostility between Italians and Slavs was unmistakable.[25]

Throughout this volatile period, the north-eastern Adriatic effectively became a battleground for competing conceptions of nationhood. They were promoted both by the Italian and the Yugoslav authorities, as well as by the Allied administration and various local interest groups. The remainder of this chapter takes a closer look at two of the most influential competing conceptions of nationhood. The first was promoted by Italian nationalist groups opposed to communism, and was based on a racialized idea of the Italian nation as the bearer of a superior civilization, destined to rule over the north-eastern Adriatic and protect it from 'slavo-communist barbarism'. The rival conception of belonging, defended by the Yugoslav authorities, was premised on the idea of Yugoslavia as a multinational federation whose unity depended primarily on common ideological affiliations and class consciousness rather than ethno-cultural ties. Both of these conceptions suggested alternatives to 'Gellnerian nationalism', yet for the border dispute to be settled, both were eventually displaced by the notion of the ethno-culturally homogeneous nation-state.

To elucidate the key elements of each of these conceptions of nationhood and sovereignty, the rest of this chapter draws on political speeches, official announcements, reports and commentaries published in major pro-Yugoslav and pro-Italian newspapers distributed in the region between 1947 and 1954, as well as on a selection of secondary sources. The pro-Italian newspapers covered here were all published in the Free Territory: they included *La Voce Libera* and *Giornale di Trieste* (otherwise known as *Il Piccolo*) and the weekly review of political affairs *Trieste*. Among these, *Giornale di Trieste* was most unequivocally in favour of the annexation of Trieste to Italy, and represented the voices of those Triestines who 'recognised themselves in [. . .] the Western, Atlantic, and European camp'.[26] The pro-Yugoslav newspapers comprise the Croatian daily *Riječki list*, later renamed *Novi list*, the Slovenian bi-weekly *Nova Gorica*, later renamed *Primorske novice*, and the Italian minority daily *La Voce del Popolo*, all published on the Yugoslav side of the border. Together with the Slovenian bi-weekly *Slovenski, Jadran* and the Slovenian minority daily *Primorski dnevnik*, both published in the Free Territory, most of these newspapers had their roots in clandestine anti-fascist, pro-communist periodicals established during World War II.[27] After the establishment of the Yugoslav federation, these newspapers were placed under the close supervision of the Communist Party of Yugoslavia, and functioned as a conduit for communist agitation and persuasion.[28]

3 Pro-Italian Newspapers: between Empire and Nation-State

Pro-Italian and anti-communist Triestine newspapers shared an unambiguous commitment to the Italian national cause, and appealed to those Italians who felt that Trieste, and the north-eastern Adriatic as a whole, formed an integral part of Italian national territory. The opening issue of *Giornale di Trieste* (6 March 1947) presented the newspaper as 'above all an Italian newspaper', whose coverage sought to 'correspond with the exigencies of a population that is largely Italian in terms of culture, language and sentiment'. According to an editorial published in the same newspaper shortly afterwards (3 May 1947) Trieste 'was and remains an Italian city', and its streets were 'our streets'. The opening editorial of *La Voce Libera* (23 July 1945) was permeated by similar sentiments, speaking about 'the love we bring to our Trieste, to the tormented Julian lands, and to the whole of Italy', thus signalling a belief in the national tie that links both Trieste and the surrounding region to Italy. Yugoslav claims to this territory, the same editorial argued, were 'clearly opposed to designs of history and culture', and were therefore not destined to last.

At first sight the notion of 'Italianness' (*Italianità*), which underpinned these writings – associated with history, culture, language and sentiment – conforms to a cultural, perhaps even 'civic' conception of national belonging, since it appears to be open to everyone, regardless of racial or ethnic descent. Yet, as Pamela Ballinger has pointed out, this interpretation is rather misleading: from the nineteenth century onwards, ideas of nationhood in Italy were characterized by a slippage between culture and race, with language and culture often standing for ethnic descent and biological 'race'.[29] The notion of *civiltà*, which blends modern ideas of culture, civilization and civility, stands at the centre of this slippage and ties modern conceptions of Italian culture and language to a hierarchy of human races. The historical roots of this notion stretch back to the ideological universe of enlightenment Venice, within which the eastern shore of the Adriatic appeared to be poised mid-way between barbarism and civilization, and so demanded the enlightened intervention of Venetian *civiltà*.[30]

Over the course of the nineteenth century, as the notion of the enlightening, assimilatory *civiltà* became one of the core elements of Italian national identity, it gradually assumed racist overtones. Admittedly these were not overtly biological: in the eyes of many Italian nationalists nothing prevented 'Slavs' from becoming civilized.

Yet they could do so only by shedding their Slavic background and assimilating fully into Italian civilization or culture.[31] In the twentieth century this racialized notion of *civiltà* was incorporated into fascist understandings of Italian identity, its imperial past and its future role as the bearer of a fascist empire. Fascists often spoke of Dalmatia, as well as the north-eastern shore of the Adriatic, as a land in need of Italian civilization, or singled out particular cities in Dalmatia as superior to other towns that were permeated by barbarism, irrationality, low levels of hygiene and a general 'balkanism'.[32] The 'new' fascist civilization was believed to be morally responsible for saving humanity, including the inhabitants of the Balkans, from the combined threats of democracy, communism and Jewish conspiracy.[33] At the same time, this civilizing mission also served to justify fascist colonial expansion and thus helped secure 'living space' for the expansion of the fascist 'New Order'.[34]

This imperial, racialized belief in the superiority of Italian *civiltà*, provided the basis for much of the reporting in the pro-Italian newspapers circulating in the region. This was particularly evident in reports from Dalmatia and those parts of Istria under Yugoslav rule, which repeatedly drew a sharp contrast between the glorious achievements of Italian civilization and the ingrained barbarity of Yugoslavs. In the eyes of *Il Piccolo* (27 October 1954) the north-eastern Adriatic was characterized by a Roman, Venetian and Italian configuration', associated with 'an unbroken progression of a two-thousand-year old civilisation' whose heritage was now being destroyed by the barbaric actions of Yugoslav communists. In a characteristic comment accompanying the photo reportage from the Istrian town of Pula/Pola, published in *Giornale di Trieste*, the town's Roman amphitheatre was used to symbolize the towering and timeless presence of 'Italianness', and to provide a stark contrast with what was described as a pitifully small and lonely group of pro-Yugoslav protesters.

Similar rhetorical constructs, based on dichotomies of past and present, imperial glory and communist barbarism, life and death, can be found in *La Voce Libera* (14 June 1948). A photo-reportage from Zadar/Zara, one of the major urban settlements on the Dalmatian coast, was composed exclusively of images of ruins, decaying buildings and empty streets. As one of the graphically most prominent subtitles suggested, the images represented a 'Venetian city', which is 'dying in a long and grey agony'. The message is clear: the Slavic inhabitants of Istria and Dalmatia have no legitimate claim to the eastern shores of the Adriatic and are incapable of preserving the achievements of Italian civilization. The presence of the Yugoslav authorities in the region is therefore an 'occupation' and evidence of 'Yugoslav expansionism' (1 April 1948). Evidently the understanding of Italianness shown in these articles has a racial boundary: the benefits of Italian *civiltà* can be generously extended to Slavs, but only insofar as they remain second-class citizens, and refrain from challenging the primacy of ethnic Italians as the only legitimate heirs of the Roman and Venetian Empires.

In several articles the contrast between Italian civilization and Slavic barbarity overlapped with the characteristic Cold War dichotomies of communism and democracy, totalitarianism and freedom. Differences in economic and political systems were presented as stemming from cultural and mental predispositions and anchored in racial differences. As the frequently-used derogatory term 'slavo-communist' suggests, Slavs were perceived as inherently prone to communist ideals, and hence to non-democratic, totalitarian modes of political rule. Such ideas were conveyed by visual elements such as caricatures and comic strips, where Slavs typically appeared rather intimidating, wearing a uniform and sometimes even barefoot and with hairy legs (e.g., *Giornale di Trieste*, 2 November 1953). Pro-Italian newspapers also frequently included reports about the cruel measures employed by the Yugoslav authorities to deal with the opposition in the newly acquired territories. Reports on various cases of '*infoibamento*' – that is, the politically motivated killings of local inhabitants opposed to communist rule, followed by the mass burial of corpses in karstic pits known as *foibe* – were particularly common. One such report was accompanied by a photo of a group of people looking at an array of human remains – bones and skulls – retrieved from one of the local pits, which served as a material 'proof' of Slav brutality (*Giornale di Trieste*, 1 April 1948). Such reports and images helped solidify the perception of Slavs as intrinsically prone to cruelty, oppression and totalitarianism.

Given the racial conception of Italian *civiltà*, and a similarly racial understanding of communism, it should not come as a surprise that pro-Italian commentators were suspicious of Yugoslav efforts to promote a multinational identity for the region. The activities of the Italo–Slav Antifascist Union, the major communist organization in the region in the early post-war years, were dismissed as being internationalist in name only: in reality they were inherently Slav and ultimately aimed at slavicizing the whole region and 'erasing, as soon as possible, every trace of Italianness in the name of the Italo–Slav fraternity' (*La Voce Libera*, 1 April 1947). Following a similar logic, communist activities in Italy were presented as inherently anti-Italian. In one editorial the newspaper linked to the local branch of the Italian Communist Party, *Il Lavoratore*, was described as 'the organ of Panslavism in Trieste' and as 'a panslavic daily' (*La Voce Libera*, 28 May 1947). Another article, published in the runup to the 1948 Italian elections, argued that the name and image of the Italian communist leader Palmiro Togliatti 'were raised on banners around the streets of Trieste by Slav communists in order to negate Italians' and suggested that communist appeals to internationalism were nothing but a cunning ploy. Yugoslavia, claimed the commentator, 'is a Slav nation' while Italy was not, and because of that, if Italy became communist, Yugoslav interests would always take precedence over Italian ones, and despite Togliatti's claims to the contrary, Trieste would not go to Italy (*Giornale di Trieste*, 10 September 1947).

It is important to note that the pro-Italian newspapers examined here were not alone in perpetuating an imperial and implicitly racialized notion of Italianness. At the time the whole of Italy was undergoing a difficult process of transition from its short-lived empire to an ethno-culturally homogeneous nation-state – a process which has often been discussed in relation to other Western states, but which is rarely acknowledged as an important part of Italy's post-war experience. Italy's democratic leaders initially fought hard to separate colonialism from Fascism, arguing that Italy should be allowed to maintain some form of temporary control over its pre-fascist colonies, and facilitate their orderly transition to independence under the aegis of the United Nations.[35] Regaining control over territories in the north-eastern Adriatic, in particular over Trieste, ranked even higher on the agenda. Many Italian observers felt that the city and the surrounding region were an integral part of Italian national territory, with historical ties with Italy which went much deeper than those of other territories.[36] Clearly the newspaper coverage analyzed here echoed such sentiments.

Yet appeals to the civilizing mission and imperial duty no longer enjoyed the kind of international support they once had. In a world organized around the global contest between the Soviet Union and the United States – both staunch supporters of decolonization movements at the time[37]– colonialist appetites and imperial models of sovereignty were falling out of favour. In addition, domestic support for colonial possessions was in decline. At a time when continental Europe was itself stumbling under the burden of post-war reconstruction, and had to resort to outside help to feed and clothe its population, the expense of colonial possessions was increasingly hard to justify.[38] In Italy the task was made even harder due to the stigma associated with Fascism. Italian citizens returning from the former colonies, including those coming from the north-eastern Adriatic, were not looked upon with much sympathy. Their new neighbours, the inhabitants of Italy's urban centres, tended to see them as both competitors for scarce resources and living reminders of a shameful fascist past.[39] Given these domestic and international pressures, Italian authorities had little choice but to forego their imperial dreams and adapt to the reality of Italy as a nation-state. By 1952 Italy had lost all its colonies, except for Somalia, and although the territorial contest over the north-eastern Adriatic took somewhat longer to settle, its outcome in the end was a rejection of Italy's claim to its former territories.[40]

In this context, territorial claims like those advanced in the Triestine newspapers were beginning to sound anachronistic, at least from the perspective of Italian metropolitan centres. Nevertheless, some elements of the imperial conception of Italianness, in particular, its racial assumptions, proved tenacious. For instance, beliefs about the deeply engrained hostility between Italians and Slavs, and about the incompatibility of their ways of life, proved influential in determining the final shape of the Italo–Yugoslav border. Faced with persistent inter-ethnic prejudice and conflicts in the area, members of the Allied Military Government were becoming more and more prone to accept that the only solution to the dispute was to make ethnicity coincide with the state border as far as possible.[41] The reports appearing in the Triestine pro-Italian newspapers at the time reinforced these ideas, and sometimes themselves explicitly resorted to ethno-national principles of border formation – for instance, when they mourned the loss of 'ethnically' Italian villages and towns annexed to Yugoslavia (e.g., *Il Giornale di Trieste*, 19 October 1954).

Ethno-racial markers also continued to play a role in assessing the eligibility of applicants for Italian citizenship from the former colonies. According to the 1947 Paris Peace Treaty, all Italian citizens who were domiciled in the territories annexed to Yugoslavia prior to World War II not only were to be automatically granted Yugoslav citizenship, but also were given the right to opt for Italian citizenship, provided that their customary language was Italian.[42] Since Slovenians and Croatians residing in the region normally spoke Italian fluently, this clause in principle gave them the possibility of opting for Italian citizenship as well. But on the Italian side this prospect prompted worries about Italian-speaking ethnic Slavs deliberately 'abusing' the provisions of the Peace Treaty to 'infiltrate' the Italian part of the region.[43] Although local authorities could not legally reject such applications, they often required the applicants to relocate to other regions in Italy, or else to register with the local authorities as foreigners.[44] Much like the imperial understanding of Italian nationhood found in Triestine nationalist newspapers, the notion of Italianness underpinning these decisions had a clear ethno-racial rationale. In this way, old ethno-racial markers were re-inscribed into the new, nation-state centred idea of Italianness. Yet the uses of the racial boundary in the two contexts differed: in the first case, racial markers served to justify territorial expansion and the inclusion of Slavs – albeit as second-class citizens – while in the second case, the boundary was used as a means of exclusion, and prevented Italian-speaking Slavs from acquiring citizenship.

4 Pro-Yugoslav Newspapers: Between Ethnic Nations and Nations of Comrades

Even a quick glance at the front pages of pro-Yugoslav newspapers in the first post-war decade shows that appeals to national belonging were an integral part of their coverage. Articles regularly addressed their readers in national terms, and some of the newspapers also featured recognizable national symbols, such as the Slovenian national coat of arms, complete with the 'national mountain' (*Triglav*) and sea waves. Yet these national references and symbols were typically combined with symbols of communism, references to the overarching 'brotherhood and unity' of Yugoslavia's nations, and appeals to non-national collectivities, in particular, to workers and peasants. Furthermore, the categories normally used to refer to the nation, such as the words '*narod*' in Serbo-Croatian, '*ljudstvo*' in Slovenian and '*popolo*' in Italian, evoked different shades of meaning. Like the English usage of 'people' they could connote simultaneously an ethno-culturally homogeneous collectivity as well as an ethno-culturally mixed group which shared a common allegiance to proletarian rule. Thus a characteristic announcement of the Communist Party of Yugoslavia on Labour Day in 1947, reproduced word-for-word in several newspapers, was addressed simultaneously to 'the peoples/nations [*narodi*] of Yugoslavia' as well as to 'workers', 'peasants', 'the intelligentsia', 'the youth', 'women', 'citizens', 'soldiers' and 'officers' (*Riječki list*, 1 May 1947). A similar array of collective subjects was invoked in an editorial in the Italian minority daily. Its author described Labour Day as

> . . . a luminous day, when the working class and the peasants, people's intelligentsia, the youth and women, all of the Croatian and Italian nations/peoples [*popolo*] of our land, along with other peoples/nations of Yugoslavia and with comrade Tito, are reconfirming their conscious and resolute effort to bring to completion all of the tasks of the five-year plan. (*La Voce del Popolo*, 1 May 1947)

This mixture of appeals to national belonging and working-class comradeship, underscored by the ambiguity of the categories of collective identity used, was wholly in line with the official socialist Yugoslav approach to nationality and statehood. Modelled on the Soviet federal system, the Yugoslav constitution recognized the existence of distinct, autonomous national identities at sub-state level while at the same time assuming a common Yugoslav identity, rooted in a shared loyalty to the communist cause.[45] The simultaneous emphasis on national distinctiveness and overarching Yugoslav working-class comradeship was presented as the only form of nationhood that was capable of guarding Tito's Yugoslavia against the shortcomings which were held to have led to its bloody inter-ethnic conflict in World War II.[46] Particular targets were the attempts by Yugoslav elites in the inter-war period to build a 'synthetic' Yugoslav culture, based on the belief that Yugoslav peoples, despite being culturally, linguistically and religiously different, in fact constituted a single national whole.[47] This understanding of Yugoslavism came to be perceived by many non-Serbs as an attempt to Serbianize the country, and despite the gradual abandonment of 'integral Yugoslavism' in the 1930s,[48] inter-war Yugoslavia was subsequently remembered as an oppressive state intent on forcibly assimilating Yugoslav peoples into a single nation.

This selective memory enabled the communist elites to construct their project of Yugoslav 'brotherhood and unity' as an entirely unprecedented endeavour to link the South Slavs together under a single political roof while at the same time maintaining their national distinctiveness. In contrast to inter-war Yugoslavia, the argument went, Tito's Yugoslavia was addressing the true causes of pre-war oppression and war-time bloodshed. These were not only limited to exploitative relations between nations, but also encompassed capitalist exploitation, nationalist antagonism between different national bourgeoisies and the continuing influence of other 'forces of the past' including feudal relationships, the Church and imperial interests.[49] Following this argument, the true solution to the Yugoslav national question could not be found solely in the continuation of the South Slav national liberation struggle. Instead the struggle had to be integrated into the international struggle of the working classes against both domestic capitalists and imperialist forces abroad. In short, the equality and brotherhood of Yugoslav nations had to go hand-in-hand with, and where necessary be subordinated to, working-class comradeship and allegiance to a communist vision of modernity.

The notion of Yugoslav 'brotherhood and unity' as a new and unique form of collective belonging was prominent in public speeches and news reports at the time. Yugoslavia, as Tito declared in an interview, was building a 'new community', a community within which 'every nation/people [*narod*] represents a specific unit on its own, yet they all together also form a strong unit' (*Glas Istre*, 6 June 1947). Eros Sequi, the first secretary of the Union of Italians and one of the few 'good Italians' trusted by the Yugoslav regime,[50] defended a similar vision of Yugoslavism, and described the new Yugoslavia as 'a state in which nationality is fully free to develop, and where economy, political power and every human activity are based on a new foundation of collaboration between humans and nations' (*La Voce del Popolo*, 1 January 1947). Italians living on the Yugoslav side of the border were regularly mentioned as equal members of the new Yugoslav nation. As one article argued, the 'great idea of brotherhood and unity', forged in the common struggle against Fascism, was capable of overcoming the hostility between Italians and Croats in Istria, and helped unite them in 'a strong front' (*Riječki list*, 2 March 1947).

It is no coincidence that none of these examples provides a particularly clear definition of Yugoslav unity. Up to about mid-1947, party officials deliberately avoided mentioning their communist credentials, and instead emphasized the equality and freedom of Yugoslav nations, the need for economic rebuilding and development and the importance of education and women's rights, etc.[51] The principal motivation for such a policy was not only the need to consolidate the position of the Communist Party at home without alienating the general population, but also the fear of damaging Yugoslavia's position *vis-à-vis* the West. Given the mounting tensions between the two superpowers, it was strategically much wiser to sound the trumpet of national liberation and equality than to provoke unwanted attention with loud proclamations of loyalty to the communist cause. Similarly, local activists involved in preparations for the visit of the international boundary commission in 1946 were asked to avoid using any symbols that would signal loyalty to the Soviet cause, and instead prepare graffiti, banners and flags that emphasized Slovenian identity and loyalty to Yugoslavia. Communist symbols such as the hammer and sickle, found on the walls across the towns and villages in the region, were to be erased immediately, and replaced with 'writings in the national spirit', such as 'Slovenians have been here from times immemorial' and 'For us, life exists only in Yugoslavia'.[52]

From about mid-1947, references to the common communist cause became more common. As a commentary published on the Day of the Republic (the anniversary of the declaration of the republic on 29 November 1943) made clear, Yugoslavia was 'a country in which its nations/peoples [*narodi*], united in brotherhood, are building for themselves a better future, building a socialist society' (*Riječki list*, 29 November 1947). Following a similar logic, 'workers' were now often singled out as the key bearers of the new Yugoslav identity. A speech delivered by Tito, reproduced in *Glas Istre* (5 September 1947), is a case in point. When talking about the five-year plan, Tito started by pointing out that the tasks of the plan were shared by 'all citizens of Yugoslavia', but then emphasized that workers were expected to bear the brunt of responsibility for fulfilling the plan, and had the duty 'to work day and night', 'selflessly', to achieve the goal. Given its leading role in the country's reconstruction, working-class comradeship was also expected to provide the connecting tissue of Yugoslav unity, tying the different nations and nationalities of Yugoslavia into a single indivisible whole. 'In our country', argued Tito, 'there is only one collectivity. . .All our working people merged into one single, huge collectivity, into a strong fist, united in thought and action'.

To be sure, these idealistic proclamations of 'brotherhood and unity' were far from the everyday reality of inter-ethnic relations in the region or in Yugoslavia as a whole. While cross-national collaboration and trust were certainly not absent, and indeed were often motivated by shared political persuasion and, in particular, loyalty to communist ideals, they were often paralleled and sometimes even outweighed by hatred and violence. This was especially true in the case of relations between Slavs and Italians. The decades of fascist rule had left a legacy of bitter memories and mutual suspicion that proved difficult to dispel, and forced many Italians to 'opt' for exile.[53] Newspapers on both sides of the border were instrumental in keeping these memories and suspicions alive. Pro-Yugoslav newspapers were full of reports about the continuing discrimination faced by the Slovenian minority in Italy, about the persistence of fascist attitudes on the other side of the border and about the devastation left behind by decades of Fascist rule in the region (e.g., *Slovenski Jadran*, 5 November 1954; *Novi list*, 29 November 1954). According to one commentator, Italians were also particularly prone to 'bourgeois' values, since their cultural capabilities were 'most ruthlessly manipulated and made deviant by decades of Fascism' (*La Voce del Popolo*, 1 January 1947). Despite frequent references to Italo–Slav fraternity, such reports and assertions did little to undermine the assumption that Italians were inherently prone to Fascism and hostile to both Slavs and communism.

At the same time, there is plenty of evidence that adherence to communism among local Slovenians and Croats did not automatically mean that ethno-national interests were subordinated to the common proletarian cause. Here too the difficulties of determining Italian citizenship among inhabitants of former Italian territories annexed to Yugoslavia after World War II serve as a useful example. As mentioned earlier, the 1947 Paris Peace Treaty technically allowed local inhabitants of Slav descent – however that was determined – to apply for Italian citizenship, as long as they could prove that Italian was their 'customary language'. However, the definition of 'customary language' was slippery, leaving the local administration considerable room for manoeuvre. In the instructions distributed to the local People's Committees in Yugoslavia 'customary language' was translated as '*domači jezik*' – literally, 'home language' – thus suggesting that in order to qualify, applicants had to use Italian not only in the public realm or at work, but also in the private sphere.[54] This translation provided the necessary grounds for refusing to grant Italian citizenship to all those applicants of non-Italian origin who were judged to be using Slovenian or Croatian language in their family environment. Thus a female applicant from Šempeter, whose husband remained on the Italian side of the border, was sent a letter explaining that the People's Committee 'cannot issue a document assigning Italian citizenship to a person who is Slovenian [. . .] since this would lead to serious consequences'.[55] Evidently, local communist officials were reluctant to accept a complete fusion between nationhood and allegiance to communism inscribed in the official version of Yugoslavism and continued to uphold the ethno-cultural conception of Slovenian identity. Yugoslav newspaper coverage, replete with references to territories that 'ethnically' belonged to

Yugoslavia, did little to discourage such views (e.g., *Slovenski Jadran*, 7 October 1954).

These different meanings and usages of Yugoslavism suggest that communist support for nationalism was not just instrumental. It may be, of course, that some party members used the rhetoric of national liberation and equality merely as a propaganda ploy to promote communist goals. Yet there is little doubt that many communist Yugoslav officials were genuinely concerned about the fate of 'their' nations and became attracted to the communist cause at least in part because of its commitment to national equality. This led the highest echelons of the Party to take every opportunity to present communist goals as entirely commensurate with particular national interests, and in fact to insist that allegiance to the proletarian cause was the only route towards the fulfillment of national liberation. For instance, according to Milovan Djilas, then one of the top leaders of the Yugoslav Communist movement, Yugoslavia was undergoing both 'a social transformation' and 'a national rebirth': 'While fighting for the freedom and independence of our nations/peoples [*naroda*] we are simultaneously building a new society, a new social order in which people will be equal' (*Riječki list*, 15 April 1947). The constant oscillation between working-class identity and national belonging was therefore more than just an exercise in manipulation. It can be seen as a compromise that made Tito's Yugoslavism appear attractive to a relatively broad range of interest groups and helped broaden the regime's popular support. Yugoslavia thus functioned – like any other nation – as a symbol with multiple meanings, which were 'offered as alternatives and competed over by different groups manoeuvring to capture the symbol's definition and its legitimating effects'.[56]

Given its malleability, it is not surprising that the double-layered nature of Yugoslavism persisted throughout the existence of communist Yugoslavia, regardless of the substantial political, economic and cultural changes that it underwent. In the years that followed the Tito–Stalin split in 1948, Yugoslavia's political leadership embraced a new set of political and economic principles, centred on the ideal of 'workers' self-management' and premised on a rejection of 'Soviet' or 'Stalinist' models.[57] The Party was expected to refrain from commanding and managing all aspects of social, political and economic life in the country, and limit its role to political education and persuasion.[58] In the aftermath of these shifts, new tropes entered Yugoslav public discourse, organized around slogans such as 'debureaucratization', 'decentralization', and of course 'workers' self-management'.[59] These shifting discourses crystallized around a new understanding of Yugoslavism, based on the idea of Yugoslavia as a meeting point of East and West, which lasted until the early 1960s and was accompanied by a renewed emphasis on a common Yugoslav culture.[60] As Tito put it in 1954, '[w]e are following our own path into socialism, and we will not allow anyone, neither those in the East nor those in the West, to make us stray from this path' (*Primorske novice*, 2 April 1954).

Despite these changes, the understanding of Yugoslavism that underpinned newspaper coverage in the northeastern Adriatic remained broadly the same: the Yugoslav nation was portrayed as a multinational community of workers, united in the support for socialism. For instance, in an editorial published in *Novi list* on the day of the Republic, both 'working class' and 'Yugoslav peoples/nations' were mentioned, perpetuating the characteristic fusion of class solidarity and nationhood (29 November 1954). In contrast, explicit proclamations of belonging to a Yugoslav community of brotherly nations and working peoples, such as those encountered in the late 1940s, were now rather rare. By the mid-1950s, the particular Yugoslav mode of belonging had, arguably, become so deeply engrained that its existence was taken for granted. In other words, the communist version of Yugoslavism had become a form of 'banal nationalism'[61]. As such, it was sustained by small, barely noticed reminders, such as references to 'us', 'our president' or 'our country', without repeatedly specifying what the 'we' referred to, or how it related to communism, nationhood and working-class comradeship.

Exceptions to this rule were those exalted moments of national celebration that accompanied major national holidays, as well as major international events involving Yugoslavia. On such occasions, explicit references to Yugoslav 'brotherhood and unity' and its particular combination of socialist values and national belonging came to the fore again. As in the late 1940s, communist officials and newspaper commentators alike insisted that communist goals were entirely consistent with particular national interests, and provided the best possible guarantee for the attainment of full national liberation. A commentary published in a Slovenian bi-weekly a few days before 25 May, which as the official day of Tito's birth, was celebrated as the Youth Day, is a case in point:

> In our struggle for national liberation, for the unification of all the parts of our national body, Slovenians of the littoral have found in Tito our most powerful supporter. His resolute words, supported by the common will and actions of all Yugoslav nations, have recently prevented great evil and a new injustice that was being prepared for us by our greedy neighbors with the support of their godfathers (*Slovenski Jadran,* 21 May 1954).

The reports accompanying the dismemberment of the FTT and the signing of the London Memorandum in 1954 are particularly telling in this respect. Once the shape of the new Italo Yugoslav border had finally been defined, the Yugoslav authorities were faced with the difficult task of justifying the 'loss' of Trieste. To do so, they not only presented Yugoslav willingness to sacrifice a part of its ethnic territory as an admirable gesture and a model for solving similar disputes elsewhere in Europe, but also repeatedly emphasized that Yugoslavia had effectively achieved everything it could realistically be expected to (e.g., *Novi list,* 7 October 1954). At the same time it was made clear that Yugoslavia was entitled to much more, and that the new arrangement of borders was not there to stay, since it did not coincide with the ethnic distribution of the population. As argued in a speech by the Slovenian writer France Bevk, reproduced in *Primorske novice* (15 October 1954), even though the London Memorandum was the best possible solution under the circumstances 'if we look into the more distant future, we should not forget that unnatural borders, which unjustly cut into the body of a nation, cannot endure'. Yet again we see that the Yugoslav formula of nationhood was capable of accommodating rather different relationships between national belonging and communist ideals. This malleability also helps explain why and how Yugoslavism could function alongside ethno-cultural principles of border legitimation, and thus help formulate a territorial arrangement that was, in no small part, underpinned by nation-state-centred ideas of sovereignty.

4 Conclusion

The notions of belonging that were fostered by pro-Yugoslav and by pro-Italian newspapers in the northeastern Adriatic both departed from the ideal of an ethno-culturally homogeneous nation-state, but did so in very different ways. The understanding of Italianness in pro-Italian newspapers was centred on the imperial notion of Italian *civiltà* as a transnational force, which gave Italy the right to expand into foreign territories and rule over populations that were considered civilizationally inferior. By contrast, pro-Yugoslav newspapers promoted a form of collective belonging and sovereignty anchored in transnational working-class comradeship and allegiance to proletarian rule. At the same time, these transnational bonds of identity and loyalty coexisted and sometimes merged with ethno-cultural and even racial notions of identity and sovereignty. Within pro-Italian nationalist discourse, *civiltà* was implicitly based on racial categories and hierarchies, most evident in portrayals of Slavs as inherently barbaric and totalitarian, and in the anxieties about granting Italian citizenship to applicants of Slavic descent. Likewise, Yugoslav 'brotherhood and unity' often drew on an ethno-racial understanding of belonging, in which Italians appeared intrinsically prone to Fascism, claims to territories in the north-eastern Adriatic were ethnically based and applicants for emigration were occasionally prevented from setting aside their Yugoslav citizenship on the grounds of their descent. These findings strengthen the view that we need to move beyond the narrow definition of nationalism as a political doctrine that requires ethnicity and polity to coincide, and instead acknowledge that the ideal of the ethnoculturally homogeneous state was just one of several available responses to manifestations of the rise of nations as political subjects. Even where it was in the end asserted, it coexisted and sometimes competed with other principles of national sovereignty and other forms of national belonging, in this case, those found in multiethnic empires and multinational communist federations.

To account for these alternative forms of nationhood and sovereignty, we need to revise the idea that nation-statehood was the only truly decisive and politically influential form of collective belonging in the modern era. Rather than being studied in isolation, the links between nationhood and political systems need to be situated in the broader context of competing projects of collective identification and popular legitimacy in the nineteenth and twentieth century, not least those based on class and racial ideology. The close proximity of class and nation is not a coincidence: they both call for an abstract sense of community in an analogous, universalistic way, and they are also both related to political power and to the state.[62] Due to these commonalities, national and class ideologies typically spread together and were often in competition for the same mass allegiance.[63] As argued here, racial categorization, sometimes disguised as 'culture' or 'ethnicity', was an integral part of the same mixture. Arguments about racial and civilizational superiority often appeared side-by-side with notions of national sovereignty and working-class allegiance and were used together with them to buttress claims to sovereignty and territory. Gender categories, though left unexplored in this analysis, were often also part of the mix. To be sure, such interlinkages were not only limited to post-war Italy and communist Yugoslavia, but also appeared, for example, in imperial and post-imperial South Africa[64] and several European countries in the inter-war period,[65] and can be seen in contemporary contexts, including contemporary immigrant societies in the West.[66] Needless to say, the encounter between these different forms of identity and loyalty, and the associated principles of legitimacy and sovereignty, was resolved in very different ways.

This discussion has also suggested that different models of nationhood and sovereignty, including those that appear logically incompatible, could often exist alongside each other. The persistence of ethno-racial prejudice in pro-Yugoslav and pro-Italian newspapers, and in everyday negotiations over citizenship in the northeastern Adriatic, provides some telling examples. In spite of official proclamations of multinational brotherhood and unity in the Yugoslav case, and proud endorsements of *civiltà* as a transnational force on the Italian side, ethno-racial perceptions of belonging and sovereignty were widespread, and occasionally received indirect endorsement in public discourse. The malleability of identity categories often contributed to that as well. As the Yugoslav case shows, the categories used to refer to the nation were often rather ambiguous. This allowed the communist notion of Yugoslavism, which appealed to a variety of interest groups and segments of the population, including some that were not particularly attracted to communist ideals as such, but could be swayed by arguments about national liberation and equality.

When considering the particular case of communist Yugoslavia, it may be tempting to interpret these ambiguities of nationhood as the result of conscious manipulation devised by the communist authorities. Yet this interpretation is too rigid to account for the range of meanings and uses attached to Yugoslavism. As Oliver Zimmer points out, scholarly observers are often too consumed by the quest for logical consistency to notice that social actors are not particularly bothered by internal paradoxes and contradictions in their perceptions of national identity.[67] The notions of belonging and legitimacy which motivated their actions and claims are often guided by disparate pragmatic considerations and tacit assumptions, including, in particular, the need to construct a national identity that makes sense and allows them to achieve particular goals within a specific local, domestic or international context. As we have seen, the negotiation of identity and loyalty in the north-eastern Adriatic was constrained by historical legacies and memories of the war and the inter-war period, the growing opposition to colonialism in the international arena, as well as the need to justify territorial demands and consolidate domestic support in a crisis-ridden situation. To this we could add the shared condemnation of Fascism and Nazism, and the need to create a distance from war-time atrocities. At some level the emphasis on transnational loyalties, whether rooted in allegiance to communism or in the notion of *civiltà*, allowed both pro-Italian and pro-Yugoslav actors to sidestep the issue of their own complicity in the advance of Fascism.

As for the Cold War, it is undeniable that from the crisis of May 1945 onwards 'high politics' significantly affected the course of the dispute. But once we take a closer look at the notions of identity and sovereignty promoted by different social actors, and the sociopolitical and historical context in which they were embedded, it becomes apparent that nationalism could not simply be manipulated at will by policymaking elites. Although numerous manifestations and competing symbolic displays of national belonging in the border region clearly were supported or carefully managed by political elites, nationalist identifications went beyond conscious manipulation. They were often guided by genuine feelings of national loyalty, which were consistent with transnational allegiances. The power of nationalist sentiments within the population as a whole should not be discounted either. To be considered legitimate any solution to the border dispute therefore had to take into account nationalist sentiments as well. The final shape of the Italian–Yugoslavian border was in the end not the product of a *Diktat* from on high but the outcome of complex negotiations in which nationalist and ethnic pressures played a central part.

Notes

[1] This chapter is based on research supported by the British Academy (SG-43957) and the Ludwig Boltzmann Institute for European History and Public Spheres, Vienna (*Border Communities* project).

[2] Karl Marx and Friedrich Engels, *The Communist Manifesto*, Oxford: Oxford University Press, 2008, 23.

[3] Walker Connor, *The National Question in Marxist-Leninist Theory and Strategy*, Princeton: Princeton University Press 1984; Martin Mevius, *Agents of Moscow: The Hungarian Communist Party and the Origins of Socialist Patriotism, 1941–1953*, Oxford: Oxford University Press, 2005.

[4] Katherine Verdery, *National Ideology under Socialism: Identity and Cultural Politics in Ceauşescu's Romania* (2nd edn), Berkeley: University of California Press, 1995; David Brandenberger, *National Bolshevism: Stalinist Mass Culture and the Formation of Modern Russian National Identity, 1931–1956*, Cambridge, MA: Harvard University Press, 2002; Jan Palmowski, *Inventing a Socialist Nation: Heimat and the Politics of Everyday life in the GDR, 1945–1990*, Cambridge: Cambridge University Press, 2009.

[5] Ernest Gellner, *Nations and Nationalism*, Oxford: Blackwell, 1983, 1.

[6] Brendan O'Leary, 'Ernest Gellner's diagnoses of nationalism: a critical overview, or what is Living and what is dead in Ernest Gellner's Philosophy of Nationalism?', in John Hall (ed), *The State of the Nation: Ernest Gellner and the Theory of Nationalism*, Cambridge: Cambridge University Press, 1991, 63.

[7] Walker Connor, *Ethnonationalism: The Quest for Understanding*, Princeton, NJ: Princeton University Press, 1994, 89–117.

[8] Daniel Chernilo, *A Social Theory of the Nation-State: The Political Forms of Modernity beyond Methodological Nationalism*, London: Routledge, 2007.

[9] Scott L. Greer, *Nationalism and Self-government: The Politics of Autonomy in Scotland and Catalonia*, New York: State University of New York Press, 2007.

[10] Marina Cattaruzza, 'Population dynamics and economic change in Trieste and its hinterland, 1985–1914', in Richard Lawton and Robert Lee (eds), *Population and Society in Western European Port Cities, c. 1650–1939*, Liverpool: Liverpool University Press, 2002, 178–9; Milan Pahor, *Slavljanska sloga: Slovenci in Hrvati v Trstu od Austroogrske monarhije do Italijanske republike*, Trieste: Založništvo TržaškegaTiska, 2004.

[11] Marina Cattaruzza, *L'Italia e il confline orientale*, Bologna: Il Mulino, 2007.

[12] Marina Cattaruzza, *Trieste nell'Ottocento: Le trasformazioni di una società civile*, Udine: Del Bianco editore, 1995, 119–66.

[13] Gianmarco Bresadola, 'The legitimising strategies of the Nazi administration in northern Italy: Propaganda in the Adriatisches Küstenland', *Contemporary European History*, 13(4), (2004), 444–6.

[14] Giorgio Negrelli, *Al di qua del mito: Diritto storico e difesa nazionale della Trieste asburgica*, Udine: Del Bianco Editore, 1978. 1978; Bresadola, Legitimising strategies, 437–39.

[15] Glenda Sluga, *The Problem of Trieste and the Italo–Yugoslav Border: Difference, Identity, and Sovereignty in Twentieth-Century Europe*, Albany: State University of New York Press, 2001, 133–55.

[16] Jean-Baptiste Duroselle, *Le conflit de Trieste, 1943–1954*, Brussels: Editions de l'Institut de Sociologie de l'Université Libre, 1966.

[17] Steven R. Ratner, *The New UN Peace-keeping: Building Peace in Lands of Conflict after the Cold War*, New York: St. Martin's Press, 1995, 98.

[18] Sluga, *Problem of Trieste*, 151.

[19] Bogdan Novak, *Trieste, 1941–1954: The Ethnic, Political and Ideological Struggle*, Chicago and London: University of Chicago Press 1970, 257–9.

[20] Marina Cattaruzza, *Socialismo adriatico: La socialdemocrazia di lingua italiana nei territori costieri della Monarchia asburgica: 1888–1915*, Manduria: Piero Lacaita Editore, 2001.

[21] Enver Redžić, *Austromarksizam i Jugoslavensko pitanje*, Belgrade: Narodnaknjiga, 1977.

[22] Novak, *Trieste*, 259.

[23] Sluga, *Problem of Trieste*, 145–53.

[24] Novak, *Trieste*.

[25] See Sluga, *Problem of Trieste*, 152–3.

[26] Guido Botteri, *Un secolo un giornale: Il Piccolo, 1881–1981*, Trieste: Il Piccolo, 1981, 43.

[27] Novak, *Trieste*, 344–7.

[28] Carol S. Lilly, *Power and Persuasion: Ideology and Rhetoric in Communist Yugoslavia, 1944–1953*, Boulder, CO: Westview Press, 2001, 35–54.

[29] Pamela Ballinger, '"Authentic hybrids" in the Balkan borderlands', *Current Anthropology*, 45 (1), (2004), 34–6.

[30] Larry Wolff, *Venice and the Slavs: The Discovery of Dalmatia in the Age of Enlightenment*, Stanford: Stanford University Press, 2001, 324ff.

[31] Glenda Sluga, 'Narrating difference and defining the nation in late nineteenth and early twentieth century "Western" Europe', *European Review of History*, 9 (2), (2004), 194–5.

[32] Wolff, 2001, 355, Glenda Sluga, 'Identità nazionale Italiana e fascismo: alieni, allogeni e assimilazione sul confine nord-orientale italiano,' in Marina Cattaruzza (ed), *Nazionalismi di frontiera: Identità contrapposte sull' Adriatico nord-orientale 1850–1950*, Soveria Mannelli: Rubbettino, 2005, 171–202.

[33] Davide Rodogno, 'Italian soldiers in the Balkans: The experience of the occupation (1941–1943),' *Journal of Southern Europe and the Balkans*, 6 (2), (2004), 125–44.

[34] *Ibid.*

[35] Christopher Seton-Watson, 'Italy's imperial hangover', *Journal of Contemporary History*, 15 (1), (1980), 169–79.

[36] Pamela Ballinger, 'Borders of the Nation, Borders of Citizenship: Italian Repatriation and the Redefinition of National Identity after World War II', *Comparative Studies in Society and History*, 49 (3), (2007), 718–19.

[37] Nils Gilman, *Mandarins of the Future: Modernization Theory in Cold War America*, Baltimore: Johns Hopkins University Press, 2003, 30–47.

[38] Tony Judt, *Postwar: A History of Europe since 1945*, London: Penguin, 278–302.

[39] Ballinger, Borders, 718–19.

[40] Seton-Watson, Italy's Imperial Hangover.

[41] See Sluga, *Problem of Trieste*, 145–53.

[42] 'Vsem krajevnim ljudskim odborom, vsem matičarjem', 1 April 1948, Pokrajinski arhiv Nova Gorica, Krajevnil judski odbor Šempeter, technical unit 3, archival unit 15, 2238/2-48-Be.

[43] Ballinger, Borders, 718–19.

[44] *Ibid*, 729.

[45] Paul S. Shoup, *Communism and the Yugoslav National Question*, New York: Columbia University Press 1968, 114ff.

[46] Dejan Jović, 'Communist Yugoslavia and its "Others"', in John Lampe and Mark Mazower, (eds), *Ideologies and National Identities: The Case of Twentieth century South-eastern Europe*, Budapest: Central European University Press, 2004, 282–5.

[47] Andrew Baruch Wachtel, *Making a Nation, Breaking a Nation: Literature and cultural politics in Yugoslavia*, Stanford: Stanford University Press, 1998, 67–127.

[48] Dejan Djokić, *Elusive Compromise: A History of Interwar Yugoslavia*, New York: Columbia University Press 2007, 171–222.

[49] Esad Zgodić, *Titova nacionalna politika: temeljni pojmovi, načela i vrijednosti*, Sarajevo: Kantonalni odbor SDP BiH, 2000, 40–2.

[50] Pamela Ballinger, *History in Exile: Memory and identity at the borders of the Balkans*. Princeton: Princeton University Press 2002, 213.

[51] Lilly, *Power and Persuasion*, 115–36.

[52] ODBA Report, 8 March 1946, Regional Archives Nova Gorica, Local People's Committee Šempeter (Krajevni ljudski odbor Nova Gorica, Pokrajinski arhiv Šempeter, technical unit 15, archival unit 97, 246/46.

[53] See e.g. Raoul Pupo, *Il lungo esodo – Istria: le persecuzioni, le foibe, l'esilio*, Milano: Rizzoli, 2005.

[54] 'Vsem krajevnim ljudskim odborom, vsem matičarjem', 1 April 1948, Pokrajinski arhiv Nova Gorica, Krajevni ljudski odbor Šempeter, technical unit 3, archival unit 15, 2238/2-48-Be.

[55] Letter sent to the applicant by the Local People's Committee Šempeter, 2 July 1948, Pokrajinskiarhiv Nova Gorica (1948b), Krajevni ljudski odbor Šempeter, technical unit 3, archival unit 15, 924/48.

[56] Katherine Verdery, 'Whither "Nation" and "Nationalism"?', in Gopal Balakrishnan (ed), *Mapping the Nation*, London: Verso, 1996, 226–33.

[57] John Lampe, *Yugoslavia as History: Twice There Was a Country* (2nd edn), New York: Cambridge University Press, 2000, 255–7.

[58] Lilly *Power and Persuasion*, 2001, 208–9.

[59] Dennison Rusinow, *The Yugoslav Experiment, 1948–1974*, London: C. Hurst & Company, 1977, 52.

[60] See Wachtel, *Making a Nation*, 128–72.

[61] See Michael Billig, *Banal Nationalism*, London: Sage, 1995.

[62] Michael Mann, *The Sources of Social Power* (vol. 2), Cambridge: Cambridge University Press, 1993.

[63] Eric Hobsbawm, *Nations and Nationalism since 1780: Programme, Myth, Reality*, Cambridge: Cambridge University Press, 1990, 124.

[64] Anne McClintock, *Imperial Leather: Race, gender and Sexuality in the Colonial Contest*, London: Routledge, 1995.

[65] Iris Wigger, 'The interconnections of discrimination: Gender, class, nation and race and the "black shame on the Rhine"', *European Societies*, 11 (4), (2009), 553–82.

[66] Flora Anthias and Nira Yuval-Davis, *Racialized Boundaries: Race, Nation, Gender, Colour and Class and the Anti-racist Struggle*, London: Routledge 1993.

[67] Oliver Zimmer, 'Boundary mechanisms and symbolic resources: towards a process-oriented approach to national identity', *Nations and Nationalism*, 9 (2), (2003), 173–93, here 189.

Bibliography

Anthias, Flora and Nira Yuval-Davis (eds) (1993), *Racialized Boundaries: Race, Nation, Gender, Colour and Class and the Anti-racist Struggle.* London: Routledge.

Ballinger, Pamela (2002), *History in Exile: Memory and Identity at the Borders of the Balkans.* Princeton: Princeton University Press.

Ballinger, Pamela (2004), '"Authentic hybrids" in the Balkan borderlands', *Current Anthropology*, 45 (1), 31–60.

Ballinger, Pamela (2007), 'Borders of the Nation, Borders of Citizenship: Italian Repatriation and the Redefinition of National Identity after World War II', *Comparative Studies in Society and History* 49 (3), 713–41.

Billig, Michael (1995), *Banal Nationalism.* London: Sage.

Botteri, Guido (1981), *Un secolo un giornale: Il Piccolo, 1881–1981.* Trieste: Il Piccolo.

Brandenberger, David (2002), *National Bolshevism: Stalinist Mass Culture and the Formation of Modern Russian National Identity, 1931–1956.* Cambridge, MA.: Harvard University Press.

Bresadola, Gianmarco (2004), 'The legitimising strategies of the Nazi administration in northern Italy: Propaganda in the *Adriatisches Küstenland*', *Contemporary European History*, 13 (4), 425–51.

Cattaruzza, Marina (1995), *Trieste nell'Ottocento: Le trasformazioni di una società civile*, Udine: Del Bianco editore.

Cattaruzza, Marina (2001), *Socialismo adriatico: La socialdemocrazia di lingua italiana nei territori costieri della Monarchia asburgica: 1888–1915*. Manduria: Piero Lacaita Editore.

Cattaruzza, Marina (2002), 'Population dynamics and economic change in Trieste and its hinterland, 1985–1914', in Richard Lawton and Robert Lee (eds), *Population and Society in Western European Port Cities, c. 1650–1939*. Liverpool: Liverpool University Press, 176–211.

Cattaruzza, Marina (2007), *L'Italia e il confine orientale*. Bologna: Il Mulino.

Chernilo, Daniel (2007), *A Social Theory of the Nation-State: The Political Forms of Modernity beyond Methodological Nationalism*. London: Routledge.

Connor, Walker (1984), *The National Question in Marxist-Leninist Theory and Strategy*. Princeton: Princeton University Press.

Connor, Walker (1994), *Ethnonationalism: The Quest for Understanding*. Princeton, NJ: Princeton University Press.

Djokić, Dejan (2007), *Elusive Compromise: A History of Interwar Yugoslavia*. New York: Columbia University Press.

Duroselle, Jean-Baptiste (1966), *Le conflit de Trieste, 1943–1954*, Brussels: Editions de l'Institut de Sociologie de l'Université Libre.

Gellner, Ernest (1983), *Nations and Nationalism*. Ithaca, NY: Cornell University Press.

Gilman, Nils (2003), *Mandarins of the Future: Modernization Theory in Cold War America*. Baltimore: Johns Hopkins University Press.

Greer, Scott (2007), *Nationalism and Self-government: The Politics of Autonomy in Scotland and Catalonia*. Albany, NY: State University of New York Press.

Hobsbawm, Eric (1990) *Nations and Nationalism since 1780: Programme, Myth, Reality*. Cambridge: Cambridge University Press.

Jović, Dejan (2004), 'Communist Yugoslavia and Its 'Others',' in John Lampe and Mark Mazower (eds), *Ideologies and National Identities: The Case of Twentieth century South-eastern Europe*, Budapest: Central European University Press, 277–302.

Judt, Tony (2005), *Postwar: A History of Europe since 1945*. London: Penguin.

Kardelj, Edvard (1953), 'Splošne pripombe k narodnemu vprašanju', *Naša Sodobnost*, 1 (5), 404–9.

Lampe, John (2000), *Yugoslavia as History: Twice There Was a Country*, (2nd edn). New York: Cambridge University Press, 2000.

Lilly, Carol (2001), *Power and Persuasion: Ideology and Rhetoric in Communist Yugoslavia, 1944–1953*. Boulder, CO: Westview Press.

Mann, Michael (1993), *The Sources of Social Power* (Vol. 2), Cambridge: Cambridge University Press.

Marx, Karl and Friedrich Engels, (2008), *The Communist Manifesto*. Oxford: Oxford University Press.

McClintock, Anne (1995), *Imperial Leather: Race, gender and Sexuality in the Colonial Contest*. London: Routledge.

Mevius, Martin (2005), *Agents of Moscow: The Hungarian Communist Party and the Origins of Socialist Patriotism, 1941–1953*. Oxford: Oxford University Press.

Mihelj, Sabina (2011) 'Imperial myths between nationalism and communism: Appropriations of imperial legacies in the north-eastern Adriatic during the early Cold War', *European Historical Quarterly*, 41 (2), 623–56.

Negrelli, Georgi (1978), *Al di qua del mito: Diritto storico e difesa nazionale della Trieste asburgica*. Udine: Del Bianco Editore.

Novak, Bogdan (2005), *Hrvatsko novinarstvo u 20. stoljeću*. Zagreb: Golden Marketing – Tehnička knjiga.

Novak, Bogdan (1970), *Trieste, 1941–1954: The Ethnic, Political and Ideological Struggle*. Chicago and London: University of Chicago.

O'Leary, Brendan,'Ernest Gellner's diagnoses of nationalism: a critical overview, or what is Living and what is dead in Ernest Gellner's Philosophy of Nationalism?', in John Hall (ed), *The State of the Nation: Ernest Gellner and the Theory of Nationalism*, Cambridge: Cambridge University Press, 1991, 40–88.

Pahor, Milan (2004), *Slavljanska sloga: Slovenci in Hrvati v Trstu od Austro-ogrske monarhije do Italijanske republike*. Trieste: Založništvo Tržaškega Tiska.

Palmowski, Jan (2009), *Inventing a Socialist Nation: Heimat and the Politics of Everyday life in the GDR, 1945–1990*. Cambridge: Cambridge University Press.

Pupo, Raoul (2005), *Il lungo esodo – Istria: le persecuzioni, le foibe, l'esilio*. Milano: Rizzoli.

Ratner, Steven (1995), *The New UN Peacekeeping: Building Peace in Lands of Conflict after the Cold War*. New York: St. Martin's Press.

Redžić, Enver (1977), *Austromarksizam i Jugoslavensko pitanje*. Belgrade: Narodna knjiga, 1977.

Rodogno, Davido (2004), 'Italian soldiers in the Balkans: The experience of the occupation (1941–1943)', *Journal of Southern Europe and the Balkans*, 6 (2), 125–44.

Rusinow, Dennison (1977), *The Yugoslav Experiment, 1948–1974*. London: C. Hurst & Company.

Seton-Watson, Christopher (1980), 'Italy's imperial hangover', *Journal of Contemporary History*, 15(1), 169–79.

Shoup, Paul (1968), *Communism and the Yugoslav National Question*. New York: Columbia University Press.

Sluga, Glenda (2001), *The Problem of Trieste and the Italo–Yugoslav Border: Difference, Identity, and Sovereignty in Twentieth-Century Europe*. Albany: State University of New York Press.

Sluga, Glenda (2004), 'Narrating difference and defining the nation in late nineteenth and early twentieth century "Western' Europe,' *European Review of History*, 9 (2), 194–5.

Sluga, Glenda (2005), 'Identità nazionale Italiana e fascismo: alieni, allogeni e assimilazione sul confine nord-orientale italiano,' in M. Cattaruzza (ed), *Nazionalismi di frontiera: Identità contrapposte sull'Adriatico nord-orientale 1850–1950*. Soveria Mannelli: Rubbettino, 171–202.

Verdery, Katherine (1995), *National Ideology under Socialism: Identity and Cultural Politics in Ceaușescu's Romania* (2nd edn). Berkeley: University of California Press.

Verdery, Katherine (1996), 'Whither "Nation" and "Nationalism"?', in Gopal Balakrishnan (ed) *Mapping the Nation.* London: Verso, 226–33.

Wachtel, Andrew Baruch (1998), *Making a Nation, Breaking a Nation: Literature and Cultural Politics in Yugoslavia.* Stanford: Stanford University Press.

Wigger, Iris (2009), 'The interconnections of discrimination: Gender, class, nation and race and the 'black shame on the Rhine', *European Societies,* 11 (4), 553–82.

Wolff, Larry (2001), *Venice and the Slavs: The Discovery of Dalmatia in the Age of Enlightenment.* Stanford: Stanford University Press.

Zgodić, Esad (2000), *Titova nacionalna politika: temeljni pojmovi, nač elai vrijednosti.* Sarajevo: Kantonalni odbor SDP BiH.

Zimmer, Oliver (2003), 'Boundary mechanisms and symbolic resources: towards a process-oriented approach to national identity', *Nations and Nationalism,* 9 (2), 173–93.

Chapter 4

Kicking Under the Table: Minority Conflict Between Hungary and Romania[1]

Martin Mevius

1 Introduction

The basic context of ethnic tensions between Hungary and Romania was created long before the Cold War by the Treaty of Trianon (1920), which meant that Hungary lost two-thirds of its prewar territory and 40 per cent of its population to Yugoslavia, Czechoslovakia and Romania. Over the following two decades, Hungarian foreign policy was completely dominated by the demand for territorial revision. Although Hungary's military destruction in World War II removed the revision of borders from the mainstream political agenda, Hungarian concerns about the minorities living beyond them remained. By the same token its neighbours continued to eye Budapest with suspicion and to see their Hungarian citizens as disloyal. Relations with Romania, which had the largest Hungarian minority (about 2 million), were especially problematic. During the Cold War Western observers found it extremely difficult to gauge the nature of this relationship. Lacking solid sources, diplomats and journalists pored over official communiqués, carefully weighing every word in order to determine its precise significance. Their findings were limited: for example, in the 1970s and 1980s, Radio Free Europe knew that Hungary and Romania were increasingly at loggerheads over the minority[2] but could not establish any details.[3] Even in the 1980s when conflicts between the two countries erupted, they found it difficult to establish motives and policies. Not surprisingly, there was also little academic work on the ethnic conflict between the two states.[4]

More recent publications have shed new light on the relationship between the two countries and their respective communist parties. They show that relations between Romania and Hungary were marred by serious conflict, not just from the mid-1980s, but throughout the Cold War. Hungarian historians Mihály Fülöp and Gábor Vincze even speak of an 'Iron Curtain' standing between the two states from 1948 to 1955.[5] According to Stefano Bottoni, the seeds of Ceaușescu's particular national communist ideology were sown in the 1956 Hungarian Revolution: the unrest this created among ethnic Hungarians deepened Romanian distrust of the minority and led to Ceaușescu's 'national megalomania.'[6] Katalin Miklóssy argues that even under the rule of János Kádár (1956–1988) Hungarian foreign policy was dictated by national interests.[7] This suggests that the charge that has often been levelled at his regime by *émigré* critics, that it was not interested in the fate of Hungarians abroad, needs to be questioned. On the contrary, the fate of the Hungarian minority in Transylvania was a constant preoccupation of the communist leadership, not least because it reflected badly on itself. Hungary attempted to influence Romania's minority policy by the use of 'quiet diplomacy' but its attempts were largely unsuccessful. Instead of leading to an improvement of minority rights it triggered further conflicts between the two states. According to György Földes, two different 'national ideologies' were involved; whereas in Hungary communist leaders attempted to differentiate between patriotism and nationalism, in Romania they actively promoted a unitary, ethnically homogeneous nation. Liberal reforms in Hungary were a threat to Romania's Stalinist regime, while the minority itself posed a threat to the centralized concept of the Romanian nation-state.[8]

On the wider question of ethnic minorities in central and Eastern Europe during the Cold War, the consensus that prevailed, at least until recently, is summarized by Benett Kovrig's view that 'ethnic discrimination and interests were laid to rest' but 'over time' nationalism once again resurfaced.[9] Shared ideology, membership of the same political-economic bloc and Soviet dominance supposedly combined to inhibit national conflicts between the two states. In the following contribution, I take a different view, arguing that there were serious conflicts between Hungary and Romania and they lasted from World War II to the fall of the Berlin Wall. I concentrate especially on the genesis of these disagreements immediately after the war, a period that has often been neglected by historians. Since both the Romanian and Hungarian communist parties wished to appear as national parties, disagreements over borders and the treatment of the Hungarian minority were probably inevitable. In the end communist ideology failed to reduce ethnic strife because ethnicity was embedded in the lives and mentalities of those who were meant to be implementing policy. Party members were not mindless automata, ruthlessly implementing policy in conformity with Leninist principles. On the contrary, their attitudes and sentiments, reflecting their milieu and recent history, were national and sometimes nationalist.

The potential for conflict can be seen in the theory and practice of the communist movement itself. The writings of Marx and Lenin presented communists with ample ammunition for either supporting or suppressing nationalism and national movements. Marx himself believed that nationalism could have a progressive function: it might forge larger economic units or, as in Poland or Hungary, foment bourgeois revolutions against dominant conservative forces. Before the working class could move towards a world revolution, it had to become 'the leading class of the nation', indeed it had to become the nation as such 'although not in the bourgeois sense of the word'.[10] Lenin too conceded that workers could develop a strong national identity, noting in 1914 that '[w]e are full of a sense of national pride'.[11] This basic notion of a progressive national identity was developed in the Soviet policy of *korenizatsiya* ('indigenisation'), which encouraged the nationalities of the USSR to use their own languages and culture in order to spread socialism. In the 1930s, appeals to broader Soviet patriotism also became more prominent. Above all the German invasion of the Soviet Union led to the rallying of the population in the 'Great Patriotic War' and an infusion of patriotism with Russian national symbols. Under the direction of the Comintern, this appeal to national sentiments was followed by other communist parties. Stalin and Georgi Dimitrov, general secretary of the Comintern, now called on all 'sections' of the Comintern to fly the flag of national liberation and downplay the call for revolution. All European parties followed this 'national line'. The dismantling of the Comintern in 1943 was meant to underline this policy, by proving that communists were not, as their enemies claimed, 'agents of Moscow'.

After the war European communist parties continued this policy and presented themselves as patriots. In seeking to square this stance with Marxism, they contrasted the 'nationalism' of capitalist states with the 'true patriotism' of communist states. Whereas the former, often labelled 'chauvinism', was based on racism and the oppression of other nations, the latter supported movements of 'national liberation' and respected other cultures. This 'socialist patriotism' was deemed compatible with 'socialist internationalism'.

2 The Hungarian–Romanian Border

Both Hungarian and Romanian communist parties followed the Comintern line as they moved from working for the resistance to becoming masters of their own states. But presenting themselves as 'socialist patriots' was not easy, and even after the disbandment of the Comintern, both parties continued to be seen as Soviet stooges. In Romania, the communists had a particularly unpatriotic reputation because they had rejected Trianon and the cession of Transylvania to Romania. Worse still, in Transylvania thousands of Hungarians had flocked to join the party and formed the largest ethnic group within it. In 1946, as many as 70 per cent of Communist Party members in Transylvania were Hungarians, Jews or ethnic Germans ('Saxons').[12] In popular perceptions the presence of so many Hungarians, alongside Jewish activists confirmed the 'alien' or 'un-Romanian' character of the party.[13] On the other side of the border, Hungarian communists had attacked the Trianon treaty from the start.

The Transylvanian question thus served as an indicator of the extent to which the two parties were prepared to make appeals to nationalism. For example, at the end of the war both parties changed their names into more patriotic-sounding ones; the PCdR (Communist Party of Romania) became the Romanian Communist Party (PCR) and the Communist Party of Hungary (KMP) was renamed the Hungarian Communist Party (MKP). Both appropriated national heroes and staunchly defended national interests. But, as the Transylvania case shows, the two 'fraternal' parties also came into conflict.

Crucially, the outcome of the dispute depended on the Soviet Union. Before the German invasion it had approved the terms of the 'Second Vienna Award' of 1940, which paved the way for the annexation of northern Transylvania by Hungary, but then it shifted towards Romania. The PCR, in exile in Moscow, was quick to pick up on the change and its underground broadcasts argued that Romania's real enemy was not the USSR, but Germany and its ally Hungary.[14] The Hungarian communists also attempted to take a national line but soon found themselves constrained by the Soviet leadership. In 1942 Georgi Dimitrov, as head of the Comintern, delayed the publication of an article by the Hungarian communist leader Mátyás Rákosi on the grounds that it was too 'pro-Hungarian'.[15] However, Stalin himself remained noncommittal. The Romanian communist diplomat Valter Román later recalled that he promised Transylvania to whichever country would switch sides earlier; when Romania abandoned Nazi Germany in the coup of 23 August 1944 Rákosi immediately 'understood that we had lost Transylvania'.[16] Yet Stalin had not yet actually made a final decision. The ceasefire agreement with Romania was itself ambiguous in that it stipulated that Transylvania 'or its greater part' was to be returned to Romania. This qualifying clause made Romanian politicians – including communists – nervous and Hungarian politicians hopeful.

Soon afterwards, the Hungarian communist leadership discussed its post-war party programme in Moscow. József Révai, the party ideologue, explicitly left open the possibility of a peaceful border revision, and also made it clear that the party would not pursue an openly revisionist policy. The main reason he gave for this restraint was not sensitivity towards his Romanian comrades but his understanding that border revisionism was a 'provocation' that could damage Soviet interests.[17] Though Révai was not explicit he may have believed that overt Hungarian nationalism could harm communist prospects in Romania, which Stalin at the time was 'bolshevizing' more speedily than Hungary. For Stalin, keeping the dispute over Transylvania unresolved was above all a useful lever in post-war power struggles. In January 1945 he told the Romanian party leader Gheorghe Gheorgiu-Dej and the Secretariat member Ana Pauker that only a 'left wing' and 'pro-Soviet' government in Romania would win Transylvania.[18] The way he used the issue to reward 'good behaviour' was shown soon afterwards. On the very day that the pro-Soviet Petru Groza government was installed (6 March 1945) the Red Army transferred the civilian administration of Northern Transylvania to the Romanian authorities.[19] In September 1945 and again in March 1946 the Soviet government repeated its support for Romania's claim at the London Council of Foreign Ministers (CFM).

Though the Soviet stance encouraged Romanian politicians, it was not clear-cut enough to discourage Hungary's leaders from pursuing border revision. Both Rákosi and Ernő Gerő (a leading member of the Secretariat) were still convinced that the terms of the ceasefire agreement gave Hungary a chance at the negotiation table.[20] Rákosi proposed to the foreign minister, János Gyöngyösi, that Hungary demand a strip of land along the eastern border, (amounting to between 4,000 and 10,000 km^2) and hinted that Stalin supported the demand.[21] This became more plausible after a meeting in Moscow on 10 April 1946 when the Soviet leader did not reject Hungarian claims out of hand but told a Hungarian delegation, including Gyöngyösi and Rákosi, that the clause in the ceasefire agreement 'gives Hungary the possibility to receive part of Transylvania'.[22] Although he made no specific promises, Stalin did offer to support further investigation of the Hungarian claims at the Paris CFM. Yet shortly afterwards Molotov assured Romanian officials that the Soviet Union fully supported the Romanian position.[23]

Molotov's assurance makes it clear that when he urged the Hungarians to initiate bilateral negotiations on the border issue on 15 April, it was a purely cosmetic exercise. The Soviet leadership wanted to pass the buck to avoid incurring unpopularity for the decision to support Romania. Nevertheless, it allowed the Hungarian delegation to return to Budapest in a mood of optimism. The Hungarian Smallholders Party (the largest party in the government coalition) now declared that the country could count on Soviet support on foreign policy issues. The communist leadership shared this optimism. On 22 April Rákosi claimed that the delegation had won Soviet 'benevolence' towards Hungarian peace aims. For the first time Hungarian communists now publicly made territorial claims on Romania, when József Révai argued in favour of limited border revision in a speech at the Budapest Music Academy. He said there was a 'strip with a Hungarian majority' along the border, for which 'we are striving in direct negotiations',[24] and mentioned specifically the cities of Satu Mare, Baia Mare, Oradea, Salonta and Arad. He added that he had reason to believe that the USSR would support the claim.[25] The speech caused uproar in Hungary, because 'everybody thought Révai's speech was based on serious promises'.[26] But in fact Révai had gone a step too far and was reprimanded for not having presented his speech to the Politburo for prior approval. In his defence, he claimed – whether correctly or not is unclear – that he had shown the speech in advance to the Soviet ambassador Pushkin.[27] For his part, Rákosi later claimed that Stalin and the 'Romanian comrades' had been critical of the speech's 'nationalist tendencies'.[28]

On 27 April 1946, the Hungarian envoy Pál Sebestyén tried to persuade the Romanian Foreign Minister Gheorge Tatarescu and Prime Minister Petru Groza to open bilateral negotiations. He insisted that Hungary had support from 'our joint great friend, the Soviet Union'.[29] The Romanians, who knew better, rejected the proposal. At a meeting with Romanian party leaders on 7 May, Gerő presented a proposal for a border change of 37,000 km² in Hungary's favour, which Gheorghiu Dej rejected out of hand.[30] On the very same day Ferenc Nagy learnt not only that the Paris CFM had decided to transfer the whole of Transylvania to Romania, but also that Molotov, in particular, had insisted on this.[31] Gheorghiu-Dej could now proudly claim that Transylvania had been given to Romania in recognition of its 'democratic' government.[32] The Hungarian communists saw things differently. As the party's Moscow representative, Rezső Szántó put it, '[w]e expected a lot from the Russians, and when the baselessness for this became clear, an anti-Soviet atmosphere was established'.[33]

None of the surviving records of the deliberations shows that either Stalin or other Soviet leaders specifically promised anything to Rákosi or Ferenc Nagy. But they did mislead them when they pointed out that the ceasefire agreement had technically left open the possibility for Hungary to 'regain' territory. Molotov then deliberately pushed for bilateral negotiations he knew to be futile. As he let slip to the Hungarians, this was little more than window-dressing, which would mean that 'the Romanians either accept or decline, but you have done your duty'.[34] Stalin and Molotov were clearly determined not to be blamed for directly rejecting Hungarian claims. But Soviet evasiveness was matched by a good dose of Hungarian wishful thinking. Foreign minister Gyöngyösi later admitted they had all exaggerated the success of the Moscow trip. According to Rezső Szántó, Rákosi and Gerő had actually been told 'clearly how far it was possible to go' but had then misrepresented the Moscow discussions on their return. Rákosi himself stated quite openly that

> our people took the notion that Hungary has the right to take up certain territorial claims. . . a little further and presented it as if the rightfulness of taking up these claims means that the Soviet Union supports these claims with all its might. Without a doubt there occurred from the returning delegation a certain exaggeration.[35]

This wishful thinking was in the end not just a lapse. It reflected the Hungarian communists' desire to represent themselves as defenders of the national interest in order to counteract the widespread view that they could not be trusted. In that sense the border dispute gives a good insight into the way nationalism worked within the Eastern bloc as a whole. Stalin used Transylvania as a bargaining tool and left his Eastern European minions guessing about his intentions. The resulting uncertainty fuelled the conflict between the Romanian and Hungarian parties.

3 The Practice of Romanian Minority Policy

Hungarian communists never pursued the goal of border revision more than half-heartedly: they could not afford to remain silent on the issue in public without incurring political embarrassment. But defending the Hungarian minority in Romania seemed an acceptable alternative and at first sight the prospects looked promising: Romania's post-war nationality legislation was certainly more liberal than that of its inter-war predecessors.[36] The (pre-communist) Rădescu government established a Ministry of Minority Nationalities, and on 6 February 1945 the Decree on the Status of Minority Nationalities laid down a range of minority rights, including provisions on language use. Rather than a 'national minority' Hungarians were now dubbed a 'co-inhabiting nationality', which implied greater equality.[37] The treatment of Hungarians under Rădescu's successor, Petru Groza, was highly praised by contemporaries and is still generally viewed positively. But in practice ethnic relations were marred by serious violence, and this in the end also affected the relationship between the Hungarian and Romanian communist parties.

Hungarian rule in Northern Transylvania from 1940 to 1944 had been far from benevolent. In 1940 Hungarian troops and vigilantes killed 158 Romanians in Ip, and four years later 93 people in Treznea.[38] When Hungarian officials left in autumn 1944 the area slid into a state of anarchy. After Romania had declared war on Germany and on Hungary (7 September 1944) Romanian paramilitary groups took advantage of the collapse of authority to wreak bloody revenge.[39] The Romanian Peasant party leader Iuliu Maniu called for the creation of voluntary military units for the reconquest of Transylvania. The communist-dominated representative body for Hungarians in Romania, the Hungarian Popular Alliance (*Magyar Népi Szövetség/* MNSz), accused these 'Maniu guards' (which it numbered at 10,000) of perpetrating atrocities against Hungarians.[40] It compiled an exhaustive list of abuses right up to 1946, and sent it to the Hungarian foreign ministry in Budapest.[41] One of the most serious abuses had taken place in October 1944 in the Székely town of Aite Seace when a self-appointed captain called Gabril Olteanu led a troop of Maniu guards from door to door to round up the townspeople. They were assembled in the school yard and forced to strip to their underwear before 26 selected men were accused of 'crimes against the Romanian army' and condemned to death. In the words of the report: '[i]n the yard of the school they erected a large scaffold. On the scaffold they first tried to execute Sándor Nagy with an axe' but 'due to the large hump on his back they didn't succeed in killing him'. The guards then shot him, killed eleven other people and started shooting into the crowd. Romanian villagers intervened and begged the guards to spare the lives of their Hungarian neighbours.

Olteanu and his band now moved on to other Transylvanian towns and villages. In Sândominic they shot several villagers, both men and women. In Gheorgheni they shot a number of people in the local brick yard. Maniu guards also murdered Hungarians in Cart, Dăneşti and Madaras. According to the MNSz, the Maniu guards were also guilty of theft, rape, beatings and robbery. István Kovács from Sfântu Gheorghe complained that Maniu guards had plundered his home and 'violated and defiled' his heavily pregnant wife. In the same town guards arrested Béla Lapikas for carrying a blue-yellow-red Romanian national armband. They beat him up and wrecked his shop. In Cozmas guards stole livestock and threatened to kill Hungarians who protested. In Miercurea/Ciucului they marched around town shouting 'this is now Romania and we have come to kill all Hungarians'. They then searched houses for weapons, pillaged them and beat up their occupants. Elsewhere, armed troops 'violated numerous Hungarian women' and set fire to the library of the primary school.

Though this detailed, day-by-day account compiled by the MNSz gives an impression of comprehensiveness, it should also be borne in mind that it was written in order to provoke a response from Budapest. This may have led some distortions. For example ordinary neighbourhood squabbles may have been 'ethnicised', while conciliatory Romanian actions, like the intervention of Romanian villagers in Aite Seace, which suggest that ethnic animosities were far from a spontaneous grass-roots upsurge, may have been ignored altogether. Overall, the inclusion of many relatively petty complaints in addition to the few examples of deadly violence in itself probably exaggerates the extent of tensions. Nevertheless, the point here is that Hungarians in the MNSz genuinely felt themselves to be collective victims. The detailed lists of anti-Rumanian complaints, which now began to circulate in Hungary, required a political response.

Abuses did not stop after the Red Army took control, the Maniu guards disbanded and authority was formally handed over to Bucharest (March 1945). Killings occurred throughout the spring and summer of 1945, though beatings were now the most common outcome. In July 1945 a staff sergeant of the gendarmerie beat up a 17-year-old boy who had failed to understand his instruction in Romanian. In Tileagd (Bihor county) 'chauvinist Romanian elements' attacked Hungarians for speaking Hungarian amongst themselves. In Ghurghiu, Romanians attacked Hungarian youths at a dance 'because they sang in Hungarian'. The murders, beatings, theft and petty violence continued into 1946.[42]

Worse than these crimes, in the view of the MNSz, was the 'mass deportation of Hungarian men', including anti-fascist and even communist activists. The MNSz newspaper *Világosság* blamed Romanians for misleading the Soviet authorities: 'malignant circles tricked the fighting Soviet troops, who hauled away the Hungarians from Cluj on suspicion of being [anti-Soviet] partisans'.[43] According to the county union secretary Pál Veres, among the 3,000 Hungarians deported by the Red Army from Cluj were 'countless communist and socialist workers'.[44] Men were also deported from smaller towns. In Sandra, having already deported the men, Soviet troops now threatened to deport the women as well. Only when the remaining children pleaded with them did local Red Army commanders intervene and release them.

The Romanian authorities also constructed several camps, with the stated purpose of detaining fascists and anti-Soviet partisans. The MNSz complained that the majority of those arrested and imprisoned in 'bestial' circumstances, without either detailed charges or a trial, were 'innocent ordinary people'.[45] The camp which had by far the worst reputation was Feldioara near Brasov, where Olteanu brought his captives from Northern Transylvania.[46] According to contemporary press reports, the camp had 6,000 inmates, many of whom died of cold and hunger. After visiting the camp, one of the prisoner's wives wrote: 'I saw how the utterly weakened prisoners were made to dig graves, but they weren't capable of digging enough graves in which to bury the daily dead'. According to another wife, 'the prisoners insisted that someone do something for them, because if not they would be destroyed'. The day she visited the camp, inmates buried 15 corpses, but had 30 fresh dead for whom they did not have the strength to dig graves. According to another correspondent, the death toll rose to between 20 and 30 per day during a typhoid epidemic. Since the camp administration did not compile statistics, no reliable figures are available of the total number of victims, but in 1993 the Romanian Defence Minister Niculae Spiroiu claimed the death toll was 298. At the time Feldioara was popularly known as a 'death camp' and the MNSz explicitly compared the Rumanian acts to Nazi genocide.[47]

There were also widespread complaints of systematic discrimination, including inequitable treatment by both Soviet Military courts
and People's Courts.[48] Economic discrimination was a further cause
for concern and here the Decree on the Control and Monitoring of
Enemy Property (CASBI) on 10 February 1945 was a particularly
painful blow.[49] The government justified it on the basis of the
Romanian-Soviet armistice of 12 September 1944, which had laid
down that enemy assets would be frozen. But its application to
Hungarians was controversial, because it meant that even though
Hungary, having declared war on Germany on 22 January 1945, was
now officially an ally, Hungarians were defined as enemy aliens.[50] To
find a way around this, Romania's (communist) Minister of Justice
introduced the legal innovation of the 'presumptive enemy', which
allowed Romanian authorities to appropriate the goods of some
30,000 Hungarians. Though formally aimed at Hungarians who had
entered Northern Transylvania after its annexation in 1940, the decree
actually affected all Hungarians who had fled from the approaching
Red Army in 1944. It is a measure of the long-term complications
caused by these expropriations that many were still unresolved
in 2005.[51] Land reform was another area of contention. According to
the MNSz, the Transylvanian Hungarians suffered 'very serious
grievances' as a result of the 'mistaken or tendentious application' of
the new law.[52] While Hungarian landlords were deprived of their land,
the beneficiaries were seldom Hungarian peasants. Instead most of
the land was divided up among newly arrived Romanian migrants.[53]

4 Hungarian Communist Reactions

By 1946 most of the positive effects of the Minority Nationality Decree
had been nullified by the violence and discrimination applied to the
Hungarian minority. The Hungarian communist leadership closely
followed the deteriorating situation and in August 1945 two young
party officials, Géza Losonczy and Sándor Haraszti, visited Transylvania
and wrote an extensive report. Although it noted that the Hungarian
minority 'enjoy precious little of the solemnly proclaimed national
rights' promised by the Groza government, it did not put the main
blame on Groza but on 'reactionary officers', 'iron guardist elements'

and 'Maniu guards', who had 'completely flooded the state apparatus' and 'openly opposed the government's intentions'. Especially in the countryside the 'serious atrocities' committed by 'reaction' had provoked much bitterness. The assault by 'Romanian chauvinism' had led to a strong Hungarian chauvinist atmosphere', so that 'the chauvinist mood has to an extent flowed over into the Hungarian workers and village toiling masses as well'.[54]

The report then described the changed stance of the Romanian party and the attitude of the Hungarian minority towards it. Before the war many Hungarians had joined the party when it had stood up for minority rights and rejected Trianon. Now the PCR applauded Trianon and even though it did not explicitly reject minority rights, it subordinated them to the 'democratic transformation of Romania'. The Bucharest party leadership had sent instructors to Transylvania in order to enforce this line 'very rigidly' and was banning any discussion in the press or in meetings of the 'daily repeated Romanian chauvinist attacks'. Transylvanian communist leaders condemned this policy of 'waiting' as 'false and incorrect'. Losonczy and Haraszti also argued that a continued failure by the Hungarian party to act would only embolden 'the Romanian reaction' and would alienate the working classes in Transylvania, 85 per cent of which, they claimed, were Hungarian.[55]

The kind of local opposition to central party authorities described in the report was not unheard of in post-war Eastern Europe. During the war, communist activists in Hungary (and elsewhere in occupied Europe) had often refused to abandon the internationalist, revolutionary line in favour of the new national line advocated by the Moscow emigration. Now some more radical Hungarian communists rejected the Romanian party's new national policy altogether. Some even called for a union with the Soviet Union, for example, at a meeting attended by 40,000 people in the Upper Tisza region. Similar demands were voiced in the Székely region but were successfully suppressed by the party leadership.

Outside the ranks of the Romanian party, this kind of separatist agitation only strengthened the conviction that communism as a whole was alien and unpatriotic. What Losonczy and Haraszti called 'these serious errors' strengthened 'the Romanian chauvinist wave'.

Conversely, the minority communist leaders who rejected the Romanian party line were 'genuinely popular with the workers and even with the party membership'. The Transylvanian communist leader Lajos Jordáki, for example, was the 'most popular man of the working class movement' because he 'gladly makes concessions to the chauvinist mood of the Hungarian masses'. This contrasted starkly with the popular assumption that the MNSz was passive or inactive in representing minority interests. In fact the MNSz did protest about atrocities and expropriations, and in the end this helped get the camps closed[56] but the protests generally took place behind closed doors. Losonzcy and Haraszti concluded that this caution had become 'untenable' since it meant that local Hungarians saw most MNSz representatives as 'traitors' and 'Romanian mercenaries'.[57]

In summary, Transylvania witnessed a growing tension between two variants of communist nationality policies. The new Romanian communist line of presenting the party as a patriotic, mass party departed from its longer-standing support for Hungarian minority rights. The Romanian party leadership condemned Hungarian protests against the new line as 'left wing exaggerations' and cracked down on local communists. The Minister of Justice Lucreţiu Pătrăşcanu told the Hungarian communists their demands for equal treatment were 'exaggerated and chauvinist'.

Despite the orthodox Marxist idiom in which it was expressed, there was also a clear ethnic dimension to this and the other purges of Hungarian leaders in Transylvania (including Jordáki). At its heart was the policy of 'Romanianising' the Communist Party, which led to an influx of new members.[58] Throughout the conflict between local Transylvanian communists and the national leadership of the PCR, Marxist analysis and ethnic (national) arguments were intertwined. For example, Haraszti and Losonczy, reflecting the view that the working classes were the engine of history, had been understandably alarmed by signs that the party was losing the support of Hungarian workers. The mirror image of their concern was the attempt by the PCR to ethnically 'reengineer' the workforce in the train assembly yard in Cluj by demanding the sacking of hundreds of Hungarian workers at the yard, and their replacement by ethnic Romanians. The combination of class and ethnic factors can also be seen in the demolition by vandals of the statue of the nineteenth-century Hungarian politician Count Tisza Kálmán in Oradea. Losonczy and Haraszti did not really know what to make of this but in the end they decided to see it as a nationalist, anti-Hungarian attack:

> Obviously Tisza Kálmán was a reactionary, but the bombing of the statue was not aimed against the reactionary, but against the Hungarian Tisza Kálmán and was therefore a chauvinist provocation of the Hungarians.

Losonczy and Haraszti themselves were treated by the Transylvanian Hungarians as Hungarians rather than communists. A speech which Losonczy gave in Cluj was greeted with tremendous approval; every time he mentioned the names of the MKP or Hungarian communist leaders such as Rákosi, the audience demonstrated its approval through an 'explosive, gigantic applause'. Losonczy saw this show of support for communists as evidence of a 'chauvinist atmosphere' as the auditorium was not only composed of workers, but members of the local bourgeoisie as well.

Regardless of this assessment it is clear that a gulf was opening up on the minority question, which would continue throughout the Cold War. While the Romanian party could not afford to appear 'soft' on the issue, the Hungarian party could not afford to be silent. This was especially the case after József Révai in effect had abandoned border revision as hopeless and shifted the focus of policy to a defence of Hungarian minority, not just in Romania but also in Slovakia, where authorities were pursuing a policy of mass deportation.[59] But Révai felt that while the MKP was ready to condemn Hungarian nationalism and attacks on Romania in public, the PCR was not reciprocating. His irritation can be seen in a letter to Vasile Luca (László Luka), a leading Romanian communist of Hungarian origin. According to Révai, while the MKP was struggling against 'Hungarian chauvinism', 'tactical considerations' forced it to break its silence about 'certain complaints of the Transylvanian Hungarians'. But he complained to Luca that 'from your statements it somehow appears as if such complaints do not exist'. This 'did not correspond to the truth' and 'would unnecessarily provoke the already sensitive

Hungarian public opinion'. As a solution he proposed a deal: '[a]s we understand your situation, understand ours as well'.[60]

5 The Cold War and Ethnic Conflict

With the hardening of the confrontation between East and West the conflict between the Romanian and Hungarian communist parties intensified. Formally, of course, the establishment of Cominform (1947) and the Treaty of Mutual Friendship and Cooperation placed the relationship between the two countries on a 'fraternal basis' yet in many ways relations actually worsened. First, conflicts over the implementation of the CASBI decrees and other expropriations increasingly soured relations. The Romanian government not only blocked Hungarian efforts to have property restituted but on 11 June 1948 went a step further by nationalizing factories and companies. The measure even included the property of the Hungarian state, now under the control of the MKP. Second, the position of the Hungarian minority deteriorated markedly. On 21 November 1948, Rákosi secretly met with Gheorghiu-Dej and Vasile Luca in the Hungarian border town of Mezőhegyes. Rákosi complained that the Hungarian minority was now 'more isolated than under Antonescu' and 'the more securely we [communists] are in the saddle, the worse this situation gets'.[61] The main points at issue were not education, cultural or language rights, about which the Romanian communists seemed to be taking a relatively tolerant line, but the orientation of the minority towards Budapest, which Romanian communists saw as evidence of disloyalty. According to Vasile Luca, 'a part of Romanian Hungarian communists expects instructions from Budapest and not from Bucharest'.[62] This attitude, which Haraszti and Losonczy had also observed, was confirmed when Hungarian embassy officials visited Transylvania. When an embassy car visited Cluj Hungarian villagers mobbed the vehicle and 'stroked' the official flag of the People's Republic.[63] They seemed indifferent to the fact that it was the flag of a communist state.

The Romanian response to these signs of 'disloyalty' was a policy of isolation. This started with a purge by the Romanian Foreign ministry not just of 'reactionaries' but also of experts on Hungarian affairs.[64]

Subsequently, representatives of the minority were forbidden to approach the Hungarian embassy in Bucharest, while other Romanian Hungarians were intimidated into keeping their distance from the embassy.[65] Ambassador Jenő Széll was personally affected by this isolationist policy when the entry of his 4 to 5 year-old children into a nursery was 'expressly sabotaged'.[66] Széll also reported that as the government tried to excise every reference to Hungary from official statements, he himself was introduced to the 1948 conference of the MNSz as 'a foreign diplomat' and mostly cold-shouldered. He also noted that although the pictures of the Hungarian national poets Ady and Petőfi were displayed at the meeting, there were none of Hungarian communist leaders: 'It was conspicuous, at least it was conspicuous to me, that Mátyás Rákosi in particular was not mentioned'.[67] Rákosi then complained bitterly to Gheorghiu-Dej that the local organizers 'very correctly elected communist leaders from Mao Zedong to Thorez into the honorary presidency, but not one Hungarian communist leader was among them'. While Hungary permitted 'unlimited' quantities of Romanian communist literature to enter the country, Romania continued to restrict literature from Hungary, even when it was communist. Rákosi also complained that it was impossible to subscribe to communist newspapers from Hungary. Neither were Hungarian classics allowed into the country, even when they were published by communist publishers after 1945. This was 'diminishing the worth of other measures that you took in the spirit of Marxist-Leninist nationality policy' and was 'grist to the mill of Hungarian nationalists'. Rákosi therefore asked the Romanian leadership to put an end to 'these damaging incidents'.[68]

His complaints had little effect. In order to further isolate the minority the Romanian government now shut down the border with Hungary altogether. Just as the Iron Curtain was 'descending across Europe' border controls between these two Iron Curtain states were being tightened. In 1948 the Romanian government proposed building a 500-metre zone along the border in which there was to be no high foliage.[69] After negotiations in Mezőhegyes the Romanians cut off low-level border traffic altogether, which, as Rákosi noted, 'affects in the first place the Hungarians, who live on both side of the border'.[70] He also complained that the Romanian authorities were not implementing the visa arrangements which had been agreed between the two countries on 16 October 1948. With a normal (i.e. non-diplomatic) passport it was now 'impossible to travel from Transylvania to Hungary or the other way round'. There were even 'armed Romanian border violations',[71] as when border guards arrested several peasants who were working on Hungarian territory in August 1947, shot four of them and beat up several others.[72] In the same year Romanian border guards shot and killed a Hungarian farmer. Afterwards, the Hungarian authorities accused the Romanians of forging official documents in order to prove he had been smuggling.[73] In April 1948 Romanian border guards wandered into Hungarian territory, arrested several people and took them back across the border.[74] Later in the year they even shot at peasants working in the field in Hungary.[75] In 1952 Romanian guards practised with live ammunition and shot across the border with it. The situation was apparently so tense that warnings had to be given to avoid shoot-outs with Romanian border guards.[76] At the same time, the term 'violent border crossing' did not always live up to its dramatic implications, and could signify no more than a single armed guard crossing the border. On 24 July 1948, for instance, Hungarian authorities opened an investigation into a 'violent incursion' by the border guard Valér Kokolean who allegedly 'crossed the border bearing weapons and there physically abused Julianna Medgyesy, an inhabitant of Garbolcs'. Kokolean denied the accusations, and stated he 'had only pushed her, but had not hit her'.[77] The Romanian justification was that as the 'forward bastion' of the USSR, Romania needed to protect its borders with particular care. This was clearly meant as an insult to the Socialist credentials of Hungary, or in Rákosi's phrase, 'not in accordance with the relationship between two People's Democracies'.[78]

In the early 1950s, as the Cold War entered its deepest freeze, relations between Hungary and Romania further worsened. Admittedly in some areas there was progress: the CASBI issue was buried, albeit only temporarily. And in 1952 Gheorghiu-Dej presented a show-piece of his nationality policy in the form of the Hungarian Autonomous Region. This was meant to offer a modicum of self-rule to some of Romania's Hungarians, albeit within the limits of Stalinist dictatorship.[79] Hungarian culture was positively promoted, along similar lines to the

Soviet policy of 'indigenization'. However, the tight grip of the PCR on the administration meant that the actual level of autonomy was lower than that of the Soviet republics.[80] And 'self-rule' in a Stalinist state was, of course, in any case a relative concept; even as the Autonomous Region was being constructed, Transylvanian Hungarians were being accused of 'espionage' in a series of show trials. The first in 1951 was the secret trial of the 'revisionists', Áron Marton, Gyárfas Kurkó and others, who were accused of espionage for Belgrade and attempting to get Hungary to re-annex Transylvania.[81] In 1954 a second show trial was held, this time of the 'Transylvanists': the former MNSz leader Edgár Balogh and the one time popular local communist Lajos Jordáki were put behind bars for having sought the re-annexation of Northern Transylvania to Hungary.[82] When Ana Pauker and Vasile Luca were purged from the Communist Party leadership in 1952, Luca was himself accused of irredentism.[83]

Above all, the major source of Hungarian complaints, namely the isolation of the minority from Budapest, was not addressed. Despite encouraging local Hungarian culture the border remained tightly sealed and access to information about Hungary was severely restricted. Though locally produced Hungarian newspapers could reach print-runs of up to 50,000 there was 'no material referring to Hungary in them'.[84] The Romanian press published few articles about Hungary. According to a Hungarian Embassy report of 1950, press coverage was not 'rich' but 'showed all the important things briefly'. The report also noted that, despite an increase in the number of articles, the Hungarian press still wrote more about Romania than the other way round.[85] Romania also continued to forbid the distribution of the Hungarian press in Transylvania and even the party newspaper *Szabad Nép* was restricted. In 1948 the newspaper had sold out within a matter of hours[86] but now only 1,000 issues were permitted for the entire country,[87] despite constant efforts by the Hungarian embassy to increase its print run (and that of other Hungarian publications). However, the embassy did not support the Hungarian government's decision to retaliate by restricting Romanian magazines in Hungary. It described this as a 'serious political mistake' since it would give Romanian party officials a further argument for restricting the distribution of Hungarian publications.[88]

6 The Hungarian Revolution and After

The 1956 Hungarian uprising was the defining moment in the relations between the two countries. It came as a 'sense of panic' was spreading within the leadership of the PCR in the aftermath of Khrushchev's 'secret speech' to the 20th Congress of the Soviet Communist Party.[89] The fears were as much about territorial revision as about liberalization. Before the revolution the Romanian diplomat Valter Román accused Rákosi of raising the possibility of population transfers and border revision.[90] Even if Román was lying (as Rákosi later claimed) his intervention illustrates how preoccupied Romania's leaders were about a possible threat to their position in Transylvania. Their sensitivity did not come out of thin air: as the situation in Hungary became increasingly volatile, anti-Stalinism in Transylvania took an increasingly national form. From the start the Hungarian population in Romania had followed developments in Budapest, like the reburial of László Rajk. The state's initial response to the first murmurs of protest was to make concessions, like admitting Hungarian authors to the Writers Union and restoring the birth house of poet Endre Ady.[91] But when the revolution threatened to cross the border the situation began to escalate. On 24 October a meeting of students in Cluj turned into a show of solidarity with revolutionaries in Budapest.[92] Then on 30 and 31 October Romanian and Hungarians teachers and students at the Timişoara Polytechnic presented a range of political and economic demands and booed officials sent by the Central Committee. In Transylvania there were spontaneous meetings at the Tîrgu Mureş University, and even in Bucharest students protested. In October and November the security services arrested 1,120 people.

The 1956 revolution cast a lasting shadow over the already poor relations between Romanian and Hungary. Although Romanians were also involved in the unrest, and some were arrested and executed, the regime chose to interpret it primarily in ethnic terms, as confirmation of the basic disloyalty of its Hungarian citizens. It also increased Romanian suspicion that irredentism was being supported from Hungary. Partly as a response Romanian nationalism as a whole became more marked. This can be seen, for example, as Stefano

Bottoni argues, in the crackdown on the Hungarian minority, which started with the fusion of the Hungarian Babes University with the Romanian Bolyai University in 1959 and led, in the following year, to the curtailment of Hungarian autonomy in the Autonomous Region.[93] Ultimately, the 1956 revolution was at the root of what Bottoni calls Ceaușescu's 'national megalomania'.[94]

The linked fear of irredentism and liberalization also helps explain the Romanian shift towards an increasingly independent stance within the Warsaw Pact. In 1961 the Plenum of the Central Committee of the PCR had already rejected its allotted role within the Eastern bloc as an agricultural producer and instead opted for a policy of autarky.[95] In the famous 'April Declaration' of 1964 it announced its independent position within the Soviet bloc. Later, Ceaușescu flirted with China and the United States and in 1968 condemned the Warsaw Pact invasion of Czechoslovakia. This policy of 'going it alone' caused further conflict with Hungary, in effect reversing the roles of the two countries within the Soviet camp. In 1958 the Soviet Union had rewarded Romania for its support in crushing the Hungarian revolution by withdrawing its troops. By the end of the 1960s it was Romania which was the pariah. Whereas Brezhnev accepted Kádár's reforms, however, grudgingly, he saw Ceaușescu as a major irritant. But rather than openly voicing criticism of Romania, the Soviet leadership devolved the task to Hungary. According to Katalin Miklóssy, although there were no explicit Soviet instructions to criticize the Romanians, Brezhnev made his disapproval of Ceaușescu abundantly clear behind closed doors. And the Hungarian leadership clearly thought they had been given a green light to criticize Romania in public.[96] Tensions were further increased by the impact of Hungarian economic reforms. Kádár's 'New Economic Mechanism', which was introduced in 1968, brought a relaxation of economic controls, which was anathema to the Romanian leaders. It provided them with a further reason to restrict contacts between the Hungarian minority and its 'kin-state'.

For all Ceaușescu's independent line, the issues which plagued the Hungarian–Romanian relationship were basically the same as before: minority rights and the isolation of the minority from Hungarian influence. In the early 1960s travel restrictions were eased on paper but in practice Hungarians wishing to visit Romania still faced huge obstacles. A secret annex to the 1961 bilateral visa agreement stipulated that they were obliged to report to the local police upon arrival.[97] Though tourism became possible in the 1960s and 1970s, visiting Hungarians complained about the behaviour of Romanian border guards, including extortion, confiscation of property (including Hungarian literature) and police brutality, including beatings. Hungarians also continued to be cut off from news about Hungary. In the early 1970s, Hungarian reports stated that the Romanian press stuck to the bare facts when writing about Hungary, omitting any analysis. The Hungarian press did not return the favour but instead toed the Soviet line, including open criticism of Ceauşescu's rapprochement towards China.[98] In the early 1980s a growing number of negative articles started appearing about both countries. At a Budapest cocktail party in 1982, Romanian diplomats loudly argued with the Bucharest correspondent of the Hungarian state press agency (MTI), complaining that '90 per cent' of Hungarian articles on Romania were negative while the comparable figure for Romanian articles on Hungary was 'only 40 per cent'.[99]

In theory the only way for Hungarians to evade these restrictions (apart from a small number of official subscribers) was through the post. However, mail tended to be intercepted and returned, which, according to the Hungarian embassy in Bucharest was something that even capitalist countries (with the apparent exception of Argentina) did not do.[100] Romania also jammed Hungarian radio and TV broadcasts.[101] In 1977, the Hungarian embassy complained once again about the way the Romanian authorities stopped publications getting through and noted that it was almost impossible to find publications from Hungary in Romanian-speaking districts.[102] The answer Hungary came up with in the 1980s was hardly fraternal: it smuggled Hungarian publications into the country. By means of this so-called 'remainders action' (*remittenda akció*) the embassy 'discretely' and 'carefully' disseminated 'politically important' unsold stock of Hungarian publishers.[103] The Hungarian foreign ministry fully supported the scheme since, even though it 'cost a lot of energy' it was an 'important' part of propaganda work.[104]

On top of these long-standing complaints, there were some new public squabbles about history and public memory. In 1961 Hungary complained about a Romanian history of Transylvania, arguing that because of its emphasis on the Romanian origins of the region it was 'nationalist'.[105] The publication in 1965 of the memoirs of Admiral Horthy caused major misgivings in Romania, and there were heated debates about it at the Romanian–Hungarian summit of July 1964.[106] Hungarian diplomats also complained that the Romanians were 'appropriating' their national heroes. One of the bitterest conflicts came with the 1970 celebration of the anniversary of Gheorghe Doja, the sixteenth-century peasant rebel. Known in Hungary as György Dózsa, he had long been portrayed by Hungarian communists as their spiritual predecessor in the struggle for national and social liberation. Hungarian embassy officials were therefore horrified when the Romanian government claimed that he was Romanian. The Hungarian state staged its own Dózsa year in 1972.

Controversies continued throughout the 1970s and reached another low point with the publication on 12 April 1982 of Ion Lancranjan's pamphlet *One Word about Transylvania*. This bitter attack on Hungary was met with extreme displeasure by the Hungarian Political Committee (Politburo), which saw it as part of the 'anti-Hungarian propaganda that has been printed in the Romanian press organs for over a year now'.[107] Another controversy was sparked by the publication four years later by the Hungarian Academy of Sciences of a three-volume *History of Transylvania*. There was an official outcry in Romania, and the debate raged far outside Eastern Europe. A paid advert in the London *Times* denounced the work as a falsification of history, and an official brochure was published condemning it as a 'conscious forgery'.[108]

Just before the Iron Curtain fell, the breakdown of Romanian–Hungarian relations was complete. Ceauşescu's bulldozing of Transylvanian villages, combined with poverty, repression and discrimination led thousands of Hungarians to flee to Hungary. Rumours of war were in the air. The Hungarian foreign minister Rezső Nyers complained to Ceauşescu that Romanian publications were clamouring for a 'military solution' to the Hungarian problem.[109] A year after he presided over the dismantling of the border fence between Austria and Hungary, Foreign Minister Gyula Horn voiced concerns over Romanian plans to build nuclear weapons and Romanian threats to Hungarian territorial integrity.[110]

7 Public Opinion and Nationalism

The disputes that hit the headlines after 1989 were not a break with the past but its continuation. The two governments had been vigorously kicking each other under the table for decades. The argument that this and similar conflicts were suppressed during the Cold War wrongly implies that communists, as internationalists, were ready to bury their national conflicts in the interest of socialist solidarity. In reality, as I have sought to show here, both regimes pursued national interests and saw the world with national eyes. This also applies to Communist Party members themselves in both Hungary and Romania. They operated within a frame of reference which was national and frequently displayed national sentiments and national resentment towards their neighbours, in short, all those feelings which were normally condemned in official propaganda as 'chauvinist'. Evidence of this can be found in the sneeringly sarcastic tone adopted by Hungarian diplomats when they derided Romanian propaganda aimed at demonstrating 'what glorious revolutionaries the Romanian people are'.[111] It is also evident in the numerous petty complaints that litter the archives of the Hungarian Foreign Ministry.[112] At the same time, they were sensitive to subtle shifts in the language of Romanian congratulatory telegrams: addressing 'the entire Hungarian people' instead of 'the friendly Hungarian people', for instance, or dropping the word 'warm' from the phrase 'warm comradely greetings'.[113] It is striking how similar this kind of close textual analysis was to that adopted by Radio Free Europe and Western diplomats in order to gain insights into Romanian politics. Evidently, the Hungarians found this world no less inaccessible.

Ordinary Hungarian party members were even more hostile. Extensive instruction about socialist patriotism and proletarian inter-nationalism seems to have had little impact. Local party secretaries frequently reported about meetings where national sentiment was freely vented. Here 'socialist patriotism', however compatible with internationalism in principle, appeared to contradict it in practice. Appeals to display pride in the 'Socialist Fatherland' often brought an implicit disparagement of other Socialist countries. 'Our agriculture is so good, that the entire Socialist community can learn from it', local party members in the Járás district boasted. In Budapest local party members took pride in the assertion that 'in western eyes our form of socialism is the most acceptable'.[114] Sometimes this sense of superiority looked more like 'socialist nationalism' than socialist patriotism.

When it came to the minority, this disparaging attitude also undercut the communist claim to have found a 'solution' to the issues that plagued the capitalist world. Hungarian propaganda had long emphasized the mistreatment of minorities in the West and especially decried the fate of blacks in the United States, which was contrasted with the supposedly progressive treatment of Hungary's Slovak minority. Yet the Hungarian public was more inclined to apply the comparison to the disadvantage of Romania. As Party members in Vas county put it:

> our mass communications whine about Negroes, Basques and Arabs, but keep quiet about the grievances of Hungarians living abroad, especially those of the minorities living in neighbouring countries.[115]

The party secretary of a factory in Budapest noted the workers' national pride in the People's Republic 'because we do not have a national question at all'. But the same workers were highly critical of Romania: '[s]everal measures by the Romanian People's Republic cause indignation, one can say, animosity'.[116] It is hard to escape the conclusion that one reason these party members were proud of Hungarian nationality policy was because it made Romania's treatment of Hungarians look bad in comparison. Elsewhere the depth of racism, anti-semitism and anti-Arab sentiments among party members emerged clearly.[117] The Vas party secretary complained about 'hidden nationalist views', which included an 'anti-Soviet attitude', and opposition to Hungary's membership of the Warsaw Pact. In Budapest, authorities noted 'especially strong worries' regarding the Romanian situation and 'nationalist and chauvinist' views among party members about the Trianon settlement, the legitimacy of which was still being questioned 30 years after the 1947 Paris Peace Treaties.[118] For some older party members, 'Transylvania and Slovakia were still "an issue"'.[119] Some expressed national pride in the beauty of Transylvania and openly said how 'great' it would be if it could be part of Hungary again. They were still bitter about the way Soviet Union had then shifted away from the Hungarian position.[120] One local party secretary noted that party members 'condemn the methods used against the minorities' in Romania and strikingly added his own view that this was 'in part with just cause'.[121] In Vas 'quite extreme opinions' about Romania were reported. Some thought the Hungarian government was too soft on Romania and wanted 'hard, decisive behaviour'.[122] By the 1980s these kinds of opinions were expressed openly at party meetings. Evidently, no one feared that criticism of Romania would get them into trouble.

8 Conclusion

On the eve of the collapse of communism, Gyula Horn wrote an appraisal of Romanian–Hungarian relations. Horn, who was a veteran of Hungarian foreign relations, did not differentiate between the pre-war Antonescu regime and communist Romania. For seven decades, he argued, Romanian politics had been was marked by 'the strategic goal of creating a unitary national state by forcibly changing ethnic composition, in order to maintain territories conquered by force of arms.' Hungarian foreign policy had failed because, through its silent diplomacy and emphasis on 'internationalist solidarity' it had 'played into the hands of realizing the Romanian leadership's goals'.[123] Under communism, Horn argued, Romania had exploited the division of the world in order to achieve its perennial anti-Hungarian aims.

Horn's memorandum illustrates how the Cold War affected Hungarian–Romanian relations and ethnic issues in general: as argued here, it did not bottle up ethnic disagreements, but actually deepened them. Though officially committed to eradicating national-ism, communist regimes in both Hungary and Romania had perpetuated it. Shared ideological ground did not prove an obstacle to this since both parties simply claimed that it was their policies that were genuinely Marxist. In private Hungarian party members voiced anti-Romanian views, which were in stark contrast to the official doctrines of internationalism. Fraternal solidarity was often invoked but in reality the bilateral relations between Romania and Hungary functioned like those of any other neighbouring nation-states with minority issues.

These issues never ceased to be a source of conflict and tension. In Romania, the Hungarian minority was feared as a source of competing communist authority or, even worse, of political liberalization. Though the Hungarian government often stated that minority policy was a Romanian 'internal affair', which it did not wish to intervene in, in practice the Hungarian party was preoccupied by it. The main explanation for this is that Romanian policies reflected badly on the standing of the MKP within Hungary. Soviet dominance of both states was unchallenged throughout the period, but this did not mean that conflict and disagreement were contained; on several occasions Soviet interference actually worsened relations. Immediately after World War II, both the Romanian and the Hungarian communist parties strove to appear as patriotic members of national front governments. This was itself a Soviet-inspired policy, designed after 1941 by Dimitrov and Stalin in order to mobilize the Russian population in defence of the German invasion. It meant that each party strove to defend its national interests and came into conflict when they diverged. In the case of the Hungarian–Romanian border, Soviet meddling also increased tensions between the two parties in 1946. Because communism in Hungary was perceived by the Romanian leadership as a threat to its own authority, the Cold War pushed Romania into greater isolation, cutting off the minority from Budapest as much as it could by tightening border controls and limiting access to information.

The 1956 uprising delivered the death blow to Romanian–Hungarian relations by establishing the Romanian view of Hungary as a source of subversive 'liberal' ideas and, by extension, of Hungarians in Transylvania as bad communists. From the 1960s Romania's independent foreign policy put an added strain on the relationship, especially as Budapest played the role of chief critic of the Ceaușescu regime. In the end Ceauşescu's virulent nationalism caused relations to collapse completely.

Throughout the period Hungarian officials operated within the logic of the nation-state rather than of the communist international. Even when their animosity was partly constrained by Soviet dominance and the need to show a united front against the common, Western enemy, there was little love lost between them and their Romanian comrades. Official attempts to instill a sense of international solidarity into the party rank-and-file failed utterly and little separated them from the rest of Hungarian society. This suggests a broader conclusion: the party exercised absolute control over education and the media, yet it did not succeed in changing basic nationalist attitudes regarding Romania. Rather than succeeding in turning peasants into Bolsheviks, the party imported nationalist attitudes and national prejudices into its ranks. It seems that by the 1970s, attitudes within and outside the party were not altogether different. Perhaps we therefore need to question some received wisdom about communist rule, not just in Hungary. Not only did communist dictatorships not exercise anything like absolute control over the minds of their subjects, but party members were themselves clearly far from devoid of national feeling.

Notes

[1] The research on which this paper is based was conducted at the University of Amsterdam and funded by the Netherlands Organisation for Scientific Research (NWO).

[2] Robert R. King and William F. Robinson, 'Romanian–Hungarian Relations: Friendship with Reservations?' Open Society Archives, Budapest (OSA), 1972, http://files.osa.ceu.hu/holdings/300/8/3/text/35-2-29.shtml. [Accessed 24 September 2009].

[3] See, for example, Patrick Moore, 'Romanian Foreign Minister in Hungary (RAD Background Report/46)', OSA, http://files.osa.ceu.hu/holdings/300/8/3/text/36-8-9.shtml [accessed 24 September 2009].

[4] A notable exception is Robert King's excellent study on disagreements among Warsaw Pact states *Robert King, Minorities under Communism: nationalities as a source of tension among Balkan Communist states*, Cambridge, MA: Harvard University Press, 1973.

[5] Mihály Fülöp and Gábor Vincze, *Vasfüggöny Keleten. Iratok a magyar-román kapcsolatokról (1948–1955)*, Debrecen: Egyetemi Kiadó, 2007.

[6] Stefano Bottoni, *Transilvania rossa. Il communismo romeno e la questione nazionale (1944 - 1965)*, Rome: Carocci, 2007; similarly Ildikó Lipcsey, (ed), *Magyarromán kapcsolatok, 1956–1958*, Budapest: Paulus Publishing, 2004.

[7] Katalin Miklóssy, *Manoeuvres of national interest: internationalism and nationalism in emerging Kadarist criticism of Romania 1968–1972*, Helsinki: Kikimora Publications, 2003.

[8] György Földes, *Magyarország, Románia, és a nemzeti kérdés, 1956–1989*, Budapest: Napvilág Kiadó, 2007, 490.

[9] Bennet Kovrig, 'Partitioned Nation: Hungarian Minorities in Central Europe', in Michael Mandelbaum (ed), *The New European Diasporas. National Minorities and Conflict in Eastern Europe*, New York: Council on Foreign Relations Press, 2000, 43.

[10] Karl Marx and Friedrich Engels, *The Communist Manifesto*, Oxford: Oxford University Press 2008.

[11] V.I. Lenin, 'On the National Pride of the Great Russians,' (Marxists Internet Archive, 1914). http://www.marxists.org/archive/lenin/works/1914/dec/12a.htm [accessed 30 November 2010].

[12] Tamas Lonhart and Virgiliu Târau, 'Minorities and Communism in Transylvania (1944–1947)', in Anne Katherine Levai Isaacs, Csaba and Vasile Vese (eds), *Tolerance and Intolerance in Historical perspective*, Pisa: Edizoni Plus, 2003, 25–45.

[13] King, *Minorities under communism*, 36.

[14] Fülöp and Vincze, *Vasfüggöny Keleten*, 313.

[15] Georgi Dimitrov, *The Diary of Georgi Dimitrov*, ed. Ivo Banac, (*Annals of Communism*). New Haven - London: Yale University Press, 2003, 249.

[16] Fülöp and Vincze, *Vasfüggöny Keleten*, 312.

[17] Archive of the Institute for Political History, Budapest. PIL 742/8, 1–11.

[18] Fülöp and Vincze, *Vasfüggöny Keleten*, 13.

[19] Islamov, Tofik and Tatiana Vladimirova Volokitina, (eds), *Transílvanskiy vopros: vengerskorumynskii territorial'niy spor i SSSR 1940–46*, Moscow: ROSSPEN 2000, 9.

[20] Fülöp and Vincze, *Vasfüggöny Keleten*, 16.

[21] Ferenc Nagy, *Struggle behind the Iron Curtain*, New York: Macmillan 1948, 204.

[22] Tatiana Vladimirova Volokitina and Tofik Islamov, (eds), *Vostochnaya Evropa v dokumentakh rossiyskikh archivov 1944–1953 gg*, vol 1. 1944–1948, Moscow: Novisibirksi' Sibir'skii Khronograf, 1997, 402–6.

[23] Mihály Fülöp, 'The Failure of the Hungarian–Rumanian Negotiations in the Spring of 1946,' *New Hungarian Quarterly*, 118, (34), (1990), 65.

[24] Draft Speech 'The Hungarian Peace' n.d. Révai Papers. Manuscript Collection of the Library of the Hungarian Academy of Sciences (MTAKK MS), 10.475/4.

[25] 'About the Hungarian Peace' MTAKK MS 4395/5.

[26] 'On the Question of the Foreign Policy of the Hungarian Communist Party,' Notes by Rezső Szántó (Russian), n.d., PIL 742/9, 63–4.

[27] Rezső Szántó, Notes and transcript, n.d., PIL 742/10, 25–41, 42–55.

[28] Mátyás Rákosi, *Visszaemlékezések 1940–1956*, ed. Istvan Feitl, Budapest: Napvilág 1997, 308.

[29] Mihály Fülöp, *Revizió vagy autonómia. Iratok a magyar-román kapcsolatok őrténetéről (1945–1946)*, Budapest: Teleki László Alapítvány 1998, 182–7.

[30] Fülöp and Vincze, *Vasfüggöny Keleten*, 17.

[31] Nagy, *Struggle behind the Iron Curtain*, 220.

[32] Fülöp and Vincze, *Vasfüggöny keleten*, 18.

[33] PIL 742/10, 25–41, 42–55.

[34] Nagy, *Struggle behind the Iron Curtain*, 210.

[35] Rákosi report to Central Committee, 17 May 1946, PIL 274.2/34, 1–35.

[36] Kovrig, 'Partitioned Nation', 45.

[37] Irina Culic, 'Dilemma's of Belonging: Hungarians from Romania,' *Nationalities Papers,* 34 (2), (2006).

[38] Maria Bucur, 'Treznea. Trauma, nationalism and the memory of World War II in Romania', *Rethinking History,* 6 (1) (2002), 35–55.

[39] Marina Blau, *Horthy's atrocities in the North of Transylvania (September 1940-October 1944),* Los Angeles, CA: Mariana Blau, 1977.

[40] 'The atrocities committed against the Hungarians of Transylvania since 23 August 1944', n.d., Hungarian National Archive (MOL), 1168–1265.

[41] *Ibid.*

[42] Zoltán Keresztes to Sándor Nékás, n.d. ('On the situation of the Hungarians in the Bánat'). MOL XIX-J-1-J-Románia-1945-1964-15d, 336/46.

[43] Report 'Consideration of the minority policy of the Gróza government', n.d. MOL XIX-J-1-J Románia-1945-1964-15d, 0032959/45.

[44] MOL XIX-J-1-j-Románia-1945-1964-14d, 1168–1265.

[45] Levente Benkő, 'A tervszerű merénylet', *Korunk* 14 (2), (2003). http://epa.oszk.hu/00400/00458/00062/oldal9616.html [accessed 8 December 2010].

[46] Maria Gál, Attila Balogh, and Imreh Gajdos, *The White Book. Atrocities committed against Hungarians in the Autumn of 1944 (In Transylvania, Romania).* Cluj: Barna Bodó 1995) [Hungarian original by the Political Section of the Acting Presidium of the Democratic Alliance of Hungarians in Romania].

[47] Benkő, Tervszerű merénylet.

[48] MOL XIX-J-1-J-Románia-1945-1964-15d, 0032959/45.

[49] Ildikó Lipcsey (ed), *Magyar-román kapcsolatok, 1956–1958.* Budapest: Paulus Publishing, 2004, 69–71.

[50] Gábor Vincze, 'A rumanizálástól az államosításig. Az erdélyi magyar iparvállalatok és pénzintézetek sorsa a magyarbarát Groza-kormány idején (1945–1948).' (Special Collection on Regional and Minority History of the University of Szeged) http://www.arts.uszeged.hu/doktar/texts/hargita.html, [accessed 6 January 2009].

[51] 'Information related to Romanian restitutions', Hungarian Embassy, Bucharest, 28 October 2005. http://www.mfa.gov.hu/kum/hu/bal/Konzuli informaciok/Utazas kulfoldre/Utazasi tanacsok/051 109 tajekoztato romaniai karpotlas.htm

[52] Domokos Gyallay-Pap, 'Subject: situation in Arad', 7 February 1946, MOL XIX-J-1-j Románia-1945-1964-15d, 295/46.

[53] MOL XIX-J-1-J-Románia-1945-1964-15d, 336/46.

[54] Sándor Haraszti and Géza Losonczy, 'Transylvanian report', n.d., PIL 274.10/71, 28–35.

[55] *Ibid.*

[56] Lonhart and Târau, 'Minorities and communism in Transylvania'.

57 PIL 274.10/71, 28–35.
58 Lonhart and Târau, 'Minorities and communism in Transylvania', 32.
59 József Révai, 'A magyarkodók ellen,'*Szabad Nép*, 13 January 1946.
60 József Révai to Gheorge Luka, 15 January 1946.' PIL 274.10/71, 61.
61 Mátyás Rákosi to Gheorge Gheorghiu-Dej, 6 January 1949. MOL 265.65/112, 1–9.
62 Report, Tamás Aladár, 6 October 1947. PIL 274.10/71, 75.
63 Iván Kalló (Hungarian Ambassador to Romania), Report on tour of Transylvania, 21 December 1950, MOL 276.65/212, 64–7.
64 'Report on trip to Bucharest', 19 December 1948. MOL XIX-J-1-j-Románia1945-1964-15d, 0342/3.
65 *Ibid.*
66 *Ibid.*
67 Jenő Szél (Hungarian Ambassador to Romania) to László Rajk', 18 December 1948, MOL 276.65/212, 4–11.
68 MOL 265.65/112, 1–9.
69 'Memorandum on issues awaiting resolution in Hungarian–Romanian relations', 15 November 1948, MOL 276.65/212, 2–3.
70 Mariana Blau, *Horthy's atrocities.*
71 MOL 276.65/212, 2–3.
72 Fülöp and Vincze, *Vasfüggöny Keleten*, 31 n. 134.
73 MOL XIX-J-1-j-Románia-1945-1964-15d, 0342/3.
74 'Continuing investigation by Romanian–Hungarian committee into the violent border crossing of organs of the Romanian border guard', 7 August 1948. MOL XIX-B-HOP-1948-IV-14, 002.
75 Report, 8 May 1948'. MOL XIX-B-HOP-1948-13 d. IV-5, 005.
76 'The arrest of András Borbély, inhabitant of Apártfalva, by organs of the Romanian border Guards', 1 September 1951. MOL XIX-B-10-HOP-1952-13d.
77 Memorandum, György Gráber, 24 July 1948, MOL XIX-B-10-HOP-1948-13d, 02.
78 MOL 276.65/212, 2–3.
79 Bottoni, , 68–9.
80 Stefano Bottoni, 'De la répression politique à la purge ethnique? L'impact de la revolution de 1956 sur le modèle communiste roumain', in Dan Catanus and Vasile Buga (eds), *Lagărul Comunist Sub impactul Destalinizării 1956*, Bucharest: Institutul National Pentru Studiul Totalitarismuslui, 2006.
81 Fülöp and Vincze, *Vasfüggöny Keleten*, 38–9.
82 *Ibid*, 39–40.
83 *Ibid.*
84 Zoltán Horváth to Népszava secretariat, 7 May 1949, MOL 265.65/212, 46–50.
85 Press political summary for November, 5 December 1950, MOL XIX-J-1-J-Románia-1945-1965-10d, 031312.
86 'Report on the Bucharest negotiations relating to the cultural agreement', n.d., MOL 276.80/8, 9–13.
87 Bottoni, *Transilvania rossa*, 94.

[88] 'Visit to book publishing and book distribution director Manescu', 10 January 1952, MOL XIXJ-1-J-Románia-1945-1964-15d, 0086.

[89] Lipcsey, *Magyar-román kapcsolatok*, 18.

[90] Fülöp and Vincze, *Vasfüggöny Keleten*, 47.

[91] Bottoni, De la répression politique', 377–8.

[92] Lipcsey, *Magyar-Román kapcsolatok*, 18.

[93] Bottoni, 'De la répression politique', 377–8.

[94] Bottoni, *Transilvania rossa*.

[95] Miklóssy, *Manoeuvres*, 78.

[96] *Ibid.*, 103.

[97] Frigyes Puja and János Péter. 'Draft Memo to the Political Committee of the MSzMP on the development of relationship between the Hungarian People's Republic and Romanian People's Republic since the meeting of the party and government delegations of both countries in 1961', 21 February 1964, MOL XIX-J-1-J-Románia-1945-1964-8d, 00664/964.

[98] László Kincses. 'The Romanian press about Hungary from 1 August to 30 December 1971', 19 January 1972. MOL XIX-J-1-J-Románia-1972-89d, 00972.

[99] Ferenc Szőcs, 'The censure of the MTI correspondent', 23 June 1983, MOL XIX-J-1-J Románia-1983-111d, 004092.

[100] Dávid Meiszter, 'Memorandum,' 12 September 1964. MOL XIX-J-1-J-Románia-1945-1964- 17d.

[101] 'Draft material for the highest level Hungarian–Romanian negotiations', 14 May 1964. MOL XIX-J-1-J-Románia-1945-1964-7d.

[102] 'The Distribution of Hungarian papers in Romania', 9 June 1977. MOL XIX-J-1-J-Románia 1977-112d, 001756/17.

[103] László Péter, 'The 1983 annual meeting of the propaganda council', 3 November 1983, MOL XIX-J-1-J-Románia-1983-121d, 005840.

[104] András Dékány, 'The evaluation of the distribution of remainders', 15 December 1983, MOL XIX-J-1-J-Románia-1983-121d, 006422. 8/11/83.

[105] Béla Köpeczi, 'Erdély története harminc év távlatából', in KislebbségkutatáS (Minorities Research) (2006). http://www.hhrf.org/kisebbsegkutatas/kk 2006 01/cikk.php?id=1332 [accessed 8 August 2008].

[106] 'Proceedings of the second day of Hungarian–Romanian negotiations', 2 July 1964, MOL XIX-J-1-J-Románia-1945-1964-8d, 06444/2. Esp pp. 261–2.

[107] 'Proposal for our statement on the Lancranjan book', 5 June 1982, MOL XIX-J-1-J-Románia 1982-120d, 003212/4.

[108] Stefan Pascu, *A conscious forgery of history under the aegis of the Hungarian Academy of Sciences*, Bucharest: Agerpress, 1987.

[109] Rezső Nyers, 'Report to the Political Organising Committee', 10 July 1989, MOL 288.11/4463, 213–15.

[110] Douglas Clarke, 'The Romanian Military Threat to Hungary', Radio Free Europe/Radio Liberty Background Report, 27 July 1989. http://www.osa.ceu. hu/files/holdings/300/8/3/text/37-6-86.shtml [Accessed 08 August 2008].

[111] László Gergán, 'Commemoration in Romania of the 125th anniversary of the bourgeois democratic revolution of 1848', 11 May 1973, MOL XIX-J-1-J-Románia-1973-92d, 002877.

[112] See, for example, Hungarian complaints that Romanians were purposely mis-translating Hungarian official communiqués in order to make them appear less friendly: 'Our Leaders' Telegram concerning the Romanian statement', 25 August 1966, MOL XIX-J-1-j-Románia-1966- 98d, 00377/10.

[113] 'Romanian leaders' greeting telegram concerning the liberation of our home-land', n.d., MOL XIX-j-1-j-Románia-1982-118d, 002966.

[114] 'The improvement of the Budapest party members theoretical level', MOL 288.22/1976/40, 70–87.

[115] 'Report on the importance of the struggle against manifestations of national-ism, anti-Sovietism and cosmopolitanism', MOL 288.22/1976/40, 116–27.

[116] 'The improvement of the party members' theoretical level', MOL 288.22/1976/36, 180–88.

[117] MOL 288.22/1976/40, 116–27.

[118] MOL 288.22/1976/40, 70–87.

[119] MSzMP Paks District Committee, untitled document, 4 June 1976, MOL 288.22/1976/37, 73–8.

[120] MOL 288.22/1976/40, 116–27.

[121] MOL 288.22/1976/37, 73–8.

[122] MOL 288.22/1976/40, 116–27.

[123] Gyula Horn, 'Informational handout on the Hungarian Romanian relation-ship and its handling', 16 June 1989. MOL 288.11/4460, 32–40.

Bibliography

Benkő, Levente (2003), 'A Tervszerű Merénylet,' *Korunk* 14 (2).

Blau, Mariana and Ruth Adomeit (1977), *Horthy's atrocities in the North of Tran-sylvania (September 1940-October 1944)*. Los Angeles, CA: Orban Mariana Blau.

Bottoni, Stefano (2006), 'De la répression politique à la purge ethnique? L'impact de la revolution de 1956 sur le modèle communiste roumain', in Dan Cata-nus and Vasile Buga (eds), *Lagărul Comunist Sub Impactul Destalinizării 1956*. Bucharest: Institutul National pentru Studiul Totalitarismului.

Bottoni, Stefano (2007), *Transilvania Rossa. Il communismo romeno e la questione nazionale (1944–1965)*, Rome: Carocci.

Bucur, Maria (2002), 'Treznea. Trauma, Nationalism and the memory of World War II in Romania', *Rethinking History*, 6 (1), 35–55.

Clarke, Douglas (1989), 'The Romanian Military Threat to Hungary', Radio Free Europe/Radio Liberty Background Report, 27 July 1989.

Culic, Irina (2006), 'Dilemma's of belonging: Hungarians from Romania,' *Nationalities Papers*, 34 (2), 175–200.

Dimitrov, Georgi (2003), *The Diary of Georgi Dimitrov*, ed. Ivo Banac, (*Annals of Communism*). New Haven-London: Yale University Press.

Földes, György (2007), *Magyarország, Románia, és a nemzeti kérdés, 1956–1989.* Budapest: Napvilág Kiadó,

Fülöp, Mihály (1990), 'The Failure of the Hungarian–Romanian Negotiations in the Spring of 1946', *New Hungarian Quarterly*, 118 (34), 61–71.

Fülöp, Mihály (1998), *Revizió vagy Autonomia. Iratok a magyar-román kapcsolatok törtenétéről (1945–1946).* Budapest: Teleki László Alapítvány.

Fülöp, Mihály and Vincze Gábor (2007), *Vasfüggöny Keleten. Iratok a magyar-román kapcsolatokról (1948–1955).* Debrecen: Egyetemi Kiadó.

Gál, Maria, Attila Balogh, and Imreh Gajdos (1995), *The White Book. Atrocities Committed against Hungarians in the Autumn of 1944 (in Transylvania, Romania).* Budapest: Barna Bodó. [originally published in Hungarian by the Political Section of the Acting Presidium of the Democratic Alliance of Hungarians in Romania].

King, Robert R. and William F Robinson (1972), 'Romanian–Hungarian Relations: Friendship with Reservations?', Open Society Archives, Budapest, [http://files.osa.ceu.hu/holdings/300/8/3/text/35-2-29.shtml].

King, Robert R (1973), *Minorities under Communism: Nationalities as a source of tension among Balkan communist states.* Cambridge, MA: Harvard University Press.

Köpeczi, ' Béla (2006), Erdély története harminc év távlatából', in *Kissebség-Kutatás* (Minorities Research), 1. [http://www.hhrf.org/kisebbsegkutatas/kk 2006 01/cikk.php?id=1332 accessed 8 August 2008].

Kovrig, Bennet (2000), 'Partitioned nation: Hungarian minorities in Central Europe', in Michael Mandelbaum (ed), *The New European Diasporas. National Minorities and Conflict in Eastern Europe.* New York: Council on Foreign Relations Press, 19–80.

Lipcsey, Ildikó (ed.) (2004), *Magyar-Román Kapcsolatok, 1956–1958.* Budapest: Paulus Publishing.

Lonhart, Tamas and Virgiliu Târau (2003), 'Minorities and Communism in Transylvania (1944–1947),' in Anne Katherine Levai Isaacs, Csaba and Vasile Vese (eds), *Tolerance and Intolerance in Historical Perspective.* Pisa: Edizoni Plus, 25–45.

Marx Karl and Friedrich Engels (2008), *The Communist Manifesto.* Oxford: Oxford University Press.

Miklóssy, Katalin (2003), *Manoeuvres of National Interest: Internationalism and Nationalism in Emerging Kadarist Criticism of Romania 1968–1972.* Helsinki: Kikimora.

Nagy, Ferenc (1948), *Struggle behind the Iron Curtain.* New York: Macmillan.

Pascu, Stefan (1987), *A conscious forgery of history under the aegis of the Hungarian Academy of Sciences* , Bucharest: Agerpress.

Rákosi, Mátyás, Istvan Feitl, Márta Gellériné Lázár, Levente Sipos (1997), *Visszaemlékezések 1940–1956.* Budapest, Napvilág.

Révai, József (1946), 'A magyarkodók ellen,' *Szabad Nép,* 13 January 1946.

Islamov, Tofik and Tatiana Vladimirova Volokitina (eds) (2000), *Transílvanskiy Vopros: Vengersko-Rumynskii Territorial'niy Spor I SSSR 1940–6.* Moscow: ROSSPEN.

Vincze, Gábor 'A romanizálástól az államosításig. Az erdélyi magyar iparvállalatok és pénzintézetek sorsa a magyarbarát Groza-kormány idején (1945–1948)' (Special Collection on Regional and Minority History of the University of Szeged). http://www.arts.u-szeged.hu/doktar/texts/hargita.html, [accessed 6 January 2009].

Volokitina, Tatiana Vladimirova Voliktinia and Islamov, Tofik, (eds), (1998) *Vostochnaya Evropa V Dokumentakh Rossiiskikh Arkhivov 1944–1953 gg,* (vol 1. 1944–1948), Moscow: Novisibirksi' Sibir'skii Khronograf.

Chapter 5

Insecurity and Control: Bulgaria and its Turkish Minority

Vasil Paraskevov

1 Introduction

The Cold War had a significant impact on the minority policies of the
Bulgarian Communist Party (Bulgarska Kommunisticheska Partiya/
BKP). At their heart was the basic sense of insecurity felt by the
country's rulers in their quest for total control. In the case of
the Turkish minority this was expressed in a deep suspicion that the
Turkish 'kin-state' might use its grievances to destabilize the regime.
The Truman Doctrine of March 1947 may have been intended by the
US government to guarantee the defence of Turkey against communist
destabilization, but in the eyes of Bulgaria's rulers it heralded US
backing for their neighbour and this was a threat. Its basis in reality
was that the radical political and social reform programme which the
BKP was implementing, was indeed provoking profound tensions
and even military resistance. For example, the 'Forest People'
(*Gorani*) continued fighting in the mountains against communist
rule well into the 1950s. Most of them were motivated by discontent
with political repression, the suppression of constitutional rights and
the collectivization of agriculture. Although the support given to
them by foreign powers was insignificant and there is no evidence
that Turkey and Greece delivered any weapons, the BCP nevertheless
concluded that the American secret services, together with the Greek
and Turkish authorities, were seeking to destabilize the regime.[1]

Bulgarian fears were strengthened when Turkey came out in
support of US policies during the Korean War and in 1952 joined

NATO. In addition to coordinating its policy with Washington, Ankara strengthened its relations with Greece and Yugoslavia by the creation of the Balkan Pact in 1953. Though this was aimed at defending member countries from Soviet aggression it too was seen in Sofia, perhaps unsurprisingly, as an act of hostility.[2] Even more significant were the fears that developing ethnic tensions in Cyprus might cause similar unrest to spread to Bulgaria's Turkish minority. Yet even though this suspicion and insecurity was never far from the Bulgarian communist 'official mind', policy towards the Turkish minority was far from consistently repressive. Broadly speaking, it evolved from an initial phase, lasting until the end of the 1950s, when cultural, religious and educational rights were supported by the state, to a period where the regime sought to 'solve' the ethnic problem by restricting minority rights and promoting assimilation.

Any understanding of the political dimensions of this insecurity has to start off with the basic reality of the country's subservience to the Soviet Union. That meant in the first case the slavish imitation of the Soviet model in every aspect of policy, including the treatment of minorities. Second, Bulgaria was completely integrated into the political, economic and military structures of the Soviet bloc, while its southern neighbour Turkey, as the Truman doctrine envisaged, received substantial political, economic and military support from the West. This basic adversarial context shaped all Bulgarian assessments of Turkey's foreign policy. Third, the Communist Party (until 1948, part of the Fatherland Front (*Otechestven Front*)), the dominant force in Bulgarian society and politics, was irreconcilably hostile towards any individuals or groups which were not under its control. This hostility was greater when, as with the Bulgarian Turks, the group had the potential to maintain contacts beyond the country's borders. Last not least, as a historically marginalized group with its own religious, cultural and educational traditions, Bulgaria's Turks were widely seen as backward. In that perspective, their orientation towards Turkey was condemned not just as subversive but also contrary to the regime's fundamental project of modernizing and 'europeanising' Bulgarian society. All in all this made the minority a source of considerable unease among Bulgarian communists as they waged their double battle; the international fight for the victory of Marxist–Leninism and the domestic struggle for radical social transformation.

The way the BKP tried to 'manage' ethnic conflict, and particularly to deal with conflicts relating to the Turkish minority has been much studied in Bulgarian historiography. There is a broad consensus that its policy emerged from the interplay of domestic and international factors, though recent studies have given more weight to the former. Scholars have also analyzed the reasons for the shifts that took place in minority policy, from the initial phase of relative 'toleration' to the more integrationist policies of the 1960s and mid-1970s, and finally to the intense assimilation of the last phase of communist rule. Several authors have recognized that the Cold War had an impact on minority policy but few have examined the relationship in any detail. For example, Evgenia Kalinova argues that the Cold War had 'direct influence on the behavior of both countries [Bulgaria and Turkey] and their policy on the migration issue'.[3] Rumyana Todorova, Jordan Baev and Nikolai Kotev have also stressed the impact of the Cold War on Turkish–Bulgarian relations, showing how badly the atmosphere of mutual suspicion, mistrust and hostility affected Bulgarian Turks.[4] Another important influence has been noted by Valeri Stoyanov, who has established a connection between the treatment of the minority and the Soviet stance on 'the national question'.[5] He has shown that Bulgaria followed the general line of Soviet politics in its attitude towards the Turkish minority. In short, policy was the outcome not just of the broad antagonisms of the Cold War but also of the country's specific relationship with the Soviet Union on the one hand and Turkey on the other.

For reasons of space, the discussion here focuses more on the relationship between the Cold War and communist policy than on the political and cultural life of the minority itself.[6] Its main argument is that Bulgaria's minority policy can be seen as a function of the country's subservient relationship with the Soviet Union and the search by the state and the Communist Party for the complete domination of Bulgarian society. In particular it seeks to extend to the earlier period Vesselin Dimitrov's argument that the assimilationist policies of the 1980s 'emerged as a result of a combination of threats and opportunities on number of levels'.[7] It argues further that the division of the world was seen simultaneously as a foreign policy *threat* (Turkey), as an *opportunity* for the government to 'deal with' ethnic minorities free of firm internal or external pressure and, last not least, as a *source of stability* in that it brought continuous political, economic and military support from the Soviet Union.

2 The Bulgarian–Turkish Context

Relations between Bulgarians and Turks have rarely been simple. At the establishment of the modern Bulgarian state after liberation from Turkish rule by the Treaty of Berlin (1878), a significant Turkish minority (usually estimated at about 10 per cent of the total population) remained within the new national boundaries. In 1900, Bulgaria had a total population of 3,744,283 of which Bulgarians made up 77 per cent (2,887,860) and Turks 14 per cent (539,656). The other important ethnic minorities were Roma (2.4 per cent), Greeks (1.9 per cent) and Jews (0.9 per cent), but in the aftermath of World War I, the number of Greeks decreased drastically to 10,564 (0.19 per cent). After World War II, the total population rose to 7,613,709 (according to the 1956 census). Of these, 85.5 per cent were Bulgarian (6,506,541), 8.6 per cent Turks (656,025) and 2.6 per cent Roma (197,865).[8]

In the Bulgarian nation-building project, which stressed the country's emancipation from its former rulers and fostered Bulgarian language and culture, the Turkish minority tended to be marginalized and sometimes feared. At the same time, its treatment was a sensitive international issue. The Treaties of Berlin and Neuilly (1919) both contained clauses guaranteeing the rights of ethnic, religious and cultural minorities (without including equivalent provisions for Bulgaria's neighbours). The wars that Bulgaria waged with its neighbours in the course of its national unification also left a legacy of bitterness, which persisted until after World War II. The most sensitive problems were posed by Macedonia and Thrace, both of which, having being part of the Turkish Empire, were incorporated into the newly established, predominantly Christian successor states. Macedonia was divided among Bulgaria, Greece and Serbia, but many Bulgarians were deeply dissatisfied with this settlement because it left about

700,000–800,000 compatriots outside the country's borders. In addition, the problem of Western Thrace, the area between the Mesta and Maritsa rivers, soured relations with Greece. While Turkey retained Eastern Thrace, Bulgaria first gained Western Thrace after the Balkans Wars but then lost it to Greece. In the course of these wars and the boundary changes that followed them about 18,000 Bulgarians were killed in Macedonia when Serb and Greek authorities entered the province. Of particular relevance here are the 280,000 Bulgarians who, out of fear of Serb, Greek and Turkish repression, migrated from these territories to the 'mother country' and kept alive national resentments about having 'lost out'.[9] Relations with Romania were also troubled: Bucharest obtained Northern Dobrudja at the Treaty of Berlin, and after the wars in the early twentieth century also gained control of Southern Dobrudja.

Nationalist revisionist agitation intensified in the inter-war period in Bulgaria, as elsewhere in Europe,[10] but there was relatively little manifest ethnic conflict, at least until the 1930s. The Bulgarian state generally observed the religious rights of the Turks and allowed Turkish-language instruction in private schools, the publication of Turkish newspapers and magazines and the participation of Turks in a range of institutions. In the early 1920s, the government of the Bulgarian Agrarian National Union (*Balgarski Zemedelski Naroden Soyuz*) allowed the minority to develop fairly successfully even though it was always kept at a low enough economic and cultural level to prevent any threat to Bulgarian predominance. Nevertheless, the spread of Kemal Atatürk's vision of Turkey as the fatherland of all Turks, in combination with the presence of a compact Turkish population at Bulgaria's southern borders, did cause significant worry to the authorities. They reacted by restricting the minority's educational rights and by increasing pressure on it to emigrate. In the mid-1930s agreement was reached with Turkey providing for the annual migration of 10,000 Bulgarian Turks. At the same time, Bulgarian nationalists exerted pressure to increase the flow. They were organized in pro-fascist organizations such as 'Fatherland Defense' (*Rodna Zastita*), which maltreated Turks, forced them to speak Bulgarian, restricted religious rights and stopped the publication of Turkish newspapers.[11]

World War II changed the context of Bulgarian minority policy fundamentally. Initially many Bulgarians saw a chance to redress what they saw as an unjust territorial settlement by joining with Nazi Germany. In 1940 the government of Bogdan Filov rejected the Soviet proposal for a pact of mutual assistance and on 1 March 1941 Bulgaria joined the Axis. Even before this the country had taken advantage of the efforts to gain its support being made by both Germany and the Soviet Union. In 1940, both powers exerted pressure on Bucharest to return Southern Dobrudja to Bulgaria because they hoped that this territorial change would ensure a favourable Bulgarian attitude.[12] In 1941 German support allowed the Bulgarian army and administration to occupy all of Macedonia as well as Western Thrace. Within the country the decline of parliamentary democracy and the rise of authoritarianism meant that fascist and authoritarian groups began to put pressure on the Turkish populations, using physical violence, burning cultural symbols such as fezzes and desecrating mosques. At the same time, officials sought to keep the level of Turkish education low enough to limit their political engagement.[13]

3 The Stalinist Model

On 9 September 1944 following a Soviet declaration of war, a communist-led *coup* overthrew Bulgaria's pro-German government. Once the tide of the war began to turn against Germany its foreign policy had become subject to mounting criticism. Now it was reversed altogether, as the country began its journey into the bloc of 'socialist brotherhood'. The trajectory was already quite clear before the end of the war, well before it was institutionalized in the Cominform (1947), Comecon (1949) and Warsaw Pact (1955). The new orthodoxy on Bulgaria's international position was encapsulated in the statement of the BKP's leadership in 1954 that '[t]he People's Democracy of Bulgaria is an indivisible part of the democratic and socialist camp led by the Soviet Union'.[14] In principle this allowed some long-standing national rivalries to be settled. Bulgaria's relationship with Rumania, which had often been tense in the past, was now – in theory – a fraternal one between two socialist neighbours. And contacts between Sofia and Bucharest over the following years were indeed good on the official level, even if there were few practical results. (This contrasted to relations with Yugoslavia, which were often soured by the long-standing Macedonian issue). The Dobrudja problem was buried when the two countries agreed in 1953 to liquidate Bulgarian property in Northern Dobrudja and Romanian property in Southern Dobrudja.[15] Conversely, Bulgaria's neighbours to the south were now part of a hostile Western camp. Turkey, which the Truman Doctrine had declared to be a threatened outpost of the 'free world', received substantial financial support from the United States in the form of Marshall Aid and other aid programmes.

At the same time, the communists consolidated their hold on power in a process that fits well the five-phase framework proposed by Joseph Rothschild: the destruction of the monarchy, the emasculation of coalition partners, the liquidation of the opposition, the internal purges of the communist leadership and finally, complete Stalinization.[16] By silencing any substantial criticism, the one-party system blocked any possibility of correcting mistakes or simply mitigating the effect of some extreme decisions.

The treatment of ethnic minorities also broadly followed the Soviet model. But in its implementation significant tensions emerged. Rogers Brubaker and others have described how Soviet nationality policy allowed some leeway to local elites, noting that the regime institutionalized 'territorial nationhood and ethnic nationality as fundamental social categories'. In practice, this created, however unintentionally, a political context in which nationalism could develop.[17] At the same time Stalin's policy of moving 'the backward nations and nationalities into the general channel of a higher culture'[18] was often not just extremely brutal but also uneven, since it was in the hands of communist elites who were themselves often nationally minded. Similarly, there was a basic tension between the Party's aspirations for the promotion of a cultural ethnic identity and its concern that this might encourage subversive nationalism. As Traicho Kostov (political secretary of the BKP) put it to the Politburo on 6 February 1945 (recording the views of the party leader Georgi Dimitrov):

To the national minorities – full rights, but with Turks – carefully. They should have the same political and citizenship rights as the

Bulgarians, possibilities for education in their own language, textbooks and mosques. But as Turks they must not represent any particular Turkish national movement because this will create conditions for Turkish agents in the country. . . We do not recognise Turkish nationalists.[19]

In line with Dimitrov's guidance, the Party gave 'full rights' to ethnic communities. After 1944 the state-sponsored Turkish private schools (which had previously been run along religious rather than secular lines) allowed publication of Turkish newspapers and magazines and gave closer attention to Turks' social and economic situation, for example, by building new factories, roads and schools. Along with this the authorities guaranteed their religious freedom, and included Turks in local committees of the Fatherland Front and local administration.[20] They also anchored minority policy in the 1947 constitution, which proclaimed that 'the national minorities have the right of education in their mother tongue and of developing their national culture' though they were also obliged to learn Bulgarian.[21] Traditionally Turks were distinguished on the basis of their language, religion, customs (e.g., dress), history and self-determination.[22] In line with the Stalinist interpretation of the national question, Turks were allowed to determine their own national identity in the new passports which were introduced in 1952. They included a special column for 'nationality' and this stayed in official documents until 1975.[23]

On the other hand, while guaranteeing the minority's cultural rights, the new power-holders were undermining its economic basis by setting up agricultural cooperatives and liquidating private property. Since most Turks lived in villages, they were disproportionately affected by these reforms. They were also offended by the atheistic aspects of communist propaganda, as well as the rhetoric (if not the practice) of gender equality. This meant that the overall outcome of this early 'progressive' project of social transformation was less than satisfactory in the eyes of the communist elite. As Trifonov has shown, after initially supporting the development of those institutions (schools, mosque, newspapers, etc.), which in one way or another 'nourish Turkish nationalism',[24] the BKP soon began to see their disadvantages.

The adversarial relationship of the Cold War intensified Bulgarian fears of Turkey. Bulgaria's rulers shared Soviet fears of a possible Anglo-American intervention, with Turkey as an instrument of an aggressive 'Western imperialism'. As the party newspaper *Rabotnichesko Delo* put it in November 1947, 'Greece and Turkey have become bases for Anglo-Saxon imperialists' and were bringing 'a permanent threat to the independence and tranquility of our country'.[25] Communist leaders did not need much persuasion to take this view or to agree with Stalin that 'the American imperialists are guiding the preparation of a new world war'. In contrast, the 'People's Democracies' were supposedly concentrating their efforts on preserving peace in the world.[26]

Bulgarian fears of Turkish destabilization were much exaggerated since, on the whole, the West actually made little effort to use the minority to subvert the regime. Yet they did contain a grain of truth: propaganda from Ankara was indeed being directed towards the Turkish minority and the Turkish mass media, in particular Turkish radio, did use the evidence of the unpopularity of communist policies to bolster their case that the internal situation in Bulgaria was unstable. Muslims were portrayed as the object of repression and assimilation while (in the sarcastic words of Bulgarian reporters) Turkey was presented as 'an earthly paradise' and 'a country of prosperity'. Turkish radio propaganda appealed to Bulgarian Turks to 'return' to 'their fatherland' and promised them welfare support.[27] According to Rumyana Todorova, this propaganda struck a chord among those Turks who were unhappy with the centralizing economic policies of the new regime and increased their readiness to emigrate.[28]

As early as 1947 a commission of the Ministry of Interior had concluded that security concerns about the Turkish population living close to the border in south-east Bulgaria meant that it should be 'diluted'.[29] Meanwhile, after a series of border incidents, tensions between Bulgaria and Turkey worsened. They reached a crisis-point in February 1948 when two Turkish military planes were brought down near Sozopol, on Bulgaria's southern coast. In September of the same year there were attacks on the Bulgarian consulate in Istanbul, which were countered by attacks on the Turkish consulate in Plovdiv.[30] In January Dimitrov had already expressed his concern that important areas of the country, such as Shumen and Razgrad, where compact Turkish communities lived, were displaying signs of nationalism and allegiance to Ankara. He also described the 'non-Bulgarian' population at Bulgaria's southern border as a 'permanent ulcer for our country'. It was the party's task to move Turks from this area and populate it with Bulgarians.[31]

An important model and counter-example here were Bulgaria's Jews. After the establishment of Israel and the establishment of diplomatic relations they were allowed to emigrate to Israel. Between 1948 and 1950 about 40,000 did so, motivated both by the pull of Israel and the push of the BKP's radical programme. The main difference between Jews and Turks in the eyes of the regime was that before the war Jews had not lived in isolation. Despite some anti-semitism they had generally been well integrated in society, had a high educational and professional level and as committed communists, many of them had, actively participated in the resistance movement against the bourgeois governments and Germans troops deployed in the country. Perhaps most importantly, Israel was not at this stage considered as part of a capitalist threat. On the contrary, the Soviet Union supported the creation of Israel and the Bulgarian party leadership naturally followed that lead in their decision to allow Jewish migration.[32]

Despite these differences, the Turkish community was led by the growth of Jewish migration to nurture similar ambitions.[33] Initially it was encouraged to do so by both Bulgaria and Turkey, albeit from entirely different motives. On the one hand, the imposition of communism affected the traditional Turkish way of life; on the other hand, Turkey's readiness to receive Turkish migrants reflected its commitment to Western values and the propaganda of the Cold War. Over time, Bulgarian fears that the border regions where Turks lived in compacted masses, could be destabilized, led the government to accept migration. At times, it even encouraged it as a useful vent for the release of pent-up social tensions.

The start of the shift was already visible in July 1949, when a Bulgarian delegation in Moscow discussed the fate of the Turkish minority with the Soviet leadership. When Stalin described the Turks as an 'unreliable' element and stated emphatically that Bulgaria should get rid of them[34] there was little scope for further discussion. On August 1949, the BCP Politburo decided to allow Turks to emigrate. In the first wave, which continued until Turkey closed its borders in November 1951, over 150,000 people left the country.[35] The number of those wanting to migrate was even greater: according to Bulgarian sources, about 250,000 Turks made special applications to the Bulgarian authorities. The BKP tried 'to stimulate the migration by all means' especially from the southern regions of Bulgaria.[36]

Although Turkey's propaganda had initially encouraged migration, its response to this influx was ambivalent. The wave of migrants put enormous pressure on the Turkish economy and, as a Turkish diplomat in Sofia put it in 1954, Turkey was also afraid of the infiltration of 'communist agents'. This led them, perhaps naively, to require migrants to sign a declaration about their political beliefs. Turkey also began to vacillate over its visa policy, repeatedly closing the borders in order to stop the flow.[37] These shifts further fuelled Bulgarian suspicions. In 1950 the Bulgarian minister in Ankara, Iordan Chobanov, declared that Turkey had no intention of solving the migration issue but was actually seeking to increase instability in Bulgaria. Their true aim, he alleged, was for the Turkish population to stay in Bulgaria but with its gaze permanently directed towards its southern neighbour.[38]

In their efforts to counteract what they saw as dangerous nationalistic tendencies, special branches of the Central Committee, *Komsomol* (the communist youth organization), and the Fatherland Front were now created in order to penetrate the Turkish community. Yet at the same time Turkish national identity was fostered by measures such as Turkish language instruction, the development of Turkish theatres, schools and nurseries, and special financial assistance to Turkish regions and the development of infrastructure. All this helped stimulate the separation of the Turkish minority from the rest of the population.[39]

4 Overcoming Stalinism through Integration

In the mid-1950s a further decisive impetus for change came from Moscow, where the direction of minority policy began to shift after Stalin's death. Two months after Nikita Khruschev's 'secret speech' in February 1956 the BKP held a plenum, which led to some important changes at the top of the party. Valko Chervenkov, the Party leader and Prime Minister, was removed and Todor Zhivkov, who, despite being first secretary, had lived in Chervenkov's shadow for the previous two years, strengthened his hold on power; Anton Iugov, who had been the Interior Minister during the communist take-over, became Prime Minister. In general the Bulgarian leadership followed the new Soviet critique of Stalinism – denouncing the cult of personality and political repressions of previous years while at the same time, trying to avoid any profound political, economic and cultural reforms that might upset the party elite.[40]

The new line on the Turkish minority also fitted in with Khrushchev's claim that the nationalities of the Soviet Union were progressively becoming integrated.[41] The Bulgarian authorities sought to lessen Turkish alienation by integrating Turks into the development of socialism. Ethnic differences were now to be eliminated by restricting religious and educational rights. Some observers saw this as meaning a policy of assimilation.[42] To soften its impact, the regime began to pay more attention to the minority's economic and social grievances.

In its new programme, the party leadership declared squarely that 'Bulgaria is not a multiethnic country' and the development of the minority's culture was to be restricted since the Turks were an 'inseparable component of the Bulgarian nation'.[43] Two years later the BKP endorsed new guidelines, which were meant to take it down the 'path of integration'. They stated explicitly that the fatherland of the Bulgarian Turks was not Turkey but Bulgaria. Imams were singled out as the main instigators of Turkish nationalist feeling; according to the State Security (*Darzhavna sigurnost*) they were responsible for disseminating rumours and thus undermining loyalty to the state. Their numbers were then drastically reduced and they were placed under the control of the security services. The level of control and the insecurities that lay behind it can be seen in a 1967 comment by Pencho Kubadinsky (a member of the Politburo) that every imam 'must be a person of the State Security. We must enter the mosques. There people are shaped. . . .' The other area where the impact of the new line was felt, was education. The party leadership noted that some Turkish pupils not only had no knowledge of Bulgarian because they had been educated only in the Turkish language but also showed no wish to learn it. From then on, all education in Bulgarian schools, teacher training institutes and universities was to be in Bulgarian only.[44] In December 1967 Zhivkov laid down the main elements of Party policy:

> we are implementing a line for the creation of a united communist nation. Lenin advocated progressive assimilation. Specifically, in our case there is a progressive assimilation of nationalities in Bulgaria, including the Turkish nationality and their fusion with the Bulgarian nation and the gradual creation of a united communist nationality.

Nevertheless, for the moment Zhivkov also emphasized that 'we do not advocate assimilation' but 'the integration of the population as an integral part of the Bulgarian nation'.[45] The party leader clearly provided the blueprint for the future – the gradual dilution of the ethnic differences between Turks and Bulgarians. Eventually, this policy was to lead to the incorporation of Turks into Bulgarian nation.

The change in direction amounted to an acceptance that the existing policy had failed. For two decades the authorities had recognized Turks as an independent ethnic group, seeking to convince them of the advantages of socialism and to overcome their pre-war marginalization through measures of economic, cultural and social progress so that ethnic differences would slowly be diluted. Now the party began to reconsider its recognition of the Turks as an ethnic group altogether, defining them instead as Bulgarians who had been assimilated by the Turks from the fifteenth to the seventeenth century. Its leaders inaugurated a massive propaganda campaign. In the 1970s and 1980s these efforts led to an increasing number of academic publications, which used old documents to prove the minority's Bulgarian origins,[46] introduced new socialist rituals to replace Muslim traditions and eventually (1984–85) replaced all Turkish for by Bulgarian names.

Not surprisingly, the new policy caused deep discontent within the Turkish minority and in the long run created a more fertile soil for Turkish nationalism. Several Turkish underground organizations were formed in the 1960s. At the same time appeals for the reestablishment of Turkish schools and for a resumption of emigration to Turkey increased, and were accompanied once again by the assertion that Bulgarian Turks were a part of the Turkish nation. Some organizations also called for autonomy and the promotion of Turkish as an official language in specific regions, such as north-eastern and south-western Bulgaria.[47] This was a direct challenge to official policy.

In parallel with these shifts in domestic policy Bulgaria's foreign policy was also undergoing significant changes, following – yet again – the Soviet lead. The new line of 'peaceful coexistence' provided an argument for enhancing contacts with the West. It also raised the difficult question of how to respond to the long-simmering conflict between Bulgaria's two western neighbours, Turkey and Greece over Cyprus.[48] In the early 1960s, Bulgaria concentrated on improving relations with Greece because it believed that this might encourage Ankara to be more flexible in the impending negotiations on migration issues. Achieving agreement in 1964 with Greece over outstanding financial debts (in particular, the 45 million dollars reparations bill that the 1947 Peace Treaty had imposed on Bulgaria), as well as several other agreements on trade, transport, tourism, etc., eased tensions between Sofia and Athens.[49]

In the light of Soviet support for Ankara in the Cyprus crisis the Bulgarian government also began to consider how to improve relations with Turkey. Discussions began on a trade agreement, and on ways of enhancing bilateral cultural and scientific contacts. But Turkish insistence on the free migration of Bulgarian Turks and on the recognition of their status as a national minority was a major sticking point. Sofia declared the Turkish position to be unacceptable and therefore did not respond.[50] The great Bulgarian fear was of a knock-on effect within their Turkish minority. In 1964, Ivan Bashev, the Bulgarian minister of foreign affairs, reported to the Politburo that the 'religious fanaticism' and 'nationalist sentiments' of the Turkish minority were providing fertile soil for anti-Bulgarian propaganda and 'attempts at interference in the internal affairs of the country'. For Bashev the mere presence of a compact Turkish population in some Bulgarian regions was a threat to the country since 'without doubt the aspirations of the Turkish reactionary circles will be increased'.[51] Yet he also judged that the resurgence of the wish to emigrate was in the country's interest. He argued that this was a suit-able moment to resolve the contradictions between the two countries since, in its response to the Cyprus crisis, Turkey had tried to main-tain good relations with the Soviet Union. The minister also believed that migration would 'decrease the basis of the Turkish government for the realization of hostile activity against our country'.[52]

In the Politburo discussion of Bashev's report in October 1964, the leadership's fear that the Cyprus crisis would increase calls for autonomy was clear to see. The Turkish definition of the minority as not merely 'ethnic' but 'national' was seen as only a step away from demanding collective rights, autonomy, independent institutions and parity with the state language. Once again, emigration was seen as the most convenient solution and it was decided to approach the Turkish government. The Turkish government, however, failed to respond to the Bulgarian suggestion for two years. When Bashev met his Turkish counterpart Ihsan Sabri Caglayangil in 1966 he signalled Bulgaria's willingness to relax restrictions on emigration but at the same time vigorously protested against Turkish advocacy of the minority's cause. Summing up, he stressed that we 'will never allow the Cyprus story in our country'.[53]

In 1968, after two years of negotiations, Bulgaria and Turkey signed a new agreement, which allowed about 130,000 Turks to migrate to Turkey between 1969 and 1978.[54] This substantial emigration clearly did help reduce ethnic tensions to some extent. But it could not 'solve' Bulgaria's ethnic issues because of the strength of pro-Turkish sentiments and Turkish nationalism among the remaining Bulgarian Muslims. Moreover, the period of expanded East–West contacts in the 1960s did not lessen Bulgarian fears of Western subversive activity. In 1966, after the Ninth Party Congress, the BKP stepped up the struggle against the impact of foreign ideologies.[55] But growing Bul-garian contacts with capitalist states meant more possibilities for Western influence and made the Turkish minority appear even more disruptive. Far from being fully integrated, many Turks appeared alienated and even hostile towards communist rule. Bashev's pessi-mistic statement summarized Bulgarian fears that Ankara might play the ethnic card in order to place Sofia in a difficult position. This kind of nervous analysis was probably reinforced by the Turkish invasion of Cyprus in 1974, and the subsequent division of the island. In 1977 State Security reports noted that Bulgaria's foreign adversaries had increased their activities to a point where it had now assumed a 'total nature'. It also stressed that Turkey was trying to prevent the fulfilment of party policy within the Turkish population and among Bulgarian Muslims, and was fostering 'migration psychoses', nationalistic sentiments, anti-Bulgarian feelings and demands for autonomy. The secret service concluded that the objective of 'bourgeois Turkey' was to use the Bulgarian Turks as a 'fifth column'.[56]

5 Bulgarianization in the Last Phase

Alongside the long-standing fear that Turkey would exploit the minority and alienate it from 'socialist developments', demographic trends helped create a particular collective *Angst*. The Turkish population had long been growing at a faster rate than the rest of the population. From about 675,500 in 1946, it grew to more than 800,000 in 1970 in spite of the emigration of around 260,000–270,000 people. For some in the BKP this was an argument for intensifying its assimilationist policies. The dilemma they faced was aptly summarized by a British diplomat who pointed out that 'within the country as a whole the main opposition to the regime is provided by the Turkish minority'. He added that Bulgaria's rulers had tried both appeasement and repression but 'under appeasement the Turks flourish and multiply, while repression . . . merely increases their attachment to their national and religious distinctiveness'.[57]

In 1971 the Politburo concluded that Turkey had altered its policy towards the Turkish diaspora in the Balkans as a whole. Instead of seeking to collect all Turks in the fatherland, the policy now seemed to be aimed at preserving Turkish identity and culture in the places where Turks were living. This prompted renewed fears that Bulgarian Turks might be 'used by the Turkish state for its objectives at an appropriate moment'.[58] In an attempt to counteract this in 1971 the new constitution declared that there were no national minorities in Bulgaria, only citizens of non-Bulgarian origin. Attacks on Muslim traditions increased and the inculcation of a patriotic and communist spirit in the education system was intensified.[59] At roughly the same time as Brezhnev developed his thesis of a 'unified Soviet nation' Bulgarian party officials introduced the term of 'the unified socialist nation'. As part of a series of wider restrictions, curbs were introduced in the cultural sphere; limitations on lifestyle choices and on Western influences and name changes for Roma and Bulgarian Muslims were imposed. They also suffered from state pressure and interference in their social and private life.[60] The BKP's aspiration to enforce the assimilation of the entire Turkish population can be seen in the 1971 party programme. As Richard Crampton puts it, 'the unified socialist nation' was

> interpreted to mean bringing about the end of the differences between rural and urban life and physical and mental labour. This would produce a nation entirely working class in its composition and thus the party of the working class, the BCP, would become the party of entire nation.[61]

Along with political, economic and cultural uniformity, it now seemed time to move to ethnic unification. In 1974, Aleksandar Lilov elaborated on this idea, placing the emphasis on the atheism, class-consciousness, patriotism and internationalist education of all Bulgarian citizens, on the development of new socialistic rituals and traditions, and of course alignment with the Soviet Union.[62] In February 1974 the BKP adopted the doctrine of the 'unified socialist nation' and intensified its efforts, not just to integrate the Bulgarian Turks but also to assimilate them completely. The new line required the Turkish minority to gradually overcome its ethnocentrism, to be ideologically and politically integrated in order to be included in 'the unified socialist nation'. The explicit goal was the final assimilation of the minority and the abolition of all features of Turkish identity. The international backdrop to this final stage was an increase in tension between East and West[63] and the establishment of the Turkish Republic of Northern Cyprus in 1983, which once again increased Bulgarian fears of Turkish intervention.[64]

The culmination of the assimilation policy was the name-changing campaign from December 1984 to January 1985, when the authorities forced about 800,000 Turks to accept Bulgarian names. The growing tensions over the following years culminated in mass Turkish protests in May 1989. The roots of Turkish resentment were the state's interference in their most private space – the choice of personal names, denunciation of Muslim customs, ban on traditional clothes, as well as banning the use of Turkish in public places. Once again the BCP sought the release of domestic ethnic tensions in increased emigration to Turkey. In June 1989, Zhivkov said that it was desirable for about 200,000–300,000 Turks to migrate.[65] However, when in the summer about 330,000 people did move from Bulgaria to Turkey the agricultural sector came close to collapse.

In contrast to other East European states, there were no mass upheavals or demonstrations in Bulgaria during communist rule. Turkish protests in the 1980s against official restrictions were clearly the exception, which proved this rule. They reached a peak of activity with the participation of Turks in terrorist acts, demonstrations, hunger strikes and dissemination of propaganda materials. In 1984, that is before the name-changing campaign, illegal Turkish groups organized explosions at Varna Airport and Plovdiv Train Station. Together with further terrorist acts, the following year they killed 8 people and injured 50.[66] But this active resistance did not produce any effective results and was easily suppressed by the security forces. However, the protests of May 1989 did have an impact on state policy. In the context of the changing international situation and the sharpening domestic ethnic and economic crisis, they pushed the BKP into allowing a new wave of emigration to Turkey. Eventually, after Zhivkov's retirement on 10 November 1989, the government allowed the resumption of Turkish names.[67] In general, Turks suffered from a range of state repressions in the late 1980s – arrests, persecutions, intimidations and casualties. According to the documents of the State Security, 19 people were killed in the name-changing campaign and protests in May 1989.[68] Passive resistance to the regime strengthened the isolation of the Turkish minority, while education in Muslim traditions turned many towards a religion and confrontation with authorities. There were also long-term repercussions for Turks on a personal level – some of them migrated to Turkey in 1989, while others began political careers in post-communist Bulgaria.

6 Conclusion

The context of the Cold War clearly marked the Communist Party's policy towards the Turkish minority on many levels. First, long-standing friction with Turkey was aggravated by the East-West conflict. In the eyes of the party leadership foreign powers such as Turkey, might use domestic problems, including ethnic issues in order to destabilize the country. At the same time, the Turkish–Greek conflict was perceived as a dangerous stimulus to Turkish separatism, regardless of the fact that both sides were in the western camp. Moreover Bulgaria's central place in the Warsaw Pact and the close relations between Sofia and Moscow meant that Turkish interference in Bulgarian affairs risked leading to a confrontation between the Eastern and Western blocs not just one limited to the Balkans.

In all this the BKP closely followed the shifts of Soviet nationality policy, starting with Stalin's theory of 'the national question'. Furthermore, as should now be clear, Bulgarian policy towards the Turkish minority oscillated between two poles, support for the development of Turkish national identity from 1944 to the mid-1950s on the one hand, and restrictions on minority cultural, religious and educational rights from the late 1950s on the other. The first approach was typical of the height of the Cold War and the Stalinist period. The demise of Stalinism led to attempts at integrating the Turkish population into Bulgarian society. Both approaches produced ethnic tensions and could not completely overcome the Turkish isolation. The Party sought an outlet for domestic problems in the migration of Turks in 1950–1951 and 1969–1978.

Last not least, communist policy has to be seen in the context of the totalitarian system. There were no alternative political views on offer that could question the communist line nor were there any social debates of sensitive ethnic issues. The Party's ethnic policy had a strong connection with its grand project for modernizing and industrializing Bulgarian society. This policy led to far-reaching changes in the economic and social status of Bulgarian Turks, without lessening either their separation or decreasing the popularity of emigration. This in turn increased the uncertainty of the party leadership and further stimulated their search for more radical solutions, which in the 1980s led them to intensify assimilation. These attempts were cut short by the collapse of communism and the end of the Cold War.

Notes

[1] Recent research suggests that the 'Forest People' emerged in the Bulgarian villages spontaneously, without a united ruling centre and instructions from abroad or Bulgarian political power. See Diniu Sharlanov, *Istoria na komunizma v Balgaria* (vol. 2), Sofia: Ciela, 2009, 111, 117; Nedyalka Grozeva, Ivanka Ivanova and Krasimira Kalcheva (eds), *Goryanite. Sbornik documenti* (vol. 1, 1944- 1949), Sofia: Glavno upravlenie na arhivite. 2001, 5, 166–7, 275.

[2] Jordan Baev, *Sistemata za evropeiska sigurnost i Balkanite v godinite na Studenata voina*, Sofia: Izdatelstvo Damyan Yakov, 2010, 60–63, 132–4.

[3] Evgenia Kalinova, 'Nauchni podhodi v izsledvaniyata za politikata kam turskoto naselenie v Balgaria v perioda 1944–1989', in Iskra Baeva and Plamen Mitev (eds), *Predizvikatelstvata na promyanata*, Sofia: Iniversitetsko izdatelstvo Sv. Kliment Ohridski, 2006, 305.

[4] Rumyana Todorova, 'Balgaro-turskite otnoshenia sled Vtorata svetovna voina (40-te – 60-te godini)' *Istoricheski pregled*, 5, 1994–1995; Jordan Baev and Nikolai Kotev, 'Izselnicheskiyat vapros v balgaro-turskite otnoshenia sled Vtorata svetovna voina', *Mezhdunarodni otnoshenia*, 1 and 2, 1994.

[5] Valeri Stoyanov, *Turskoto naselenie v Balgaria mezhdu poliusite na etnicheskata politika*, Sofia: LIK, 1998.

[6] There is a significant literature on the Turkish minority under communism. See for example Staiko Trifonov, 'Miusiulmanite v politikata na balgarskata darzhava (1944–1989)', in *Stranitsi ot balgarskata istoria. Sabitiya, razmisli, lichnosti* (vol. 2), Sofia: Prosveta, 1993, Evgenia Kalinova and Iskra Baeva, *Balgarskite prehodi 1939–2002*, Sofia: Paradigma. 2002; Ibrahim Yalamov, *Istoria na turskata obshtnost v Balgaria*, Sofia: IK Ilinda-Evtomov, 2002; Stoyanov, *Turskoto naselenie* Mikhail Gruev and Aleksei Kalionski, *Vazroditelniyat protses: Miusiulmanskite obshtnosti i komunisticheskiyat rezhim*, Sofia: Ciela, 2008.

[7] Vesselin Dimitrov, 'In Search of a Homogeneous Nation: The Assimilation of Bulgaria's Turkish Minority, 1984–1985', *Journal of Ethnopolitics and Minority Issues in Europe*, 23, (2000). [http://www.ecmi.de/jemie/download/JEMIE01Dimitrov10-07-01.pdf] [accessed on 8 February 2011].

[8] Richard Crampton, *Bulgaria*, Oxford: Oxford University Press, 2007, 424–5.

[9] Dimitur Sazdov, Radoslav Popov and Ljudmil Spasov, *Istoria an Balgaria 681–1944*, (vol. 2), Sofia: Sofi-R, 2003, 549.

[10] Mark Mazower, *Dark Continent: Europe's Twentieth Century*, New York: Alfred A. Knopf. 1999, 41–3.

[11] Stoyanov, Turskoto naselenie, 57–87; Yalamov, Istoria na turskata obshtnost, 121; Evgenia Kalinova, 'Nasilieto v politicata na balgarskata darzhava kam balgarskite turtsi 30-te – 80-te godini na XX vek', *Istoria, 3*, (2004), 52–64.

[12] Nikolaï Genchev, *Vanshnata politika na Balgaria 1938–1941,* Sofia: Vektor. 1998, 95–183.

[13] Stoyanov, *Turskoto naselenie,* 88–90.

[14] Central State Archive (Centralen Darzhaven Arhiv/CDA), fond (f.) 1 B, opis (op.) 5, arhivna edinitsa (a.e.) 132, 23.

[15] Georgi Markov, Istoria na balgarite (vol 3, Ot Osvobojdenieto (1878) do kraya na Studenata voina (1989)), Sofia: Knigoizdatelska kashta Trud., 2009, 623.

[16] Joseph Rothschild, *Return to Diversity. A Political History of East Central Europe since World War II,* New York and Oxford: Oxford University Press. 1989, 115. The most detailed Bulgarian studies of the Communist takeover are Mito Isusov, *Politicheskiyat zhivot v Balgaria 1944–1948,* Sofia, Akademichno izdatelstvo Prof. Marin Drinov. 2000; Lubomir Ognyanov, *Darzhavno-politicheskata sistema na Balgaria 1944–1948* (2nd edn), Sofia: Standart, 2007.

[17] Rogers Brubaker, *Nationalism Reframed: Nationhood and the National Question in the New Europe,* Cambridge: Cambridge University Press, 1996, 17, 36–40.

[18] Robert Service, *Stalin. A Biography,* London: Pan Books, 2005, 99.

[19] Cited in Baev and Kotev, 'Izselnicheskiyat vapros, 19.

[20] Stoyanov, *Turskoto naselenie,* 94–101; Trifonov, Miusiulmanite, 211.

[21] Veselin Metodiev and Lachezar Stoyanov (eds), (1990), *Balgarski konstitutsii i konstitutsionni proekti,* Sofia: Izdatelstvo Dr Petar Beron, 1990.

[22] Antonina Zhelyazkova, 'Turks', in Anna Krasteva (ed), *Obshtnosti i identichnosti v Balgari,.* Sofia: Petekston, 1998, 371–83.

[23] Mikhail Gruev and Aleksei Kalionski, *Vazroditelniyat protse,* 123; Stoyanov, *Turskoto naselenie* 122–3.

[24] Trifonov, *Miusiulmanite,* 211.

[25] *Rabotnichesko Delo,* 18 November 1947.

[26] CDA, f. 1 B, op. 5, a.e. 113, p. 60, 117.

[27] Ognyanov, *Darzhavno-politicheskata* sistema na Balgaria 1944–1948, 129.

[28] Todorova, Balgaro-turskite otnoshenia 35–6.

[29] *Ibid.*

[30] Baev and Kotev, Izselnicheskiyat vapros, 1, 18; Todorova, Balgaro-turskite otnoshenia, 39; Stoyanov, *Turskoto naselenie,* 104–5.

[31] Trifonov, Miusiulmanite, 211.

[32] Boika Vasileva, Evreite v Balgaria 1944–1952 g, Sofia: Universitetsko izdatesvo u. Kliment Ohrdski 1992, 159–60; Crampton, *Bulgaria,* 434–5.

[33] Stoyanov, *Turskoto naselenie,* 108.

[34] Kalinova and Baeva, *Balgarskite prehodi,* 115.

[35] Liubomir Ognyanov, *Diplomativata na savremenna Balgaria* Shumen: Universitetsko izdatelstvo Episkop Konstantin Preslavsky, 2006, 130, 133.

[36] Baev and Kotev, Izselnicheskiyat vapros, 21–5.

[37] Baev and Kotev, Izselnicheskiyat vapros, 1, 21–5; Todorova, 1994–1995, 40–46; Kalinova and Baeva, *Balgarskite prehodi* 115–16.

[38] Veselin Bozhkov, *Zaplahata ostava.* Sofia: Programni produkti i sistemi. 50, cited in Kalinova and Baeva, *Balgartskite prehodi,* 50, footnote 73.

[39] Trifonov, Miusiulmanite, 213.

[40] Liubomir Ognyanov, *Darzhavno-politicheskata sistema na Balgaria 1949–1956,* Sofia: Standart, 2008, 86–95.

[41] Stoyanov, *Turskoto naselenie*, 124–5, 143, 158–9.

[42] See Gruev and Kalionski, *Vazroditelniyat protses*, 112; Dimitrov, Homogenous Nation, 5.

[43] Stoyanov, *Turskoto naselenie*, 126.

[44] Trifonov, Miusiulmanite, 213–15; Yalamov, *Istoria na turskata obshtnost*, 328–30; Notification on the Orthodox Church and Muslem Clergy, cited in, Veselin Angelov (ed), *Strogo sekretno. Dokumenti za deinostta na Darzhavna sigurnost (1944–1989)*, Sofia: Smolini, 2007, 352.

[45] Vulkan Valkanov, *Istoria na Balgaria (1944–1989)* (vol. 1), Varna: Universitetsko izdatelstvo Chernorizec Hrabar, 2006, 267–8. Similarly in November 1967 Zhivkov stated that 'we are implementing a line not for the differentiation of the Turkish population in Bulgaria but for its integration', cited in Trifonov, Miusiulmanite, 215. For the gradual assimilation of the Turkish community see Gruev and Kalionski, *Vazroditelniyat protses*, 112–14.

[46] Dimitrov, Homogenous Nation, 8; Ch Marinov, 'Ot "internacionalism" kam nacionalism. Komunisticheskiyat regim, Makedonskiyat vapors i politikata kam etnicheskite i religiozni obshtnosti', in Ivailo Znepolski (ed), *Istoria na Narodna republika Balgaria*, Sofia: Ciela, 2009, 512–13.

[47] Trifonov, Miusiulmanite, 215–16.

[48] See Tony Judt, *Postwar. A History of Europe since 1945*, London: Pimlico, 2007, 509–10.

[49] Georgi Daskalov, *Balgaria i Gartsia. Ot razriv kam pomirenie 1944–1964*, Sofia: Universitetsko izdatelstvo Sv. Kliment Ohridski, 2004, 423–93.

[50] Kalinova and Baeva, *Balgarskite prehodi*, 210.

[51] *Ibid*, 209.

[52] *Ibid*, 210–11, note 109.

[53] Baev and Kotev, Izselnicheskiyat vapros, 2, 50–1.

[54] Stoyanov, *Turskoto naselenie*, 151.

[55] Vladimir Migev, *Prajkata prolet'68 i Balgaria*, Sofia: Iztok-Zapad, 2005, 85–7.

[56] Archive of the Ministry of Interior/Arhiv na Ministerstvoto na vatreshnite raboti, Fonds 22, op. 1, a.e. 57, 24, 27.

[57] J. L. Bullard to Goulding, 8 February 1973, National Archives London, Foreign and Commonwealth Office (FCO), 28/2239.

[58] Baev and Kotev, Izselnicheskiyat vapros, 2, 55.

[59] Gruev and Kalionski, *Vazroditelniyat protses*, 115–16.

[60] Mikhail Gruev, *Mezhdu petolachkata i polumesetsa Balgarite miusiulmam i politchestiyat reshim 1944–1959*, Sofia: Kuta, 2003; Hugh Poulton, *The Balkans – Minorities and States in Conflict*, London: Minority Rights Group, 1991, 111–15; Georgieva, Pomatsi, 286–94.

[61] Crampton, *Bulgaria*, 356; Stoyanov, *Turskoto naselenie* 143.

[62] Stoyanov, *Turskoto naselenie* 148–9.

[63] Vladimir Zubok, *A Failed Empire. The Soviet Union in the Cold War from Stalin to Gorbachev*, Chapel Hill: University of North Carolina Press, 2007, 265.

[64] Kalinova, Nasilieto v politicata na balgarskata darzhava, 59–60.

[65] CDA, f. 1 B, op. 68, a.e. 3670, p. 11, 44.

[66] 'Report on the Activity of the State Security during the 1980s', cited in Angelov, *Strogo sekretno*, 665–6.

[67] Dimitir Ludjev, *Revoliutsiyata a v Balgaria 1989–1991* (vol. 1), Sofia: Izdatelstvo Dr Ivan Bogorov, 2008, 308–9.
[68] 'Report on the Activity of the State Security during the 1980s', Angelov, *Strogo sekretno*, 665–6.

Bibliography

Angelov, Veselin (ed) (2007), *Strogo sekretno. Dokumenti za deinostta na Darzhavna sigurnost (1944–1989)*. Sofia: Smolini.

Baev, Jordan. and Nikolei Kotev (1994), 'Izselnicheskiyat vapros v balgaro-turskite otnoshenia sled Vtorata svetovna voina', *Mezhdunarodni otnoshenia*, 1 and 2.

Baev, Jordan (2010), *Sistemata za evropeiska sigurnost i Balkanite v godinite na Studenata voina*. Sofia: Izdatelstvo Damyan Yakov.

Bozhkov, Veselin (2001), *Zaplahata ostava*. Sofia: Programni produkti i sistemi.

Brubaker, Rogers (1996), *Nationalism Reframed: Nationhood and the National Question in the New Europe*. Cambridge: Cambridge University Press.

Crampton, Richard (2007), *Bulgaria*. Oxford: Oxford University Press.

Daskalov, Georgi (2004), *Balgaria i Gartsia. Ot razriv kam pomirenie 1944–1964*. Sofia: Universitetsko izdatelstvo Sv. Kliment Ohridski.

Dimitrov, Vesselin (2000), 'In Search of a Homogeneous Nation: The Assimilation of Bulgaria's Turkish Minority, 1984–1985', *Journal of Ethnopolitics and Minority Issues in Europe 23*, [http://www.ecmi.de/jemie/download/JEMIE01Dimitrov10-07-01.pdf] [accessed on 8 February 2011].

Genchev, Nikolaï (1998), *Vanshnata politika na Balgaria 1938–1941*. Sofia: Vektor.

Georgieva, Tsvetana (1998), 'Pomatsi – Balgari Miusiulmani', in Anna Krasteva (ed), *Obshtnosti i identichnosti v Balgaria*. Sofia: Petekston.

Grozeva, Nedyalka, Ivanka Ivanova and Krasimira Kalcheva (eds), (2001), *Gorianite. Sbornik documenti* (vol. 1, 1944–1949). Sofia: Glavno upravlenie na arhivite.

Gruev, Mikhail (2003), *Mezhdu petolachkata i polumesetsa. Balgarite miusiulmani i politicheskiyat rezhim 1944–1959*. Sofia: Kota.

Gruev, Mikhail and Aleksei Kalionski (2008), *Vazroditelniyat protses: Miusiulmanskite obshtnosti i komunisticheskiyat rezhim*. Sofia: Ciela.

Isusov, Mito (2000), *Politicheskiyat zhivot v Balgaria 1944–1948*. Sofia, Akademichno izdatelstvo Prof. Marin Drinov.

Judt, Tony (2007), *Postwar. A History of Europe since 1945*. London: Pimlico.

Kalinova, Evgenia and Iskra Baeva (2002), *Balgarskite prehodi 1939–2002*. Sofia: Paradigma.

Kalinova, Evgenia (2004), 'Nasilieto v politicata na balgarskata darzhava kam balgarskite turtsi 30-te – 80-te godini na XX vek', *Istoria*, 3, 52–64.

Kalinova, Evgenia (2006), 'Nauchni podhodi v izsledvaniyata za politikata kam turskoto naselenie v Balgaria v perioda 1944–1989', in Iskra Baeva and Plamen Mitev (eds), *Predizvikatelstvata na promyanata*. Sofia: Iniversitetsko izdatelstvo "Sv. Kliment Ohridski", 302–7.

Ludjev, Dimitir (2008), *Revoliutsiyata v Balgaria 1989–1991* (vol. I). Sofia: Izdatelstvo Dr Ivan Bogorov.

Marinov, Ch. (2009), 'Ot "internacionalism" kam nacionalism. Komunisticheskiyat regim, Makedonskiyat vapors i politikata kam etnicheskite i religiozni obshtnosti', in Ivailo Znepolski (ed), Istoria na Narodna republika Balgaria. Sofia: Ciela.

Markov, Georgi (ed) (2009), *Istoria na balgarite* (vol 3, *Ot Osvobojdenieto (1878) do kraya na Studenata voina (1989))*. Sofia: Knigoizdatelska kashta Trud.

Mazower, Mark (1999), *Dark Continent: Europe's Twentieth Century*. New York: Alfred A. Knopf.

Metodiev, Veselin and Lachezar Stoyanov (eds) (1990), *Balgarski konstitutsii i konstitutsionni proekti*. Sofia: Izdatelstvo Dr Petar Beron.

Migev, Vladimir (2005), *Prajkata prolet'68 i Balgaria*. Sofia: Iztok-Zapad.

Ognyanov, Liubomir (2006), *Diplomatsiyata na savremenna Balgaria*. Shumen: Universitetsko izdatelstvo Episkop Konstantin Preslavsky.

Ognyanov, Lubomir (2007), *Darzhavno-politicheskata sistema na Balgaria 1944–1948,* (2nd edn), Sofia: Standart.

Ognyanov, Liubomir (2008), *Darzhavno-politicheskata sistema na Balgaria 1949–1956,* Sofia: Standart.

Poulton, Hugh (1991), *The Balkans – Minorities and States in Conflict*. London: Minority Rights Group.

Rothschild, Joseph (1989), *Return to Diversity. A Political History of East Central Europe since World War II*. New York and Oxford: Oxford University Press.

Sazdov, Dimitur, Radoslav Popov and Ljudmil Spasov, (2003), *Istoria an Balgaria 681–1944,* (vol. 2), Sofia: Sofi-R.

Service, Robert (2005), *Stalin. A Biography*. London: Pan Books.

Sharlanov, Diniu (2009), *Istoria na komunizma v Balgaria* (vol. 2). Sofia: Ciela.

Stoyanov, Valeri (1998), *Turskoto naselenie v Balgaria mezhdu poliusite na etnicheskata politika*. Sofia: LIK.

Todorova, Rumyana. (1994–1995), 'Balgaro-turskite otnoshenia sled Vtorata svetovna voina (40-te – 60-te godini), *Istoricheski pregled,* 5.

Trifonov, Staiko (1993), 'Miusiulmanite v politikata na balgarskata darzhava (1944–1989)', in *Stranitsi ot balgarskata istoria. Sabitiya, razmisli, lichnosti* (vol. 2). Sofia: Prosveta.

Valkanov, Vulkan (2006), *Istoria na Balgaria (1944–1989)* (vol. 1). Varna: Universitetsko izdatelstvo Chernorizec Hrabar.

Vasileva, Boika (1992), *Evreite v Balgaria 1944–1952 g.* Sofia: Universitetsko izdatestvo Sv. Kliment Ohridski.

Yalamov, Ibrahim (2002), *Istoria na turskata obshtost v Balgaria*. Sofia: IK Ilinda-Evtomov.

Zhelyazkova, Antonina (1998), 'Turks', in Anna Krasteva (ed), *Obshtnosti i identichnosti v Balgaria*. Sofia: Petekston.

Zubok, Vladimir (2007), *A Failed Empire. The Soviet Union in the Cold War from Stalin to Gorbachev*. Chapel Hill: The University of North Carolina Press.

Chapter 6

South Tyrol: Ethnic Winner in the Cold War

Günther Pallaver

1 Introduction

At the start of the Cold War South Tyrol could already look back on decades of acute ethnic conflict. When the southern part of the Austrian province of Tyrol was allocated to Italy after World War I, the treatment of its overwhelmingly German-speaking population became an international *cause célèbre*. Nationalist and democratic parties in Italy, Austria and Germany – as well as lobbies as far away as Britain – disputed the fairness of the decision, and discussed the possibility of revising it. Mussolini's policy of intense Italianization increased the arguments and after 1933 important parts of South Tyrol's political elite gravitated towards National Socialist Germany. But in 1939, in an attempt to remove the bone of contention, the two dictators came to an agreement. A euphemistically named 'option' would give South Tyroleans the chance to choose either German citizenship and move to Germany, or Italian citizenship, which would mean remaining in Italy but without any minority protection.[1] This was meant to bring a definitive resolution of the problem but in fact it triggered further conflict between 'those who wanted to stay' (*Dableiber*) and 'those choosing to leave' *(Optanten)*. By the end of 1939, approximately 86 percent of the population (ca. 200,000) had decided to resettle to Germany and only the course of the war prevented them from doing so.[2] When the Italian surrender in September 1943 brought the 'Pact of Steel' to an abrupt end, triggering the German occupation of Northern Italy, South Tyrol was placed under direct German administration (along with Trento and Belluno) as part of the 'Operational zone of the Alpine foothills' (*Operationszone Alpenvorland*). In this last phase of the war, though there was some (limited) resistance activity, both the *Wehrmacht* and the Nazi rule were accepted by most of the population.

When Germany finally surrendered in May 1945 representatives of the Italian resistance movement (*Comitato di Liberazione Nazionale*) assumed power under the aegis of the U.S.-led Allied Military Government and at the start of 1946 South Tyrol was returned to Italian administration. Later in the year the Paris Agreement was negotiated between Austria and Italy. It was a compromise with Austria confirming the 1919 Brenner border in return for an Italian guarantee of extensive autonomy. The implementation (or lack of it) of this agreement became the central point of dispute in the conflicted ethnic politics of the following decades. Only in 1992 was an agreement on the implementation of autonomy finally brokered by the United Nations in a way which was considered satisfactory to both the German-speaking population and the Austrian government.[3] In the intervening decades, ethnic issues and rights were much debated and disputed between Bozen/Bolzano, Vienna and Rome, and between South Tyrol's German-speaking and Italian-speaking populations. In the 1960s these differences erupted into violence including bomb attacks.

As can be seen, the conflict raged – with varying degrees of intensity – at the same time as international politics was marked by the Cold War. How were the two related? Two historians' comments provide an initial point of orientation. First, there is Rolf Steininger's view of Tyrol as 'the first victim of the Cold War'. In this perspective 'South Tyrol became prematurely caught up in the millstones of the Cold War, and this – and only this – ultimately decided South Tyrol's fate'.[4] A related perspective is implied by Mark Mazower's observation that

> On each side of the Iron Curtain, potentially destabilizing disputes were managed bilaterally, under the gaze of the presiding super-power. Neither Austro–Italian differences over South Tyrol nor Hungarian–Romanian disputes over Transylvania were allowed to jeopardize bloc cohesion.[5]

Both comments see ethnic politics as in some sense at the disposal of 'high politics' but they differ in their focus. Steininger empathizes with the frustration of regional leaders, apparently powerless in the face of the decisions of international power-brokers, while in Mazower's synoptic view the Cold War appears as a 'system' of equilibrium, in which ethnic conflict is dysfunctional.

The argument presented here, by contrast, is that the leadership of South Tyrol's minority often played an important active part in the decisions that affected them and that the Cold War sometimes represented as much an opportunity to them as a threat (or a millstone). While anti-communism did sometimes determine the mobilization against ethnic grievances, the relationship between high politics and regional politics was more complex than either Steininger or Mazower suggests.

One key to this understanding is that while, as Mazower rightly suggests, the South Tyrol dispute brought into conflict two states which were both within the Western 'bloc' in terms of values, economic organization and parliamentary democracy, there were also significant differences between the two; their trajectories out of the war, their position in the burgeoning East–West conflict and in the institutions of Western Europe.

2 South Tyrol within the Western 'bloc'

Although Italy formally remained in a state of war after September 1943, diplomatic relations were soon re-established with the three main Allies. The fact that Italians had, at least on one interpretation, liberated themselves and then fought alongside the Allies for almost two years, decisively influenced the Allies in their favour. Although this did not stop Italy being held to account for its alliance with Nazi Germany, President Truman expressed the wish for it to become a full member of the United Nations.[6] The terms that were then unilaterally offered nevertheless seemed harsh to many Italians: the country lost its fleet, all of its African colonies, some small border areas in the West and in the East, and all of Istria including the Dalmatian coast.[7] This put all the more pressure on Rome to defend the Brenner border against calls for its revision. On this point all Italian political parties were virtually united.[8]

By contrast, when the first crucial discussions about South Tyrol were taking place at the London Council of Foreign Ministers (September 1945) Austria did not yet even have a recognized government. The 'State Government' that had been established in Vienna under Soviet protection in April 1945 was mistrusted by the West and boycotted for several months. Admittedly, under the terms of the Moscow Declaration (1943) Austria's independence was to be restored, but the form or speed of the process was not laid down in any detail. The relative weakness of Austrian resistance to Nazi rule meant that Allied attitudes to Austrian sovereignty were even more ambivalent than towards Italy. Like Germany, though less punitively, the country was to be occupied and subject to measures like denazification and re-education. Though the basic aim of weakening Germany was common ground among the occupying powers, this did not lead to any particular support for Austria's call for a border revision in Tyrol. There was no consensus that it was vital either for Austria's independence or its democratic future.

Most importantly, even at this early stage, Western policy was strongly influenced by the fear that Communist parties in Italy and Austria could exploit the post-war malaise to increase their influence and ultimately take power. At the end of the war, the Soviet Union had an occupation zone in Eastern Austria but no military presence in Italy at all. Though Western policymakers felt uncertain about the long-term future of both countries, their conclusions differed. In the case of Italy, the precariousness of the government was seen as a reason for not inflicting on it the 'loss' of South Tyrol with all the unpopularity this would bring. As a result, the West shifted its ground. When the future of South Tyrol had first been discussed in 1944, the British Foreign Office had not excluded the possibility of a border revision, which would return it to Austria, and Roosevelt had positively supported the idea.[9] But as decision-making entered a more concrete phase, Western support ebbed. When the newly established South Tyrol People's Party (*Südtiroler Volkspartei*/SVP) called for South Tyrol to be returned to Austria in May 1945 there was little resonance in London or Washington.

While Western calculations not only involved the imponderables of two countries which were potential allies, but might also become part of a threat, Soviet calculations were apparently more straightforward. South Tyrol played only a minor role in its strategy, at best serving as a possible bargaining chip to be used against either Austria or Italy or as a way of persuading them to accept Yugoslavia's territorial claims.[10]

Nevertheless, there is reason to question Steininger's view of South Tyrol as the 'first victim of the Cold War' and his related hypothesis that if there had been no East–West conflict, South Tyrol would have been 'returned' to Austria. Though Western wishes to strengthen Italy against communist influence clearly played a major part in its decision-making, this argument pays insufficient weight to the broader anti-German climate in which the decision was made. To put it in general terms: in 1945 any population that could be seen as ethnically German or connected Germany had a weak hand. Not only was there a widespread aversion to all things German, but there was also a deep suspicion of any claims for the collective rights of German (or 'German-speaking') minorities including the 'right of self-determination'. The echoes of Hitler's tactics of legitimizing German expansion into Central Europe, and in particular the misuse of minorities, such as the Sudeten Germans was clear. And the decision of the Potsdam Conference to agree the expulsion of some 14 million Germans from the eastern territories showed that the Allies, notwithstanding their misgivings about the methods adopted, basically endorsed the goal of creating homogeneous nation-states in Eastern and Central Europe. Against this benchmark, the outcome for the South Tyroleans could almost be seen as fortunate. Despite the basic similarity of their situation to that of German minorities further east, they successfully evaded the logic of ethnic cleansing and expulsion.

A look at South Tyrol's 'war record' underlines the point. The decision of the overwhelming majority of the population to resettle in Germany should not of course be equated with unconditional approval of the Nazi regime. Yet in the climate of post-war Europe, it might easily have been. In the light of Nazi atrocities and the experience of occupation, Allied decision makers and publics were rarely able or were willing to make distinctions. The Italian government and media for their part were certainly all too ready to label those who had chosen to leave in 1939 as Nazis. Those calling for them to be deprived of Italian citizenship or even removed them from the country could be found in the higher ranks of the Christian Democracy such as De Gasperi, as well as in the Italian Communist Party (Togliatti).[11] Unfair though this was, it had some basis in reality: first, a broad majority of South Tyrol's political elite had indeed openly endorsed National Socialism; second, when National Socialists seized power in South Tyrol they had been assisted by local Nazis; and third, local Nazis had participated in atrocities including the extermination of Jews and 'euthanasia' killings, atrocities in the Bolzano transit camp and other acts of persecution. All this suggest at least the probability that – with or without the Cold War – the Austro-Italian border would have remained unchanged and that South Tyrol's 'missed chance' should therefore not be ascribed to the Cold War.

But the argument can be taken further: in some ways South Tyrol positively benefitted from early Cold War tensions. It is at least arguable that without the West's fear of Soviet encroachment, it would not have exerted the pressure that resulted in the Paris Agreement. In the summer of 1946 Vienna's South Tyrol policy appeared to be in ruins.[12] There was no Plan B now that 'Plan A' (border change on the basis of self-determination) had failed. At this point, Western policy shifted in favour of Austria. Perhaps the most important difference to the previous autumn was the outcome of Austria's first post-war parliamentary elections in November 1945, where the Austrian Communist Party (*Kommunistische Partei Österreichs*/KPÖ) had performed disastrously. The strength of Austrian anti-communism was reflected in the dominance of the new coalition government by the People's Party (*Österreichische Volkspartei*/ÖVP) and Socialists (*Sozialistische Partei Österreichs*/SPÖ) (with the Communists reduced to a minor role). In the deepening crisis, the continuation of this coalition seemed vital to the West. The British Foreign Office feared that unless Austria's Foreign Minister Karl Gruber could demonstrate that his South Tyrol policy had achieved some success he would be under threat. This apparently weighed more than any particular concern for minority rights and led the Foreign Office to apply great pressure on both Italy and Austria to come to an agreement. Above all, it made it clear to the Italian Government that it was also in Rome's interest for Austria to be favourably disposed towards it. Unless it could extract something from the ruins of its South Tyrol policy, it might be driven to a more pro-Soviet line. The high expectations of the Austrian public had been shown by numerous demonstrations held in South and North Tyrol and the petition signed by 155,000 South Tyroleans and presented to the Austrian Chancellor Leopold Figl. When their demand was finally rejected by the four allies on 24 June 1946,[13] it paved the way for an agreement based on 'internal self-determination,' i.e., autonomy, instead of 'external self-determination.' Thanks to the British initiative, an understanding was reached within weeks and on 5 September 1946 the Paris Agreement was signed (later integrated into the Italian Peace Treaty).[14] This was followed in 1948 by the passing by the Italian Parliament of the First Autonomy Statute, which meant that unlike in the 1920s, South Tyrol could not be treated as a merely internal Italian matter. Austria was given the special legal status of a 'protecting power.'

3 The Disappearance of Ethnic Politics?

As the division of Europe deepened, both Italy and Austria became part of the Western 'community of values,' in the sense that they had multi-party parliamentary systems and capitalist economies. Both benefitted heavily from Marshall Aid and were members of the OEEC and its successor organizations (EPU, OECD). Austria's integration into Western Europe's economy was as crucial to its post-war recovery as it was to Italy but Austria, as an occupied country, operated under more constraints. Unlike Italy, it could not join NATO or the Western European Union, although in many ways – some of them covert – it was a *de facto* member.

In this period of Western integration and Cold War tension, South Tyrol virtually disappeared from the international horizon in what some have called a 'South Tyrolean lull' (*Südtirolflaute*). It also hardly featured in the media or in public discussion in Italy or Austria. In the run-up to the 1948 election campaign Italian politics was dominated by the confrontation between Christian Democrats and the Popular Democratic Front (*Fronte Popolare*), which included Communist and Socialists. Over the following decade, the Austrian media for its part, focused primarily on the four power Treaty negotiations and the burdens of the continuing occupation. Apart from Austrian disappointment at the failure to 'regain' Tyrol, there was a widespread feeling that neither the Italian government (nor other Western governments) should be upset at a time when their support was needed against Soviet pressure on the West.[15] If the South Tyrol conflict was addressed at all, it was not as part of a bilateral conflict between Italy and Austria, but rather in the context of the East–West confrontation.[16] The only major exception to Austria's softly-softly approach came in 1953. After Italy's Prime Minister Giuseppe Pella had demanded a plebiscite for Trieste the Austrian government responded with a note to Paris, London, and Washington calling, unsuccessfully, for the right of self-determination to be applied to South Tyrol.[17]

South Tyrol may have come off the international agenda but ethnic politics did not disappear. On the contrary, ethnic actors adjusted to the new international context, seeking to turn it to their advantage. The continuation of ethnic politics in a new key can be seen in the stance of the SVP, which was the dominant regional party from its foundation in 1945 and consistently won an absolute majority of seats in provincial elections with a share of the vote ranging from 67.6 per cent (1948) to 48.1 per cent (2008).[18] To understand this success it is essential to see the way that, as an ethnic 'catch-all party' it successfully gained support from all social classes.

At the same time, it successfully operated in and exploited a political culture which was emphatically conservative and Catholic. In the Cold War the anti-socialist and anti-communist dimension to this culture led the SVP to give top priority to maintaining a conservative hegemony at provincial and national levels.[19] In its support for an anti-communist front with the Christian Democrats (*Democrazia Cristiana*/DC) its leadership was also prepared to accept the implementation of the Paris Agreement, even when, from an ethnic perspective, there was a good reason to challenge the way the DC was sabotaging it.

A major milestone in this process was the 1948 Italian election campaign, in which the DC, together with other conservative parties, united against the 'popular front' of the communists and socialists.

The elections were viewed in Western capitals as a crucial test of anti-communist mobilization. South Tyrol's leading Catholic, Bishop Johann Geisler, called it a battle between 'Christ and anti-Christ,' between 'Rome and Moscow,' and between 'Freedom and Bondage.'[20] He went on to explain that

> out of all the parties running in my Diocese, there are only two whose programmes conform to the demands of the Church authority: namely, the *Südtiroler Volkspartei* and the *Democrazia Cristiana*. From a religious point of view, believers can – with a good conscience – cast their votes for either of these two parties.[21]

In the pursuit of anti-communist unity some Catholic figures outside the SVP even attempted to convince the party not to put up any candidates at all, and instead give their votes *en bloc* to the DC.[22] Though not willing or able to go this far, Erich Ammon, the SVP chairman, did signal to the second provincial conference of the SVP that it would make common cause with the DC:

> We will fight the (Italian) government only in those places and at those times where our national interests may be harmed. We should not forget, however, that *this* Italian government has fought for the consolidation of the state as well as for the Christian and European spirit. Electoral campaigns notwithstanding, there should be no doubt whatsoever that in this battle we are on their side.[23]

The anti-communism, which underpinned this strategy, under the slogan of 'Edelweiss Unity' ('*Einheit im Edelweiss*') was, admittedly also later aimed at the neo-fascist right but its prime targets were any groups which appeared, or could be portrayed as being left-of-centre: socialists and social-democrats were all lumped together and labelled communist. Indeed, anyone who questioned the need for the ethnic unity of the South Tyrolean German population risked being labelled in the same way. This meant that all forms of political dissent or debate tended to be discredited.

As Geisler's comment suggests, this anti-communism was strongly supported by the Catholic Church.[24] It reached new heights in Bishop

Josef Gargitter's pastoral letter of 1955 titled 'The dangers of communism in our country':

> Christendom and communism are opposites like heaven and hell, like God and the Devil. (. . .) all those belonging to the Communist party and their doctrine, and all those who encourage it, are excommunicated – that is, they will remain excluded from the community of the Church and from the graces of the Church's sacraments.

For Gargitter, communism was also a threat to South Tyrol's ethnic identity (*Volkstum*):

> A leftist government with pro-communist tendencies in their politics, economics and cultural life is incompatible with political party programmes based on the bedrock of Christianity. Every connection with communism is a betrayal of the highest values of our ethnic way of life.[25]

Until the beginning of the 1970s the Catholic Church worked hand-in-hand with the secular leadership of the SVP, whose main concern was to preserve their business interests. The two converged around the defense of the 'old order' resting on the two pillars of the Church and the Catholic Party. The values the party upheld were those of a conservative 'naturally' hierarchical social order (education aimed at elites, traditional woman's role, etc.) and the rejection of industrialization, because of the danger of increasing working-class strength.

Here the ethnic cleavage (German-speaking vs. Italian) largely reinforced the confessional one (catholic vs. anti-clerical) since despite the shared confession it was the national or ethnic factor, which was declared to embody primary values.

The SVP invoked this ethnic primacy to argue in favour of minority protection and provincial autonomy while Catholic conservatism was directed against the communist enemy. While ideological elements were subjected to strong fluctuations, and tended to be activated when there was a real, or presumed danger of the Left taking over government, ethnic elements were a constant. Left-of-centre German-speaking parties or candidates were attacked on both counts; they were accused of both splitting the ethnic community and supporting communism. This two-pronged approach can be seen in the accusations levelled in 1966 against the South Tyrol Social Democrats under Egmont Jenny and later against the Social Progress Party (*Soziale Fortschrittspartei*). The Communist Party itself, despite its electoral insignificance in South Tyrol (it never won more than six per cent of the votes in provincial elections between 1948 and 1973) was an object of constant attack. This did not change as it softened its class struggle rhetoric in the 1970s and gave more emphasis to minority rights and the implementation of the 'package.'[26] Neither did the evolution of the Italian Communist Party as it evolved towards reformist 'eurocommunism' significantly soften the anti-communism of the SVP. In August 1975 the SVP Senator Peter Brugger, apparently irritated by Communist electoral successes in Italy, even went so far as to say that the SVP would 'demand the right of self-determination for South Tyrol, should Italy fall into the hands of Communism.'[27]

4 South Tyrol Returns to the International Agenda

At the end of the 1950s, South Tyrol became an international issue once again. One likely explanation for this 'reappearance' was the changes in relationship between Austria and Italy following the Austrian State Treaty of 1955. The restoration of Austrian sovereignty was accompanied by the declaration of 'permanent neutrality,' which cemented Austria's position outside NATO. Neutral Austria, together with neutral Switzerland, now formed a wedge in NATO's southern flank, leading to some disgruntled Western observers to see this as a rupturing of what the Western Defence Union (WEA) had joined together only the year before.[28] Two years later, Italy became a founder member of the European Economic Community (EEC) while Austria, constrained by neutrality, joined the less ambitious British-led European Free Trade Association (EFTA). Nevertheless, despite economic contacts with its Eastern European neighbours, Austria's dependence on West European trade and investment and its integration with the West Germany economy was the key to its growth

over the following decades. The implications of Austrian neutrality
emerged more clearly after the 1956 Hungarian Uprising as the
Austrian government sought to make a clear distinction between
'neutralization,' which it rejected as an unacceptable departure from
basic liberal democratic values, and a desirable neutrality. Especially
after Bruno Kreisky took over as foreign minister, Austrian governments also began to display greater self-confidence on the international stage. This new assertiveness was seen in more forceful calls for
minority rights to be implemented in South Tyrol. At the same time,
in the region itself the political and economic situation deteriorated.
A first pointer to things to come was a bomb explosion in 1956. The
following year, the SVP organized a mass protest demonstration in
which 35,000 people demanded autonomy, separate from the
Italian-speaking province of Trentino. But there was no indication
that Italy was prepared to move towards implementing the autonomy
required by the Paris Agreement.

In 1960, faced with Italy's flat rejection of Austrian complaints,
Kreisky decided to raise the South Tyrol question in the UN General
Assembly. The decision was far from easy since it cut across the
established East–West division, which dominated the UN. Not
only was Italy an important member of the Western bloc but the
Italian–American lobby was also a powerful factor in U.S. politics.
Italy gained further US support by declaring that it was ready to
station NATO's nuclear weapons in South Tyrol. Since it required
the area to be politically stable, this reinforced American interest in
maintaining Italian control there.

Fearing that the Soviet Union would profit from the dispute, the
Western powers asked Italy and Austria to resolve their differences
bilaterally. In effect, they meant that Austria should withdraw its
appeal to the UN. Despite being subjected to tremendous pressure,
Kreisky resisted and instead sought to 'sell' the idea of South Tyrol's
rights by giving them a European dimension.[29] Specifically, he linked
them to the Social Democratic policy on Germany, which was to
support 'the peaceful reunification of Germany in freedom and the
establishment of a European security system based on the restoration
of freedom and self-determination for all European peoples.'[30] Only
by overcoming the forced division of Germany and Europe would

real détente and enduring peace be possible. Kreisky thus portrayed South Tyrol as a part of this wider project for overcoming the European Cold War.

The response of the Western powers to Kreisky's initiative was lukewarm. Admittedly, Britain was particularly active, partly because the Paris Agreement had been substantially the result of a British initiative and partly because Britain was the leading state of the European Free Trade Area to which Austria also belonged. British 'Tyrolophile' traditions probably also played a part. This partly offset the energetic calls from the Italian government for support from its NATO partners. But Denmark was the only NATO member-state to come out openly against Italy[31] and overall Western pressure on Italy was probably less decisive than the pleas of non-aligned states, including Ceylon/Sri Lanka, Cyprus, India, Indonesia and Ghana. Ireland, as a non-NATO state, played a decisive role in mobilizing Third World support for Austria.

Contrary to Western fears, the Soviet Union did not get involved. In the logic of the Cold War it might have seen the conflict as a 'windfall,' which could be used to attack Italy, for failing in its democratic duty. In fact, it acted with great restraint. There are several likely explanations for this: first, the Soviet government was presumably reluctant to draw attention to its own numerous ethnic or national minorities and their various discontents. Second, it was probably also reluctant to champion the rights of a German-speaking minority at a time when the expellee organizations in West Germany were vociferously asserting their claims. This was reflected in the DDR position that South Tyrolean demands for self-determination were tantamount to right-wing extremism.[32] The Austrian and Italian Communist parties took a similar line.[33] Perhaps most important was the reluctance of the Soviet bloc to make an issue of a post-war border at a time when one of its main foreign policy concerns was to legitimize the frontiers established at the end of World War II (e.g., the absorption of the Baltic States, the division of Germany and the Oder–Neisse line).

In response to two UN resolutions Italy and Austria eventually began bilateral negotiations but they made slow progress.[34] In South Tyrol this caused disappointment and disaffection with the SVP leadership and led some militants to resort to armed violence in the hope of 'bombing South Tyrol into self-determination.' International public opinion was meant to force Italy to make concessions.[35] On the night of 11 June 1961, later christened the 'night of fire' (*Feuernacht*), the group blew up 37 electricity pylons located all over South Tyrol.[36]

These attacks made national headlines in Italy as well as Austria but their international impact was much less than the 'bombers' had hoped. The world's attention was fixed on the building of the Berlin Wall (11 August 1961) and the Cuban missile crisis. In comparison, the South Tyrol conflict hardly seemed decisively important. Furthermore, the Italian response to the bombing campaign was less repressive than the bombers hoped. Admittedly, Rome did send 7,000 soldiers and *carabinieri* to South Tyrol and it also set up the so-called 'Commission of 19,' comprising federal, provincial Tyrolean and regional Trentino–South Tyrolean representatives. The commission was given the task of coming up with a set or 'package' of measures meant to implement far-reaching legislative and administrative autonomy. This response reflected an important long-term shift in Rome from coalitions of the centre to the centre-left. Underpinning this was a broader process of transformation and democratization within Italian society and politics. At its centre was the gradual softening of the deep antagonism between the Communist Party and the Christian Democrats, which eventually paved the way to the 'historic compromise.'

5 South Tyrol as a Secret Service Playground

While 'world opinion' was hardly touched by the 'night of fire,' one group of Cold War actors did begin to get involved in South Tyrol more seriously: the secret services. From both sides of the Iron Curtain they began to use the province as a testing ground. Their involvement, which took many South Tyrol activists by surprise, fostered a wider process of radicalization and escalation. Whereas the first wave of bombings had largely been the work of home-grown perpetrators or 'dynamiters' (*dinamitardi*), a wider circle now became involved. And unlike the first generation, which had taken care not to endanger human life, the second and third generations, most of whom came from extreme right wing circles in Austria and Germany, were less fussy. And they were ready to carry out attacks beyond South Tyrol's borders.

The Austrian State Police and West Germany's Federal Intelligence Service, who had followed the activities of the 'Liberation Committee of South Tyrol' (BAS) from the start, now, stepped up their surveillance.[37] Then the Italian Armed Forces Intelligence Service/*Servizio Informazione Forze Armate*, which had initially been taken by surprise by the bombings, began to infiltrate the BAS. Here they were able to test the methods, which they later used in their subversive 'strategy tension' (*strategia della tension*) against the Italian state, including the use of *agents provocateurs*, simulated terrorist attacks, kidnappings, disinformation and even – as in the case of Luis Amplatz – the assassination of terrorist opponents.[38] How far they were prepared to go was later shown by the (failed) coup attempt by Carabinieri-General Giovanni de Lorenzo in 1964.

Alongside conventional Western diplomatic representatives, who closely followed these developments, the U.S. secret service was also involved.[39] The CIA had actually been present at the foundation of the BAS and Fritz Molden, the Austrian media tycoon and son-in-law of CIA Director Allen Dulles, acted as a link to the activists and organized their finance. Leopold Steurer has argued that the activists were themselves little more than pawns of the U.S. government, which was once again seized by the fear that the left might gain power in Rome. The fear was triggered by the fall of the Tambroni government in 1961, which had been supported by the neo-Fascists Movimento Sociale Italiano. This opened up the possibility that the left might join a government coalition. According to Steurer, the USA tolerated the bombings in the hope that the crisis would boost the Italian right.[40] Here at least the prospect of increased tension between the two Western neighbours, Italy and Austria, did not appear to be a consideration.

However, the involvement of West German and Austrian neo-Nazis also seems to have increased Soviet interest, and that of East German and Czech secret services. The KGB contacted some South Tyrol terrorists in the mid-1960s. It even offered them logistical support but, in line with their militant anti-Communism, the terrorists refused it.[41] The main Soviet aim was apparently less an interest in South

Tyrol politics *per se* than the wish to drive a wedge between Italy and West Germany.[42] They may have been encouraged by Italian media descriptions of the first wave of bombings as the 'first German military action since the end of the war.' In similar vein the Italian media accused Germans of 'anti-Italian rabble-rousing propaganda, revanchism and militarism.' *La Stampa* wrote that 'by carrying out the bombing attacks in Italy, German nationalists are stirring up public opinion in favour of a revision of lost territory in the East – namely: Prussia, Pomerania, Silesia and the Sudetenland.'[43] In addition, the Soviet government may have hoped to divert international interest from events in Czechoslovakia.[44] Whatever its exact motivations, the Soviet secret services went so far as to work out a detailed plan to blow up the oil pipeline that ran through the Lake Constance, and then lay the blame on Italian extremists.

By the end of the 1960s the Soviet involvement had achieved little. Neither the West German nor the Italian governments showed any interest in allowing their relations to deteriorate over South Tyrol.[45] Increased international tensions following the invasion of Czechoslovakia and the US turmoil over Vietnam were much stronger countervailing consideration. Most importantly, neither terrorism nor secret service activities were able to derail the negotiations that now began between the Italian government and the SVP. The 1969 package they agreed to, including 137 measures to protect the German and Ladin minorities, was followed in 1972 by the Second Autonomy Statute, which contained far-reaching stipulations such as ethnic proportional representation and compulsory bilingualism in the public domain. There was a surge of optimism in both language groups and the neighbouring states and for a time nearly all violence ceased.[46] It seems likely that the foreign secret services now suspended operations in South Tyrol.

6 Détente and the End of the Cold War

The 'Spring' that followed the 1969 agreement did not last long. When the first measures of minority protection were implemented in the mid-1970s they triggered a backlash within the Italian population, which thought their privileges were threatened. Their sense of vulnerability was increased by a serious crisis that developed in regional industry and one of the largest employers of Italian workers in South Tyrol.[47] On the German side there were complaints that progress towards autonomy was too slow. A minority group thought the measures did not go far enough and returned to the demand for self-determination and 'reunion' with Austria. In 1984, as both North and South Tyrol celebrated the 175th anniversary of the Tyrolean uprising of 1809, a new wave of terror began, instigated by an Austrian splinter group called 'One Tyrol' (*Ein Tirol*).[48]

The secret services also resumed their machinations, in particular the Italian secret services' 'tension strategy.' Here the interests of the Italian state coincided with the aim of Italian nationalists to discredit the separatist movements that had emerged in North Tyrol in particular. This convergence of interests led to tacit co-operation between rogue elements of the Italian Secret Service and the Italy's Far Right. 'Primula' was a special unit of the shadowy top-secret 'Gladio' organization, which in the 1950s had been part of the co-operation between the Italian secret services and the CIA.[49] Even though 'Gladio' had supposedly long since been disbanded, there is clear evidence that it was involved in the new wave of attacks, which targeted both Italians and Germans.[50] The *Stasi* also returned, pursuing similar goals to those of the 1960s.[51] At one point its interests even converged with those of the Italian secret services (supported by the United States) and the right-wing extremists who had infiltrated it. Some double agents even worked simultaneously for both the Italian and East German secret services. Their shared ground was the wish to see the idea of self-determination tarred with the brush of right-wing extremism,[52] and more fundamentally, the concern to maintain the territorial *status quo*.

The 1975 Helsinki Final Act, which declared Europe's borders to be 'inviolable,' is generally seen as the highpoint of European détente. The revival of concerns about human rights, which marked the late 1970s, an unintended or at least unexpected consequence of it, fed into sharpening East–West tensions to create what some have called the 'second Cold War.' The military aspect of this deterioration was the crisis that followed the 1979 NATO decision to deploy a new generation of intermediate nuclear missiles (Cruise and Pershing) supposedly in order to catch up with the earlier Soviet build-up of SS-20 missiles. Opposition to the NATO decision escalated into a broad social mobilization against both NATO and the Warsaw Pact and included both neutral Austria and the NATO member, Italy. Municipal governments on both sides of the Iron Curtain declared themselves nuclear-free zones, forming an 'East–West quadrangle' of Italy, Austria, Yugoslavia and Hungary. Though towns in Tyrol (North and South) did not join this initiative, there were cross-border initiatives and demonstrations calling for the closure of NATO camps and missile bases, including those in South Tyrol.[53]

Nevertheless, when the Cold War did finally end, there was a moment when politics seemed to be returning to an earlier pre-war mode. The independence of the Baltic States, Ukraine and Belarus and the reunification of Germany brought the issue of right of self-determination back to the forefront of discussion and showed that 'inviolability' did not preclude an agreed revision of state borders. For one group within the SVP this revived the vision of reunification. There was also talk of the 'Slovenian path,' i.e., a relatively painless separation from Italy. On 15 September 1991 a huge rally was held near the Brenner Pass under the slogan of 'Break off from Rome – regional unity now' (*Los von Rom – Landeseinheit jetzt*).[54] Though the 'realists' in the SVP quickly regained the upper hand, their concern to take the wind out of these 'utopianist' sails did lead to a final push for agreement on the last outstanding points on implementation of the package.

In 1992 both Austria and Italy formally presented a 'declaration of conflict settlement' (*Streitbeilegung*) to the United Nations,[55] formally ending the thirty-year-old dispute. Over the following decade, after Austria joined the European Union (1995), frontier barriers at the Brenner Pass were removed. South Tyrol now serves as a model for the successful resolution of ethnic minority conflicts.[56]

7 Conclusion

As the case of South Tyrol shows, the interaction between the 'high politics' of the Cold War and the ethnic politics of the region could be very complex. Nevertheless, five broad conclusions can be drawn here:

First, the German minority of South Tyrol was in many respects a winner from the Cold War. As tensions between the East and West were starting to increase, it received the protection of international law in the form of the 1946 Paris Agreement. Even though its implementation took several decades, this was in marked contrast to the treatment of ethnic Germans in Eastern and Central Europe.

Second, the Cold War provided the SVP with the powerful weapon of anti-communism. This was used with great effect against any political dissent from left-of-centre. Here the Cold War appears as something that regional ethnic politicians could use for their own ends, as much as *vice versa*. And, as politics of the 1960s and 1970s showed, it was a weapon they were reluctant to give up, even when the notion of a genuine communist threat appeared increasingly implausible.

Third, anti-communism was not just an instrument. Especially until the 1960s it was embedded in the world-view of Tyrol's elites. That applied both to Church leaders or those close to the Church and to the secular leaders of the SVP. It meant that at the height of the Cold War the SVP acted loyally towards Christian Democrat Italian governments and was ready to overlook the inadequacies of minority protection because it saw it as a bulwark against communism. Conversely, the SVP was unable or unwilling to recognize that it actually shared much ground with South Tyrol's left-wing or secularist parties. Although this might suggest that Cold War ideology (or religion) could and often did trump ethnicity, it should be stressed that most South Tyroleans saw no tension between the two.

Fourth, the Eastern bloc's readiness to exploit the conflict propagandistically was quite limited. Even after it was internationalized, the Soviet government probably felt too vulnerable about its own nationality policies to do so and, more importantly, was committed to maintaining the post-war territorial *status quo*. A partial exception came with the interventions of East European secret services (in particular, the East German *Stasi*), which sought to destabilize Italy as a NATO member and foster dissent between it and its NATO partner,

West Germany. But even though this sometimes produced a strange alignment with far-right elements in the Italian secret service, there was never much likelihood that the SVP would abandon its ideological objection to communism in order to extract concessions from the Italian state.

Fifth, ethnic politics disappeared from the international agenda in the 1940s and most of the 1950s and returned when Austria took it to the United Nations in 1961. But both the disappearance and re-emergence were illusory in the sense that ethnic politics and, in particular, ethnic grievances had remained a central reality throughout the period. The anti-communist alignment of the SVP with the DC had not stopped the SVP mobilizing ethnic resentments or fears.

Mark Mazower's claim that 'ethnic disputes were not allowed to jeopardize bloc cohesion' therefore seems only partly valid in the case of South Tyrol. The implication that coercion or pressure (through the invocation of the Soviet threat) was exerted from above by the superpowers or by national governments is undermined by the complexity of national and regional political interactions. And, as the violence in the 1960s shows, there were clear limits to the abilities of the superpowers to impose stabilization on a region where a large part of the population felt – or was persuaded – that it was suffering a basic 'ethnic injustice'.

Notes

[1] See Günther Pallaver and Leopold Steurer, *Deutsche! Hitler verkauft euch! Das Erbe von Option und Weltkrieg in Südtirol*, Bozen: Raetia, 2011.

[2] See Karl Stuhlpfarrer, *Umsiedlung Südtirol* (2 vols), Vienna: Löcker, 1985 and 'Südtirol 1939–45. Option, Umsiedlung, Widerstand, in *Föhn*, 6/7, (1980), 53.

[3] See Rolf Steininger, *Autonomie oder Selbstbestimmung. Die Südtirolfrage 1945/46 und das Gruber–De Gasperi Abkommen*, Innsbruck-Vienna-Bozen: Studienverlag 2006, (revised edn).

[4] Rolf Steininger, *Südtirol im 20. Jahrhundert. Vom Leben und Überleben einer Minderheit*, Innsbruck-Vienna: Studienverlag, 1997, 237.

[5] Mark Mazower, 'Minorities and the League of Nations in Interwar Europe', in *Daedalus*, 126, (2), (1997), 47–63.

[6] Leopold Steurer, 'Südtirol 1943–1946: Von der Operationszone Alpenvorland zum Pariser Vertrag', in Hans Heiss and Gustav Pfeifer (eds), *Südtirol – Stunde Null? Kriegsende 1945–46*, Innsbruck-Vienna-Munich: Studienverlag, 2000, 48–116.

[7] Karl-Heinz Ritschel, *Diplomatie um Südtirol. Politische Hintergründe eines europäischen Versagens,* Stuttgart: Seewald Verlag, 1966, 213.

[8] Heinz-Rudolf Othmerding, *Sozialistische Minderheitenpolitik am Beispiel Südtirol von den Anfängen des Konflikts bis heute,* (2 vols), University of Hamburg PhD, 1984.

[9] Steurer, *Südtirol,* 68.

[10] Steurer, *Südtirol,* 70.

[11] See Claus Gatterer, *Im Kampf gegen Rom. Bürger, Minderheiten und Autonomien in Italien,* Vienna-Frankfurt am Main-Zurich: Europaverlag, 1968; Klara Rieder, *Silvio Flor. Autonomie und Klassenkampf. Die Biographie eines Südtiroler Kommunisten,* Bozen: Edition Raetia, 2007, 88–91.

[12] Rolf Steininger, *Los von Rom? Die Südtirolfrage 1945/46 und das Gruber-De Gasperi-Abkommen,* Innsbruck: Studienverlag, 1987.

[13] See Steininger, *Südtirol im 20. Jahrhundert,* 246–51.

[14] Steininger, *Südtirol im 20. Jahrhundert,* 363.

[15] Claus Gatterer, '35 Jahre nach dem Pariser Vertrag. Das Südtirol-Problem aus der Sicht eines Südtirolers in Österreich', in Claus Gatterer, *Aufsätze und Reden,* Bozen: Edition Raetia, 1991, 210–11.

[16] Josef Berghold, *Italien – Austria. Von der Erbfeindschaft zur europäischen Öffnung,* Vienna: Eichbauer Verlag, 1997, 183.

[17] Gatterer, *Im Kampf gegen Rom,* 1013.

[18] See Anton Holzer, *Die Südtiroler Volkspartei,* Thaur: Kulturverlag, 1991; Günther Pallaver, 'The Südtiroler Volkspartei: from Irredentism to Autonomy', in Lieven De Winter, Margarita Gómez-Reino and Peter Lynch (eds), *Autonomist Parties in Europe: Identity, Politics and the Revival of the Territorial Cleavage* (ICPS, vol. 2). Barcelona: Aleu, 2006, 161–88; Günther Pallaver, 'The Südtiroler Volkspartei', in Anwen Elias and Filippo Tronconi (eds), *From Protest to Power. Autonomist parties and the challenges of representation,* Vienna: Braumüller, 2011, 171–93.

[19] Südtiroler Volkspartei, *Programm und Statut der SVP, genehmigt auf der Landesversammlung vom 11. February 1947,* Bozen 1947, 34, 37.

[20] Sophie G. Alf, *Leitfaden Italien. Vom antifaschistischen Kampf zum Historischen Kompromiß,* Berlin: Rotbuch Verlag, 1982, 96.

[21] *Volksbote,* 23 January 1947.

[22] Günther Pallaver and Leopold Steurer, *Ich teile das Los meiner Erde - Condividerò la sorte della mia terra. August Pichler 1898–1963,* Bozen: Edition Raetia, 1998, 112.

[23] *Ibid,* 112.

[24] See Joachim Goller, *Die Brixner Richtungen. Die Südtiroler Volkspartei, das katholische Lager und der Klerus,* Innsbruck-Vienna-Bozen: Studienverlag, 2008.

[25] *Katholisches Sonntagsblatt,* 9 September 1955.

[26] Othmerding, *Sozialistische Minderheitenpolitik,* 926.

[27] *L'Adige,* 5 August 1975.

[28] See William L. Stearman, *Die Sowjetunion in Österreich 1945–1955,* Bonn: Siegler, 1962; Manfred Sell, *Die neutralen Alpen,* Stuttgart: Seewald Verlag, 1965.

[29] Steininger, *Südtirol im 20. Jahrhundert,* 448; Rolf Steininger, *Südtirol zwischen Diplomatie und Terror 1947–1969* (vol. 2), Bozen: Athesia 1999, 167ff.

[30] Klaus Berchtold, *Österreichische Parteiprogramme 1868–1966*, Munich: Verlag für Geschichte und Politik, 1967.

[31] Friedl Volgger, *Mit Südtirol am Scheideweg. Erlebte Geschichte*, Innsbruck: Haymon-Verlag, 1984, 232.

[32] Julius Mader, 'Südtirol – Exerzierfeld westdeutscher Revanchistenverbände', in *Deutsche Außenpolitik*, 1 (1964), 54–9.

[33] Othmerding, *Sozialistische Minderheitenpolitik*, 671.

[34] Alexander von Egen, *Die Südtirol-Frage vor den VereintenNationen. Rechtsgeschichte und Dokumente, mit einer Zusammenfassung in italienischer und englischer Sprache*. Frankfurt am Main: Peter Lang, 1997.

[35] Elisabeth Baumgartner, Hans Mayr, and Gerhard Mumelter (eds), *Feuernacht. Südtirols Bombenjahre. Ein zeitgeschichtliches Lesebuch*, Bozen: Edition Raetia, 1992.

[36] Michael Gehler, '. . .daß keine Menschenleben geopfert werden sollten – das war der Plan'. Die Bozner, Feuernacht 'und die Südtirol-Attentate der 1960 er Jahre', in Michael Gehler and René Ortner (eds), *Von Sarajewo zum 11. September. Einzelattentate und Massenterrorismus*, Innsbruck-Vienna-Bozen: Studienverlag, 2007, 205–56; Hans Karl Peterlini, *Südtiroler Bombenjahre. Von Blut und Tränen zum Happy End?*, Bozen: Edition Raetia, 2005; Manuel Fasser, *Ein Tirol – zwei Welten. Das politische Erbe der Südtiroler Feuernacht*, Innsbruck-Vienna-Bozen: Studienverlag, 2010.

[37] Christoph Franceschini, 'Spielwiese der Geheimdienste. Südtirol in den 60er Jahren', in Gerald Steinacher (ed), *Im Schatten der Geheimdienste. Südtirol 1918 bis zur Gegenwart*, Innsbruck-Vienna-Munich-Bozen: Studienverlag 2003, 223.

[38] *Ibid*, 223.

[39] *Ibid*, 222; Siegfried Stuffer, 'The Alto Adige-Question. Der Südtirol-Konflikt aus der Sicht der USA', in Baumgartner, Mayr and Mumelter (eds), *Feuernacht*, 332–6.

[40] *Il Mattino*, 22 June 2001, 6.

[41] *Alto Adige*, 11 April 1992, 20 November 1999, 14.

[42] Franceschini, Spielwiese, 222–4.

[43] *La Stampa*, 11 September 1963.

[44] *Il Mattino*, 15 October 1999, 17.

[45] Steininger, *Südtirol zwischen Diplomatie und Terror* (vol 1), 798–866.

[46] Michael Gehler, 'Vollendung der Bilateralisierung als diplomatisch-juristisches Kunststück: Die Streitbeilegungserklärung zwischen Italien und Österreich', in Sieglinde Clementi and Jens Woelk (eds), *1992: Ende eines Streits. Zehn Jahre Streitbeilegung im Südtirolkonflikt zwischen Italien und Österreich*, Baden-Baden: Nomos-Verlag, 2003, pp. 17–82.

[47] See Günther Pallaver, 'Südtirols Konkordanzdemokratie. Ethnische Konfliktregelung zwischen juristischem Korsett und gesellschaftlichem Wandel', in Sieglinde Clementi and Jens Woelk (eds), *1992: Ende eines Streits. Zehn Jahre Streitbeilegung im Südtirolkonflikt zwischen Italien und Österreich*, Baden-Baden: Nomos-Verlag, 2003, 177–203.

[48] Hans Karl Peterlini, 'Die Achse am Brenner. Die Rolle der Geheimdienste seit den 70er Jahren. Südtirol zwischen Gladio und Stasi', in Gerald Steinacher (ed), *Im Schatten der Geheimdienste. Südtirol 1918 bis zur Gegenwart*, Innsbruck-Vienna-Munich-Bozen: Studienverlag, 2003, 229–64.

[49] Peterlini, Die Achse am Brenner, 203.

[50] Peterlini, *Ibid*, 237, 2005, 319–43.

[51] Mader *Südtirol* 1964.

[52] Peterlini, Die Achse am Brenner, 237.

[53] Günther Pallaver, 'L'erba del vicino. Italien-Österreich. Nachbarn in Europa', in Michael Gehler and Rolf Steininger (eds), *Österreich und die europäische Integration 1945–1993. Aspekte einer wechselvollen Entwicklung*, Vienna-Cologne-Weimar: Böhlau Verlag, 1993, 230.

[54] Steininger, *Südtirol im 20. Jahrhundert*, 542.

[55] See Andrea Di Michele, Francesco Palermo, and Günther Pallaver (eds), *1992. Fine di un conflitto. Dieci anni dalla chiusura della questione sudtirolese*, Bologna: il Mulino, 2003.

[56] See Günther Pallaver, 'South Tyrol's Consociational Democracy: Between Political Claim and Social Reality', in Jens Woelk, Francesco Palermo and Joseph Marko (eds), *Tolerance through Law. Self Governance and Group Rights in South Tyrol* (European Academy Bozen/Bolzano), Leiden-Boston: MartinusNijhoff Publishers, 2008, 303–27.

Bibliography

Alf, Sophie G. (1982), *Leitfaden Italien. Vom antifaschistischen Kampf zum Historischen Kompromiß*. Berlin: Rotbuch Verlag.

Baumgartner, Elisabeth, Mayr, Hans and Mumelter, Gerhard (1992) (eds), *Feuernacht. Südtirols Bombenjahre. Ein zeitgeschichtliches Lesebuch*. Bozen: Edition Raetia.

Berchtold, Klaus (1967), *Österreichische Parteiprogramme 1868–1966*. Munich: Verlag für Geschichte und Politik.

Berghold, Josef (1997), *Italien – Austria. Von der Erbfeindschaft zur europäischen Öffnung*. Vienna: Eichbauer Verlag.

Di Michele, Andrea, Palermo, Francesco and Pallaver Günther (eds) (2003), *1992. Fine di un conflitto. Dieci anni dalla chiusura della questione sudtirolese*. Bologna: il Mulino.

Egen, Alexander von (1997), *Die Südtirol-Frage vor den Vereinten Nationen. Rechtsgeschichte und Dokumente, mit einer Zusammenfassung in italienischer und englischer Sprache*. Frankfurt am Main: P. Lang.

Fasser, Manuel (2010), *Ein Tirol – zwei Welten. Das politische Erbe der Südtiroler Feuernacht*. Innsbruck-Vienna-Bozen: Studienverlag.

Franceschini, Christoph (2003), Spielwiese der Geheimdienste. Südtirol in den 60er Jahren, in Gerald Steinacher (ed), *Im Schatten der Geheimdienste. Südtirol 1918 bis zur Gegenwart*. Innsbruck-Vienna-Munich-Bozen: Studienverlag, 187–223.

Gatterer, Claus (1968), *Im Kampf gegen Rom. Bürger, Minderheiten und Autonomien in Italien*. Vienna-Frankfurt am Main-Zürich: Europaverlag.

Gatterer, Claus (1991), '35 Jahre nach dem Pariser Vertrag. Das Südtirol-Problem aus der Sicht eines Südtirolers in Österreich', in Claus Gatterer, *Aufsätze und Reden*. Bozen: Edition Raetia, 210–11.

Gehler, Michael (2003), 'Vollendung der Bilateralisierung als diplomatisch-juristisches Kunsstück: Die Streitbeilegungserklärung zwischen Italien und Österreich 1992', in Sieglinde Clementi and Jens Woelk (eds), *1992: Ende eines Streits. Zehn Jahre Streitbeilegung im Südtirolkonflikt zwischen Italien und Österreich.* Baden-Baden: Nomos-Verlag, 17–82.

Gehler, Michael (2007), ' . . . daß keine Menschenleben geopfert werden sollten – das war der Plan. Die Bozner Feuernacht und die Südtirol-Attentate der 1960er Jahre', in Michael Gehler and René Ortner (eds), *Von Sarajewo zum 11. September. Einzelattentate und Massenterrorismus.* Innsbruck-Vienna-Bozen: Studienverlag, 205–56.

Goller, Joachim (2008), *Die Brixner Richtungen. Die Südtiroler Volkspartei, das katholische Lager und der Klerus.* Innsbruck-Vienna-Bozen: Studienverlag.

Holzer, Anton (1991), *Die Südtiroler Volkspartei.* Thaur: Kulturverlag.

Mader, Julius (1964), Südtirol – Exerzierfeld westdeutscher Revanchistenverbände, in *Deutsche Außenpolitik,* 1, 54–9.

Mazower, Mark (1997), 'Minorities and the League of Nations in Interwar Europe. in *Daedalus,* 126 (2), 47–63.

Mumelter, Gerhard (1999), 'Das deutscheste aller deutschen Länder. Briefe und Bomben. In einer umfassenden Geschichte Südtirols werden die Spannungen zwischen Rom und Bonn aufgearbeitet', *Süddeutsche Zeitung,* 6 December 1999.

Othmerding, Heinz-Rudolf (1984), *Sozialistische Minderheitenpolitik am Beispiel Südtirol von den Anfängen des Konflikts bis heute,* (2 vols), University of HamburgPhD, 1984.

Pallaver, Günther (1993), 'L'erba del vicino. Italien-Österreich. Nachbarn in Europa', in Michael Gehler and Rolf Steininger (eds), *Österreich und die europäische Integration 1945–1993. Aspekte einer wechselvollen Entwicklung.* Vienna-Cologne -Weimar: Böhlau Verlag, 226–66.

Pallaver, Günther (2003), Südtirols Konkordanzdemokratie. Ethnische Konfliktregelung zwischen juristischem Korsett und gesellschaftlichem Wandel, in Sieglinde Clementi and Jens Woelk (eds) *1992: Ende eines Streits. Zehn Jahre Streitbeilegung im Südtirolkonflikt zwischen Italien und Österreich.* Baden-Baden: Nomos-Verlag, 177–203.

Pallaver, Günther (2006), 'The SüdtirolerVolkspartei: from Irredentism to Autonomy', in Lieven De Winter, Margarita Gómez-Reino and Peter Lynch (eds), *Autonomist Parties in Europe: Identity, Politics and the Revival of the Territorial Cleavage* (ICPS, vol. 2). Barcelona: Aleu, S.A., 161–88.

Pallaver, Günther (2008), 'South Tyrol's Consociational Democracy: Between Political Claim and Social Reality', in Jens Woelk, Francesco Palermo and Joseph Marko (eds), *Tolerance through Law. Self Governance and Group Rights in South Tyrol* (European Academy Bozen/Bolzano), Leiden-Boston: Martinus Nijhoff Publishers, 303–27.

Pallaver, Günther (2011), 'The SüdtirolerVolkspartei', in: Anwen Elias and Filippo Tronconi (eds), From Protest to Power.Autonomist parties and the challenges of representation, Vienna: Braumüller, 171–93.

Pallaver, Günther and Steurer, Leopold (2011), *Deutsche! Hitler verkauft euch!. Das Erbe von Option und Weltkrieg in Südtirol.* Bozen: Raetia.

Pallaver, Günther and Steurer, Leopold (1998), *Ich teile das Los meiner Erde - Condividerò la sorte della mia terra. August Pichler 1898–1963.* Bozen: Edition Raetia.

Peterlini, Hans Karl (2003), Die Achse am Brenner. Die Rolle der Geheimdienste seit den 70er Jahren. Südtirol zwischen Gladio und Stasi, in Gerald Steinacher (ed), *Im Schatten der Geheimdienste. Südtirol 1918 bis zur Gegenwart,* Innsbruck-Vienna-Munich-Bozen: Studienverlag, 229–64.

Peterlini, Hans Karl (2005), *Südtiroler Bombenjahre. Von Blut und Tränen zum Happy End?* Bozen: Edition Raetia.

Rieder, Klara (2007), *Silvio Flor. Autonomie und Klassenkampf. Die Biographie eines Südtiroler Kommunisten.* Bozen: Edition Raetia.

Ritschel, Karl Heinz (1966), *Diplomatie um Südtirol. Politische Hintergründe eines europäischen Versagens.* Stuttgart: Seewald Verlag.

Sell, Manfred (1965), *Die neutralen Alpen.* Stuttgart: Seewald Verlag.

Stearman, William L. (1962), *Die Sowjetunion in Österreich 1945–1955.* Bonn: Siegler.

Steininger, Rolf (1987), *Los von Rom? Die Südtirolfrage 1945/46 und das Gruber-De Gasperi-Abkommen.* Innsbruck: Studienverlag.

Steininger, Rolf (1997), *Südtirol im 20. Jahrhundert. Vom Leben und Überleben einer Minderheit.* Innsbruck-Vienna: Studienverlag.

Steininger, Rolf (1999), *Südtirol zwischen Diplomatie und Terror 1947–1969* (3 vols), Bozen: Athesia.

Steininger, Rolf (2006), *Autonomie oder Selbstbestimmung. Die Südtirolfrage 1945/46 und das Gruber – De Gasperi Abkommen.* Innsbruck–Vienna–Bozen: Studienverlag (new edn).

Steurer, Leopold (2000), 'Südtirol 1943–1946: Von der Operationszone Alpenvorland zum Pariser Vertrag', in Hans Heiss and Gustav Pfeifer (eds): *Südtirol – Stunde Null? Kriegsende 1945–46.* Innsbruck-Vienna-Munich: Studienverlag, 48–116.

Stuffer, Siegfried (1992), 'The Alto Adige-Question. Der Südtirol-Konflikt aus der Sicht der USA', in Elisabeth Baumgartner, Hans Mayr and Gerhard Mumelter (eds), *Feuernacht. Südtirols Bombenjahre. Ein zeitgeschichtliches Lesebuch.* Bozen: Edition Raetia, 332–6.

Stuhlpfarrer, Karl (1985), *Umsiedlung Südtirol,* (2 vols), Vienna: Löcker.

Südtiroler Volkspartei (1947), *Programm und Statut der SVP, genehmigt auf der Landesversammlung vom 11. February 1947.*

Volgger Friedl (1984), *Mit Südtirol am Scheideweg. Erlebte Geschichte.* Innsbruck: Haymon-Verlag.

Chapter 7

Sorbian Ethnic Interests, the GDR State and the Cold War

Peter Barker

1 Introduction

The Sorbs of Upper and Lower Lusatia in south-eastern Brandenburg and eastern Saxony are the last remaining representatives of the Slavonic tribes which moved westwards beyond the Oder and in the fifth or sixth century established settlements in the area up to the Elbe and beyond. During their subsequent history, which was marked by close proximity to Germans, they have been subject to a range of influences, which have directly affected both their demographic structure and their ethnic identity. In the tenth century, along with other Slav tribes, they were defeated by the Franks and henceforth lived in a state of submission to the dominant German political and economic power. At the Congress of Vienna in 1815 the whole of Lower Lusatia, as well as parts of Upper Lusatia, were ceded to Prussia from Saxony. Prussian policy towards the Sorbs was for the most part more repressive than that of Saxony. After 1815, Prussia attempted to remove teaching in Sorbian in schools, and many Sorbian-speaking priests were replaced by German speakers. Lower Lusatia was also subject to much stronger economic pressures during the process of industrialization in the latter part of the nineteenth century. The development of opencast mining for lignite after World War I also led to the destruction of many Sorbian communities. Only two Slav groups managed to maintain their separate cultural and linguistic identity into the twentieth century: the Upper and Lower Sorbs in Lusatia.

The Nazi takeover in 1933 led to an immediate deterioration in the Sorbs' position. Nazi policy was governed by their general view of the cultural and racial inferiority of all Slavs. They therefore had to treat the Sorbs as inferior citizens and restrict any attempts they made to assert their independent identity. In 1937 the *Domowina* (Homeland), the main Sorbian cultural organization since its foundation in 1912, was banned, and except for certain religious publications, all Sorbian publications were closed down. Sorbian teachers and priests were transferred to other parts of the Reich and by the end of 1938 no more Sorbian was taught in schools. In 1940 plans were drawn up by Himmler to deport the Sorbian population to the *Generalgouvernement* in Poland but Hitler intervened to defer any transfers, and in the end no action was taken. The Nazi period certainly had a negative effect on the strength of Sorbian identity, language and culture. However, it is difficult to assess accurately the precise impact of Nazi policies on their demographic development. The official census of 1933 produced a figure of only 57,000 Sorbs, while a private survey carried out under Nazi rule by O. Nowina between 1936 and 1938 arrived at a figure of 111,000.[1] Both figures clearly failed to reflect the real numbers but whatever the precise effect of these years of Germanization one thing is clear about the end of the war: the majority of Sorbs welcomed the Soviet, Ukrainian and Polish troops who reached Lusatia in April 1945 as fellow-Slav liberators.

Outside Lusatia, the literature on the Sorbian ethnic minority is sparse. The major work has been done by the Sorbian institutions themselves, in particular the Sorbian Institute in Bautzen, created in 1951. In the GDR this meant, however, that Sorbian historians were subject to the ideological restrictions imposed by the official Marxist view of history. This applied in particular to the four-volume history of the Sorbs produced in the 1970s by the Institute.[2] Much of the work since 1990 has concentrated on revising the historical view presented during the GDR period. This has meant approaching sensitive areas such as the effect of opencast mining on the demography of the bilingual area.

The end of World War II was a major turning-point in Sorb-German relations; the social, economic and material dislocation which accompanied it was particularly acute in Lusatia. From the middle of

April 1945 it was caught up in the last battle for Berlin, and there was fierce fighting in Bautzen and other towns. After the cease-fire, the area was also directly affected by the agreements made at the Yalta and Potsdam conferences. The eastern part of Görlitz was placed under Polish administration, so that towns like Zittau, Görlitz and Cottbus were now frontier towns, cut off from their hinterland. The Germans from these areas immediately started crossing the Neiße, even though almost all the bridges had been destroyed, and streamed into these towns, where they remained for several months. All the towns shared one major problem, the chaos in the supply system, and many were also victims of the indiscriminate and destructive activities of Soviet troops. Overall, Lusatia had to endure severe material damage as well as immense human suffering: widespread rapes, summary executions and indiscriminate maltreatment by the occupation forces. The fact that the Sorbs were Slavs did not stop them from being mistreated in a similar fashion to the German population.

In this immediate post-war period, the region was particularly affected by the re-drawing of frontiers; its sudden close proximity to Poland and Czechoslovakia meant that it was forced to accommodate huge waves of German refugees, triggered by the 'wild' expulsions that preceded the Potsdam Conference. The stretch of land 200 km to the east of the Oder–Neiße line was one of the first areas from which Germans were expelled after the cease-fire. In this first period of expulsions over 300,000 Germans were driven out of Silesia and after Potsdam in August the expulsions were swiftly reactivated even before the plan for 'organized' expulsions under the supervision of the Control Council for Germany was signed on 17 October 1945.[3]

'Wild' expulsions from the Sudetenland in May and June 1945 also had a major impact. According to the census of October 1946, the Soviet zone took nearly forty per cent of all refugees and expellees, officially designated resettlers (*Umsiedler*) after the establishment of the Central Administration for Resettlers (*Zentrale Verwaltung für Umsiedler*) in September 1945. By 1948 they accounted for just under a quarter (24.2 per cent) of the population of the Soviet zone. This dramatic change in the demographic structure of the Soviet zone had a particular impact on bilingual communities in the eastern parts of Lower and Upper Lusatia. From October 1945 to March 1946

Saxony was designated not as a reception and resettlement area for expelled Germans, but only as a staging-point on the route to eastern Brandenburg and Mecklenburg. However, the situation could not be controlled by purely administrative measures and many refugees did succeed in settling in Saxon villages. By the end of 1946, 17 per cent of the population in Saxony were refugees, which was still a much lower figure than the 43.4 per cent in Mecklenburg.[4] Only villages and small towns were designated to take these large numbers of refugees and expellees, because the need for workers was greatest in the countryside. More than half of those resettled in the Soviet zone were accommodated in villages and small towns with less than 2,000 inhabitants. Then in March 1946 the Soviet Military Administration (SMAD) altered its decree and designated Saxony as a settlement area for deported Germans. Since the majority of the bilingual villages lay in Saxony, they were affected especially badly by this measure. In 1946 the *Domowina* put together sets of statistics for the Sorbian area. They make clear that the refugees who were accommodated in the villages of the Sorbian language area often made up more than 20 per cent of the population; in some villages the proportion soon reached over fifty per cent.[5] The head of the *Domowina*, Paul Nedo, had already warned in 1945 of serious economic and cultural consequences for the bilingual area: in his view Germanization, which was already far advanced in some areas, would be accelerated by these demographic changes.[6]

2 The Sorbs at the Start of the Cold War

Since the Sorbian area was in the Soviet Zone of Occupation (SBZ), it was inevitable that minority policy would be influenced by the cooling of the international climate. Particular moments of tension, whether within occupied Germany or more widely within the Eastern bloc, tended to have a negative effect on Sorbian institutions and leaders. The Sorbs were, after all, a Slav minority in a German environment controlled by the Soviet Union. This meant that their leaders were torn between seeking an international solution through the post-war Conferences of Foreign Ministers (CFM), where they hoped for Soviet support, and looking for alliances with whatever

German groups emerged from the new power structures of the Soviet zone. The Soviet Union saw advantages in presenting their policy towards the Sorbian minority as a positive model of how ethnic minorities should be treated. This also applied to an extent to the leaders of the Socialist Unity Party (*Sozialistische Einheitspartei Deutschland*/SED) which was founded in 1946 as a fusion of the KPD and parts of the SPD, although in the early post-war years this positive dimension was not immediately apparent. Despite the fact that both Lenin and Stalin put class before minority interests, some SED leaders were highly sceptical about applying Leninist nationalities policy to the Sorbs, especially in Brandenburg. In the Soviet Union this had given non-Russian ethnic groups some cultural rights, although emphasizing that the right of self-determination could and should not serve as an obstacle to the dictatorship of the working class. Stalin had presented the outline of this policy in 1923 in the theses for the Twelfth Congress of the Russian Communist Party (Bolsheviks) on 'National Factors in Party and State Affairs.'[7]

The development of policy was not helped by divisions within the Sorbian leadership. An acute conflict developed between those Sorbian leaders in the Lusatian National Committee (*Łužiskoserbski narodny wuběrk*) based in Prague, who were pressing for political separation from Germany, and the *Domowina*, which by the summer of 1946 had moved to a position of qualified cooperation with the SED. The leader of the Domowina, Paul Nedo, who had resumed the position he had held before 1937, is the most prominent example of a Sorb leader torn between the competing pressures of ethnic and national politics. The fact that he had joined NSDAP organizations as a school teacher in the 1930s and then in 1945 became a member of the KPD clearly exposes him to a charge of opportunism. Yet from the perspective of minority interests he could reasonably claim that he was seeking to get the best possible outcome for the Sorbs in a situation where they had precious few options. The National Committee in Prague, by contrast, favoured the international route to finding solutions to the 'Sorbian question.' In September 1945 the two organizations set up jointly the Lusatian National Council (*Łužiskoserbska narodna rada*), and in this early period both were keen to gain support from 'Slav' countries. Until March 1946 the *Domowina*, in reaction to being denied the status of a political organization by the Soviet authorities, pursued a line independent of the KPD and was therefore prepared to support the efforts of the National Committee on the international stage. But by the autumn of 1946 it had joined forces with the SED and agreed to put up candidates on a joint list for local and state elections. This decision signalled the definitive failure of the *Domowina*'s campaign to establish an independent political role for itself inside Germany. It was also a recognition of the reality that the SED was going to be the dominant political force in the Soviet zone. The inevitable result of this 'realism' was to alienate those Sorbs linked to the Christian Democrats (CDU) and the Liberals (LDPD), who tended to look to the National Committee in Prague for support.

By October 1946, when the Slav Committee in Bautzen was re-established, the split between the *Domowina* and the National Committee had become obvious. Though National Committee members were excluded, they still travelled as a delegation to Belgrade on 4 December for the first post-war All-Slav Conference. They were followed on 13 December by members of the *Domowina* as the official delegation. The arrival of two Sorbian delegations made it clear to the other delegations that the Sorbian leadership was deeply split. Nevertheless, the Yugoslav government agreed to represent Sorb interests at the forthcoming German Peace Treaty discussions at the London and Moscow CFM.

Differences between the two organizations continued during the preparations for these talks and although the two sides did attempt to work together their standpoints remained very different. *Domowina* leaders were more constrained by the need to work with the SED, while the Prague leaders were relatively unaffected by these internal constraints and were able to concentrate on international lobbying. Then in February 1947, frustrated by the lack of agreement over the inclusion of minority protection in articles in the Saxon and Brandenburg constitutions, the *Domowina* changed its line again. The obstructive attitude towards other Sorbian cultural and political interests taken by all political parties, including the SED, as well as the Soviet administration led the *Domowina* to reduce co-operation with the authorities and turn again to the Allies. But the attempt to involve the Moscow CFM (March to April 1947) failed, despite the support of the Yugoslav delegation. The Soviet Union had no time for ideas of an independent Lusatia, mainly because this would result in a reduction of the territory of their zone. It therefore put pressure on its satellites not to support Sorbian claims and expressed its anger at Tito's support for the Sorbs. The Sorbian question was only raised once by the Yugoslavs at the preparatory CFM meeting in London in January 1947. At the Moscow CFM itself the Soviet Union blocked any discussion and the issue was not raised again at subsequent meetings.

Meanwhile, the National Committee submitted a separate memorandum with more radical demands. The helplessness of Nedo's position is a classic example of the difficulties faced by ethnic politicians seeking to influence international decisions, but caught between ethnic and national politics. The 'Truman Doctrine' of March 1947 promised to support any free nation seeking to defend itself, but it was not intended to cover ethnic minorities like the Sorbs. When Sorbian leaders attempted to lobby Western governments there was little response. Apparently, the West regarded the Sorbian case as an internal matter, to be left to the Soviet authorities.

3 Sorbs and the SED

After the Moscow conference, hostility between the *Domowina* and the National Committee grew. Nedo described the Committee as reactionary because it refused to co-operate with any German political forces and was demanding the expulsion of German expellees from the Sorbian area. The conflict was resolved by a combination of natural causes and outside political events: the two main Sorbian leaders in Prague, Pastor Jan Cyž and Jurij Cyž both died in the course of 1947 (of natural causes) and the Communist take-over in Prague in February 1948 led to the dissolution of the National Committee's office there. This meant that the organization, which had most vigorously represented the fears of Sorbian farmers about political developments in the Soviet zone, especially the moves towards collectivization and the anti-church measures, no longer existed. As a result, a large section of the Sorbian community became alienated from the political process altogether.

From late 1947 to March 1948 the *Domowina*'s policy of putting pressure on the SED and the Soviet administration began to bear fruit. In May 1947 it received permission from the Soviet authorities to set up a Sorbian printing firm and moves were also set in train to pass a Saxon Law on Sorbian rights. In October 1947 the *Domowina* was recognized as the sole representative of Sorbian interests and was able to influence the drafting of the law. However, not all of its demands were met. For example, at the end of November 1947 in the course of a meeting with the SED leadership in Berlin, including the joint chairmen of the SED, Otto Grotewohl and Wilhelm Pieck, its call for a separate state of Lusatia was rejected. The Sorbs were also denied recognition as a 'nation' (*Volk*) by the SED and were described instead as a 'part nation' (*Volksteil*) because they did not fulfil the requirement of economic independence according to the Stalinist definition of a nation contained in the theses of 1923. On the other hand, the meeting did give some support to Sorbian cultural interests. In March 1948 a law passed by the Saxon parliament granted the Sorbs a number of rights, such as the right to set up bilingual schools in areas designated as bilingual, and the right to use Sorbian in local administration.

In Lower Lusatia, where Germanization was much more advanced, the situation was very different. By 1945 Lower Sorbian was in the process of dying out as a living language, except in a few villages south of Cottbus. The SED, in particular Friedrich Ebert, their leader in Brandenburg, showed no interest in supporting Sorbian cultural interests. Here the activities of the National Committee, in particular their demands for the separation of Lusatia from Germany, caused damage. They helped make the German population very hostile to those Sorbs who supported the *Domowina*, which was not allowed to operate there until January 1949. It was only after pressure from the Soviet authorities and the SED in Berlin that local SED functionaries reluctantly introduced measures to support Sorbian culture in Lower Lusatia. But those many Sorbs who preferred to use the older German term 'Wends' (*Wenden*) were suspicious of the links between Upper Lusatia and Czechoslovakia and, more widely, of the international activities of Sorbian institutions. Their weaker sense of ethnic identity had already led to greater integration with the German population.

Furthermore, as Protestants the Lower Sorbs were (and still are) suspicious of the strong position of the Catholic Church in Upper Sorbian villages.

There were close relations between Sorbian leaders and institutions in Bautzen with Poland and Czechoslovakia but both countries had their own political and territorial preoccupations and this rapidly faded. By contrast, the Yugoslav military mission in Berlin continued to follow Sorbian activities with great interest. In August 1946 their representatives addressed the first post-war meeting of Sorbian students, the *Schadźowanka*. The head of the mission, General Avšič, then started a campaign to encourage Sorbian work brigades to come to Yugoslavia to work on projects like the building of the railway line between Brčko and Bamovići. The first brigade, led by Jan Nali, left Bautzen in October 1946 and took part in the World Youth Congress in Belgrade and the World Student Congress in Zagreb. It was awarded various medals and prizes for its contribution to the work project and further visits were planned for 1947. These took place in the summer of 1947, during which the Sorbian Youth groups also participated in political activities.

Sorbian brigades were then invited to the next project in 1948, along with the youth wing of the SED, the Free German Youth (*Freie Deutsche Jugend*/FDJ). The Sorbian youth organization, '*Serbska Młodźina*,' led by the Sorbian writer Jurij Brězan, was still separate from the FDJ and was not a member of the international communist youth movement, the World Federation of Democratic Youth (*Weltbund der Demokratischen Jugend*). A group of Sorbian young people, organized by the *Serbska młodźina*, left to work on the building of the Zagreb–Belgrade railway line in June 1948 and won the prize for the best foreign brigade. But the group was criticized by the Yugoslavs for concentrating too much on the Sorbian question and not displaying enough class consciousness.[8] The Yugoslavs also thought they were too preoccupied with ethnic identity and were not internationalist enough.

While the group was still in Yugoslavia the situation in Berlin changed dramatically. The tensions between the Soviet Union and the Western powers turned into a major crisis. Apart from the Soviet attempt to isolate West Berlin economically, the development that immediately impacted on the Sorbian brigade was the currency reform: the creation of a separate West German Mark, followed almost immediately by the introduction of an East German Mark (*Ostmark*), left it stranded without funds. As a result, the group had to be helped to get home by the Yugoslav authorities.

4 The Cominform Dispute and Surveillance

Soon afterwards the Cominform passed a resolution accusing Yugoslavia of harbouring an anti-Soviet attitude, of representing bourgeois nationalist positions and of betraying the international working-class movement. The resolution, which was the culmination of a series of arguments with the Soviet Union and was supported by most communist parties of the eastern bloc, was followed by a wave of anti-Tito propaganda throughout Eastern Europe, a blockade of Yugoslavia from the middle of 1949 and a large number of arrests for 'Titoist' activities. Another casualty of the sharpening tensions within the eastern bloc was the independent Sorbian youth organization, which in December 1948 was forced to merge with the FDJ. Up to the summer of 1949 Sorbian members of the FDJ still had bilingual membership cards and were allowed to wear a badge in the Sorbian national colours, blue-red-white, with the inscription '*Łužica*' (Lusatia). But these marks of separateness were now abolished and Sorbian youth identity was totally swallowed up by the FDJ as part of the overall incorporation of Sorbian organizations into SED institutions.

While the first Sorbian brigades were still in Yugoslavia, Poland and Czechoslovakia had retreated from their formal support for Sorbian demands for political autonomy, leaving their host government as the only 'eastern bloc' country to support them. Yugoslav support had admittedly been fairly consistent since the end of the war, but now Tito's main motive in presenting himself as a facilitator of Sorbian interests was really to use the Sorbian question in his growing disagreement with Moscow. In December 1947 the *Domowina* had praised Yugoslavia as a 'land of peace and progress' (*Land des Friedens und Fortschritts*).[9] But the Cominform split transformed the context and led to the condemnation of Tito as a traitor, pursuing a personality cult and militarism. Then followed the trials of Hungarian Minister of the Interior, László Rajk, and the Bulgarian Deputy Prime Minister, Traicho Kostov, as well as the arrest of members of the Cominform.

The recent Sorbian links with Yugoslavia were now viewed with suspicion. Members of the returning Sorbian brigade (which had claimed, rather implausibly, that it had only heard of the Cominform resolution in Prague after it had left Yugoslavia) found themselves under political pressure and in January 1950 were forced to give back their medals 'as a protest by Sorbian youth against the criminal policies of the Tito clique.'[10] Some of its members, like the leader Jan Nali, were accused of being agents of Yugoslavia and put on trial. In 1951 Jurij Rjenč, the Sorbian representative in Belgrade, was put on trial for treason and sentenced to 25 years' imprisonment.[11]

From the end of 1951 to 1953 the *Domowina* itself came under close surveillance by the SED, culminating in an investigation by the Central Party Control Commission (ZPKK), which was responsible for party discipline. Erich Mielke, the deputy head of the state security organization (*Stasi*), had ordered regional offices in Dresden and Cottbus to monitor closely the activities of Sorbian leaders and institutions.[12] During an interrogation on 3 August 1953 by the ZPKK, Kurt Krjeńc, a communist who had succeeded Nedo as head of the *Domowina* in December 1950, was questioned about his colleagues and his own actions. The purpose of the investigation seems to have been to find evidence of close links between certain members of the *Domowina* and Czechoslovakia, in particular with the group, which had been put on trial in Czechoslovakia in November 1952 on the charge of being Zionist, nationalist traitors. Krjeńc was himself strongly criticized for his links with former SED members who had been recently purged, and for his submission of a map to the Politburo, which had suggested the creation of a Lusatian district (*Bezirk*) after the forthcoming abolition of the eastern states (*Länder*) in 1952. He was also accused of favouring the idea of a Sorbian Communist Party with membership books in Sorbian; all these charges Krjeńc vehemently denied.[13] It has to be remembered that Krjeńc was a loyal SED member who had been put in charge of the *Domowina* in 1950 to keep an eye on Sorbian nationalist activities. It is therefore clear that at the very time when a series of measures were being put in place by the SED with the declared intention of putting

Sorbian language and culture on an equal basis with German in Lusatia, some in the inner circles of the party were treating all Sorbs, whether Communists or not, as potential enemies. They suspected 'Sorbian nationalists' of maintaining close links with 'reactionary' circles in Czechoslovakia and Poland following the failure of moves towards a separate Sorbian state. Even after the change in the leadership of the *Domowina* the secret police complained that the proletarian group on the executive committee under Krjeńc was being overshadowed by bourgeois, nationalist Sorbs. In particular, they resented the active role of Church leaders, both Protestant and Catholic, in the running of the *Domowina*.[14] Above all, the secret police complained of its inability to maintain strict control of Sorbian-language publications. Since the central press censorship office in Berlin was not in a position to exercise this control itself, it was forced to depend on the *Domowina*, which it did not wholly trust.[15]

The suspicion that Sorbian functionaries and institutions were engaged in anti-state activities deepened after the 1953 June uprising. After the interrogation of Krjeńc in August 1953 the ZPKK followed up its investigation of Sorbian institutions with further secret police raids on the offices of the *Domowina* and the Institute for Sorbian Ethnic Research. They found copies of the maps and memoranda that had been used between 1945 and 1947 by the Lusatian National Council and the *Domowina* to lobby the Allies in their autonomy campaign. The Control Commission was particularly suspicious of the memorandum which the Council had sent in January 1946 to the foundation meeting of the United Nations in London, because it contained a map of Lusatia which extended beyond the Oder–Neiße frontier agreed at Potsdam. In a letter written to Hermann Matern, the Politburo member responsible for Party discipline, the Commission made it clear that it was particularly suspicious of the Director of the Institute, Pawoł Nowotny. They knew he had had contacts with the Polish secret police during the war, and they had always suspected the leadership of the *Domowina* of putting Sorbian national interests before the building of socialism in the GDR.[16] But, as the regime now made clear, the point of its 'nationalities policy' was to give Sorbs more social equality, not national or ethnic rights.

Suspicion continued through the 1950s and in 1955–56 even led to an active operation by the Ministry for State Security (MfS) to investigate whether three leading Sorbs, Pawoł Nowotny, the writer Jurij Brězan, and the former head of the *Domowina*, Paul Nedo, had been involved in 'anti-state activities.' Despite being very critical of their behaviour, the investigation came to the conclusion that it had not been treasonable, and active surveillance was terminated in 1956.

In the more liberal atmosphere that followed Khrushchev's denunciation of Stalin's 'mistakes' at the Twentieth Party Conference of the Soviet Communist Party (February 1956) the *Domowina* attempted to enter into discussions with the Churches. They hoped to persuade them to soften their view of the 'communist' *Domowina* and to challenge the opinion of the Catholic Church, in particular its view that only the Churches could lead the Sorbian people. Leaders of the *Domowina* were also allowed to take up invitations to visit West Germany and to attend a congress of the Federal Union of European Nationalities (FUEN) in Austria. But the Hungarian revolution of October 1956 brought this 'liberal' period to an end. The latter part of the 1950s saw the final split between the *Domowina* and the Churches, the rejection by the government of any notion of a bilingual Lusatia and the intensification of the collectivization of agriculture, which affected Sorbian farmers particularly badly.

The repression of those Sorbs who refused to accept the constraints of SED nationalities policy tended to be harshest at times of wider ideological and political tension. Thus in the period from 1958 to 1960, when the SED was increasing the tempo of forced economic and political change, as well as hardening its attitude towards the nationalities policy, there was an increase in the number of prosecutions of individual Sorbs. An editor of the Sorbian newspaper *Nowa Doba*, Hinc Šołta, who had been under surveillance by the secret police since 1956, was regarded by the secret police as an enemy of socialism and suspected of using his position within the newspaper to produce a series of ambiguous reports. He was accused of having strong links with Polish and Hungarian reformers and dismissing the official nationalities policy as no more than an instrument to further the interests of the SED. After arrest and interrogation, he was sentenced on 20 October 1958 to fourteen months' imprisonment.

Although this persecution was perhaps more a result of Šołta's generally negative attitude towards political developments than his Sorbian identity, in the case of Pawoł Nali the ethnic element was clearly crucial. Nali had been regarded with suspicion because of his support for a separate Sorbian state in the 1940s and because he had studied in Yugoslavia from 1948 to 1950. In the late 1950s he attracted the attention of the secret police because he spoke out publicly against the formation of agricultural co-operatives in Lusatia. He regarded the destruction of small Sorbian family farms as evidence of further repression of Sorbian culture. He also attacked the creation of the energy complex 'Black Pump' (*Schwarze Pumpe*) (see below) because he regarded it as part of an SED campaign to promote Germanization. Last and not least, he was suspected of having links with the American secret service and RIAS, the American broadcasting station. He was arrested on 14 July 1960 and in April 1961 was sentenced to three-and-a-half years' imprisonment.

After the political turbulence, which followed the building of the Berlin Wall in 1961 a more stable period began, although the SED became worried in the mid-1960s about the effect of the 'Prague Spring' on the Sorbian intelligentsia. Between 1969 and 1972 the secret police carried out an active investigation of a number of leading Sorbian intellectuals, including Dr Jan Cyž, the former chief administrative officer (*Landrat*) of Bautzen, and Pawoł Nowotny, the director of the Institute for Sorbian Ethnic Research. The authorities were aware of their critical attitude towards the Warsaw Pact invasion of Czechoslovakia and of their close links with Czech intellectuals. But they were unable to establish that a group hostile to the state had been formed in the Institute for Sorbian Ethnic Research, and the action was suspended.

5 Minority and International Politics

Both superpower relations and tensions within the eastern bloc were a major influence on the formulation and implementation of the GDR's nationalities policy as well as on the careers of particular Sorbian leaders. It should be remembered that the international background of ethnic politics was one of unremitting tension, punctuated by dramatic crises and only occasional moments of relaxation. The German–German border was the front line of the global confrontation, with the BRD and the GDR being incorporated into their respective military blocs, NATO and the Warsaw Pact. Perhaps most importantly for the Sorbs, the course of the Cold War greatly affected the opportunities for Sorbian institutions to establish relations with parallel institutions outside the GDR. Whereas Sorbian institutions were used by the GDR to set up cultural links with Slav countries, especially with Poland and Czechoslovakia, the actual links between them and ethnic minorities in eastern bloc countries were restricted. One particular reason in the case of Slovakia, Hungary and Rumania was the very different position of their respective ethnic minorities. Unlike the Sorbs, the Hungarian minorities in Czechoslovakia and Rumania, for example, did have a 'kin-state,' which they could, at least in principle, look to for support. Similar situations existed in the relations between several other Eastern bloc countries and were a constant source of friction. The Sorbs were seen not so much as dangerous in themselves as for the destabilizing example they might set. As a result, open discussion and the exchange of views between ethnic minorities in different countries were restricted.

As for West Germany, contacts were complicated by the activities of German expellee groups there. The toleration of these groups by successive West German governments was regarded by the SED as evidence of West Germany's desire to revise the frontier changes agreed at Potsdam and of its failure to come to terms with its national socialist past. The GDR, in contrast, wished to link its ideological claim that Leninist nationalities policy provided positive support for the minority with its 'German claim' that it was dealing more effectively with the legacy of National Socialism than its West German competitor. In any case, the actual links with the West were highly restricted. It was not until 1954 that the GDR government allowed two delegations from the Danish minority in Schleswig-Holstein to visit Bautzen. An official report commented that 'both delegations studied with great amazement the democratic and cultural freedoms experienced by the Sorbian minority.'[17] In return, the *Domowina* was allowed to accept an invitation in 1955 to take a delegation to Flensburg to study the situation of the Danes.

However, links with the Federal Union of European nationalities (FUEN), founded in 1949 and based in Flensburg, were strongly discouraged and the *Domowina* was not allowed to become a member. The secretary of the Union, Professor Skadegard, wrote to the *Domowina* in 1954 expressing interest in the bilingual school system in Lusatia, but the *Domowina* was not allowed to invite a delegation from the FUEN because the GDR government considered it to be under Western influence and supported financially by the Americans. In the more liberal atmosphere of early 1956 the FUEN tried again but this time problems over the involvement of German expellee organizations, to which the SED objected, complicated the issue. The department in the Central Committee responsible for foreign affairs sent a memo to the department responsible for the Sorbs noting that the FUEN was 'an organisation which has close connections to the European movement (in particular to the Council of Europe) and was in general not kindly disposed towards the socialist states. It works closely together with West Germany and with the emigré organisations based in West Germany.'[18]

Although the *Domowina* was then allowed to invite Professor Skadegard to Bautzen, it was told that there was no question of it joining the FUEN until the latter changed its attitude towards the GDR.[19] When the FUEN then invited the *Domowina* to attend the next FUEN congress in neutral Austria (Carinthia) in the summer of 1956 the Foreign Policy Department conceded that it would not be a bad idea for Krjeńc to attend. However, they insisted that if the German groups from the 'Sudetenland' started agitating against Czechoslovakia, he had to leave immediately. Krjeńc then made a speech at the Congress criticizing the expellee groups and, according to his report, made little contact with most of the other groups attending. The only group that the *Domowina* delegation met formally was the left-wing Carinthian Slovene group linked to the Yugoslav government (the 'Democratic Front of Working People').[20] The events of October 1956 in Hungary put a stop to any further links with the FUEN and West Germany. Professor Skadegard did manage one more visit to Bautzen in June 1959, but further contacts with the FUEN were blocked.[21]

Visits to other NATO countries at the end of the 1950s were used primarily for undercover purposes. When a Welsh delegation consisting of education officials visited Bautzen in April 1958, the secret police report revealed satisfaction at the positive reaction of the visitors to the bilingual school system, but they were kept under very strict control.[22] In return, a Sorbian delegation, led by Wilhelm Koenen, the head of the National Front, and Krjeńc, was allowed to visit Wales in May 1959, but, if the secret police report is to be believed, the visit was primarily used to establish contact in London with left wing, pro-GDR Labour MPs like Ian Mikardo and Konni Zilliacus.[23]

Nevertheless, there were some interesting visits in the 1960s. One came in October 1966 when for the first time since 1948 a *Domowina* delegation was finally allowed to visit Yugoslavia. But overall in the mid- to late-1960s, external relations were negatively influenced by the growing unease of the GDR government at developments in Czechoslovakia. In February 1967 Klaus Sorgenicht, the official responsible for the *Domowina* in the Central Committee, wrote a memorandum to his counterpart in the Politburo, Hermann Axen, titled 'External relations of the *Domowina*,' which shows how susceptible the activities of the *Domowina* were to the regime's foreign policy concerns. It starts by saying that the *Domowina* should not be allowed to widen its contacts with foreign countries. Contacts with Poland could be continued, but only as long as they were under strict political control. Contacts with Czechoslovakia should be curtailed and the Domowina should only be allowed to have contact with the Museum in Prague, which exhibited material about the Sorbs. There were to be no further contacts with Yugoslavia or with Switzerland (which Krjeńc had also visited in 1966). The same applied to the FUEN.[24] These restrictions stayed in place into the 1970s, although the situation became more flexible after the GDR signed the Helsinki Final Act in 1975.

6 Culture and Economic Development

The restrictions on the *Domowina*'s external relations in both Western and Eastern Europe were in contrast with the growing cultural autonomy it was granted within the GDR. Between 1950 and 1958, in particular, the SED took the ethnic concerns of the Sorbs seriously, seeking to import Leninist nationalities policy and create the cultural institutions and bilingual schools that were central to it. But, at the same time it emphatically asserted the primacy of socialist reconstruction: the collectivization of agriculture, the nationalization of the economy and the domination by the SED of all institutions (except the churches). The main figure in Sorbian affairs during this period was the SED Politburo member, Fred Oelßner, who was responsible for policy towards the Sorbs until he was thrown out of the Politburo by Ulbricht in February 1958. Oelßner developed the policy of a bilingual Lusatia, while at the same time coming down hard on what he saw as Sorbian chauvinism, which was seen as undermining the political and economic policy of the SED. Under his supervision, new structures were introduced along the lines of 'democratic centralism' and in 1952 the *Domowina* recognized the leading role of the SED, along with other non-SED institutions. The role assigned to the *Domowina* was a dual one: the SED saw its role primarily as winning over the Sorbian population to the socialist reconstruction of the GDR, especially in the areas of industrialization and the collectivization of agriculture. But although Oelßner was responsible for the policy towards the Sorbs, his emphasis on Lusatia becoming bilingual also assigned to the *Domowina* the role of principal supporter of Sorbian cultural interests.

Parallel to this two-pronged policy was economic development, in the form of a massive expansion of lignite mining and the creation of large power stations, notably the 'Black Pump' (*Schwarze Pumpe*) near Hoyerswerda. Lignite was the only major energy resource in the GDR, and from 1955 the state sought to exploit its resources in central Lusatia, a predominantly Sorbian area, which had the highest grade of the fuel. Many Sorbs found work in the new plant, but the majority of the workforce was recruited from other parts of the GDR. This meant an influx of German workers whose children then went to bilingual schools. These workers, including SED functionaries, objected to their children being forced to learn Sorbian in school and started to write protest letters to the SED leadership. There were attempts at the plant to provide outlets for the Sorbian language, but these also met opposition from the German workforce and the SED leadership in the plant. No brigades (the main labour unit in GDR factories and cooperative farms) were formed from Sorbs, which had been a major demand of the *Domowina*. As a result, almost inevitably, German became the language of the workplace. Hoyerswerda, the nearest town, which up to the mid-1950s had a population of 7,700, (one thousand of whom were Sorbs), grew rapidly. By the 1980s, it had become an exclusively German town with a population of over 70,000.

The rapid expansion of opencast mining was followed in the 1960s by the building of several more power stations in central Lusatia. In these later projects, no attempt was made at all to support Sorbian language and culture or to avoid the destruction of Sorbian villages. Only in the 1970s and 1980s did some muted criticism of this policy become possible, expressed primarily in the literary works of writers, such as Jurij Koch (*Die Landvermesser*, 1977) and Kito Lorenc (*Flurbereinigung*, 1972). By the end of the 1980s, over 70 villages had been destroyed completely and the populations resettled in towns such as Cottbus and Weißwasser.[25]

The other side of assimilation was the collectivization of agriculture. Ever since it was first announced by the SED in 1952, the policy was strongly resisted by the Sorbs because the family farm was the only unit where Sorbian was predominantly spoken. The SED did not allow the formation of Sorbian cooperatives and where the Sorbs predominated in a particular agricultural cooperative (*Landwirtschaftliche Produktionsgenossenschaft*/LPG) they either appointed German managers, who banned the use of Sorbian in their presence, or they amalgamated the LPG with one that had a higher proportion of Germans. As a result, the Sorbs lost the only workplace area where Sorbian was still the main language. The collectivization process was intensified in 1958 when the SED proclaimed the goal of complete collectivization, although it did make an exception for Church-owned farms, one of which was in the Sorbian area.

In this period the alienation between ordinary Sorbs and the *Domowina* reached its lowest point. When the latter was forced to help persuade reluctant Sorbian farmers to accept collectivization, many turned to the Churches for support. As the *Domowina* was also prevented from criticizing the SED's industrialization policy, it ceased to exist at all as a viable organization and it lost its position as the main representative of Sorbian cultural interests. It had to accept its social and political role as the transmitter of SED policy to the Sorbs and was seen as having betrayed Sorbian interests. Although it did recover some members in the 1970s and 1980s as it attempted to resume its role as a defender of Sorbian cultural interests for as long as the GDR lasted, it was never able to escape from its image as the 'red *Domowina*.' Part of the *Domowina*'s attempt to rehabilitate itself in the late 1980s was to resume a dialogue with the Churches, which had effectively ended in the mid-1950s. Many Church members had left the *Domowina*. So had a number of priests with official functions in it, who openly preached against socialist measures like collectivization, especially in the Catholic areas to the north-west of Bautzen where language usage was strongest.

7 Conclusion

Between 1958 and 1971, the SED successfully asserted the primacy of Communist goals over the concerns of ethnic politics. This became clear as the original nationalities policy, which had supported Sorbian cultural interests (within the limits of Leninist doctrine), was progressively undermined by state repression. After 1958, the slogan, 'Lusatia will become bilingual' was declared to be false, Oelßner was removed by Ulbricht from the Politburo, and Sorbian interests within the political system were now represented by a functionary of the Ministry of the Interior. The demotion of any consideration of Sorbian interests could hardly have been made clearer. The *Domowina* was told to concentrate on its political duty to build socialism and on its social roles. Attempts to support Sorbian linguistic and cultural interests were denounced as 'nationalism.'

In the 1960s several measures in educational policy undermined the position of Sorbian in schools. In 1962 the use of Sorbian in 'A schools,' i.e., those in which Sorbian was the mother tongue of most pupils and where most subjects had been taught in Sorbian, was restricted. Henceforth, all scientific or technical subjects were to be taught in German, and Sorbian was to be restricted to the humanities. In 1964 it was decreed that in the 'B schools', where Sorbian was the second language of most pupils (including a number of German pupils) Sorbian would be optional for both Sorbian and German pupils. In any case, the implementation of the policy had varied widely between different areas: in some, such as the district of Bautzen, Sorbian had been compulsory for both Sorbian and German pupils, while in others there had been little pressure on German pupils. The result of the 1962 measure was a massive drop in the number of pupils taking Sorbian, from 12,800 in 1962 to 3,200 in 1964. By the end of the 1960s the number had fallen to under 3,000, although it did rise again to over 6,000 by the 1980s. While the number of pupils being taught in Sorbian in the 'A schools' remained fairly constant, the main drop was in the 'B schools.'[26] By the time Erich Honecker became head of the SED in 1971, policy towards the Sorbs had degenerated into the hollow repetition of political slogans.

In conclusion, the history of the Sorbian minority during the Cold War clearly points up the tension between international, national and local ethnic politics, which in this case led to the almost complete subjugation of local interests to national and international interests. Despite the introduction of a network of cultural institutions, the end result was accelerated assimilation. Admittedly in the late 1940s and early 1950s, the SED, under pressure from the Soviet administration, did at first embark on a policy of support for Sorbian culture and language through the creation of a network of Sorbian cultural institutions. Support also came from neighbouring Slav countries until 1948, especially from Czechoslovakia and Yugoslavia. But with the Sovietization of the GDR in the 1950s and the impact of the Cold War, any emphasis on Sorbian cultural interests came to be denounced as 'nationalism' or even 'Titoism.' Ethnic politics became subordinated to national and international politics, and Sorbian leaders had little choice but to accept this, or face the consequences.

In the sense that they consistently emphasized the primacy of socialist politics, the SED was therefore responsible for overseeing the continuing Germanization of the Sorbian population. Between 1945 and 1990 the Sorbian-speaking population was roughly halved. This decline was not reflected in the official figure of 100,000, which the SED used right up to 1989. (It declined to publish Ernst Tschernik's demographic survey of 1955–56 because it already showed a decline to about 80,000).[27] But this assimilation can also be seen as the almost inevitable result of the 'modernization' of the economy and social structures, in particular the move from a predominantly rural to an urban or semi-urban population. Though the broad phenomenon of assimilation was in that sense separate from the nature of the regime, the way it was imposed by the state and the brutality with which its consequences were 'managed', cannot be separated from the national and international politics of the GDR.

The strength of the GDR state and the ideological commitment of its leaders meant that in the end Sorbian leaders were powerless to counteract these trends. The *Domowina* succumbed to the pressures of national policy and the policy requirements of the SED. Although the Sorbs benefited from Soviet and SED support in institutional terms, their ethnic aspirations were always subordinated to the political and economic aims of the SED. The Cold War constrained the external activities of the *Domowina*, especially those which affected, or could be seen as affecting the German–German conflict. The only structures that were able to provide the minority with significant support were the Churches, in particular the Catholic Church. At grass-roots level, where a Sorbian identity was equated with the Catholic religion, Sorbian identity could still be cultivated. By the same token, the political structures, which marginalized religion, were rejected by an overwhelming majority of Sorbs.

Notes

[1] Ernst Tschernik, *Die Entwicklung der sorbischen Bevölkerung von 1832 bis 1945. Eine demographische Untersuchung*, Berlin: Akademie Verlag, 1954, 43.

[2] Klaus J. Schiller, and Manfred Thiemann, *Geschichte der Sorben. Von 1945 bis zur Gegenwart* (vol. 4), Bautzen: Domowina Verlag, 1979.

[3] Philipp Ther, 'Expellee policy in the Soviet zone and the GDR', in David Rock and Stefan Wolff (eds), *Coming Home to Germany? The Integration of Ethnic Germans from Central and Eastern Europe in the Federal Republic*, New York and Oxford: Berghahn, 2002, 58.

[4] Unless otherwise stated, all the statistics in this paragraph are taken from *Ibid*, 60. For population statistics relating to the Sorbs before 1945, see Tschernik, *Entwicklung*.

[5] 'Sorbenstatistik 1946', assembled by the *Domowina*, Archive of the Sorbian Institute/Sorbisches Kulturarchiv (SKA), Bautzen, MS/XVII/3.

[6] Paul Nedo, Memorandum on the German–Sorbian relationship, SKA/ZM XXIII/26 E, Mikławš Krječmar Papers.

[7] Joseph Stalin, *Works* (vol. 5), Moscow: Foreign Languages Publishing House, 1953, 184–96.

[8] For details of the work brigade visits to Yugoslavia, see Piotr Pałys 'Die Arbeitsbrigaden der sorbischen Jugend', *Lětopis* 54, (2), (2007), 56–64.

[9] Meeting of board and committee of *Domowina*, 25 February 1947, SKA/D/ II/1.6.A, 61–2.

[10] Resolution by members of the Sorbian Work Brigades 1946–1948, 7 January 1950, SKA D II 7.7, C (II), 232.

[11] *Domowina* Report to Fred Oelssner, 1 November 1951, Bundesarchiv, Stiftung Archiv der Parteien und Massenorganisationen der DDR (SAPMO), BA/ SAPMO, DY30 IV 2/13/377.

[12] Mielke, Memorandum, 'Nationalist and Titoist subversion amongst the Sorbs,' (Nationalistische und titoistische Umtriebe unter den Sorben), Directive no. 4/51, 13 December 1951, Commissioner for State Security Files (Bundesbeauftragte für Stasi-Unterlagen/BStU), MfS (Ministerium für Staatssicherheit)/GVS (Geheime Verschlußsache), 42/51.

[13] See 'On the investigation in the case of Kurt Krenz' ('Zur Untersuchung in der Angelegenheit Genosse Kurt Krenz'), 3 August 1953, BA/SAPMO, DY30 IV 2/4/268, 1–33.

[14] Secret police. Bautzen District office, Analysis of the Sorbian question-*Domowina*, (Analyse über die Angelegenheit der Sorben – Domowina), 20 November 1956, BStU, MfS/BV Dresden, KD Bautzen 2007, 12.

[15] *Ibid*, 13.

[16] See letters from Arthur Ullrich (Head of the local Control Commission office, Bautzen) to Hermann Matern (responsible for internal security in the Politburo), 21 September 1953, BA/SAPMO, DY30 IV 2/13/377 and 22 September 1953 in BA/ SAPMO, DY30 IV 2/13/379.

[17] Discussion between the *Domowina* and the *Sektor Gesamtfragen*, Berlin, 3 February 1955, BA/ SAPMO, IV 2/13/380.

[18] Foreign Policy Department (Abteilung Außenpolitik) to Klaus Sorgenicht (Head of the State and Law Department (Abteilung Staat und Recht)), 2 March 1956, BA/SAPMO, IV 2/13/381.

[19] *Ibid.*

[20] Report, 29 August 1956, BA/SAPMO, IV 2/13/380.

[21] See Ludwig Elle,'Domowina und FUEV in den 1950er Jahren', *Europa Ethnica*, 50 (3), (1993), 132–35.

[22] Report, 11 April 1958, BA/SAPMO, IV 2/13/383.

[23] Report on visit to Wales, 3 August 1959, BA/SAPMO, IV/2/13/384.

[24] Sorgenicht to Axen, 6 February 1967 (Auslandsbeziehungen der Domowina), in BA/SAPMO, IV A2/13/131, 203–4.

[25] Figures from Frank Förster, *Verschwundene Dörfer*, Bautzen: Domowina Verlag, 1995, 18–19.

[26] See the tables in Peter Barker *Slavs in Germany. The Sorbian Minority and the German State since 1945*, Lewiston-Queenston-Lampeter: Edwin Mellen Press, 2000, 87, 108.

[27] Ernst Tschernik, *Ausführlicher Abschlussbericht: Die gegenwärtigen demographischen, volkskundlichen und sprachlichen Verhältnisse in der zweisprachigen sorbischen Lausitz*, (1954), SKA XXXII, 22D.

Bibliography

Barker, Peter (2000), *Slavs in Germany. The Sorbian Minority and the German State since 1945*. Lewiston-Queenston-Lampeter: Edwin Mellen Press.

Elle, Ludwig (1993), 'Domowina und FUEV in den 1950er Jahren', *Europa Ethnica* 50, (3), 132–5.

Förster, Frank (1995), *Verschwundene Dörfer*. Bautzen: Domowina-Verlag.

Pałys, Piotr (2007), 'Die Arbeitsbrigaden der sorbischen Jugend', *Lětopis*, 54, (2), 56–64.

Pech, Edmund (1999), *Die Sorbenpolitik der DDR 1949–1970. Anspruch und Wirklichkeit*. Schriften des Sorbischen Instituts 21, Bautzen: Domowina-Verlag.

Schiller, Klaus J. and Thiemann, Manfred (1979), *Geschichte der Sorben. Von 1945 bis zur Gegenwart* (vol. 4). Bautzen: Domowina Verlag.

Schurmann, Peter (1998), *Die sorbische Bewegung 1945–1948 zwischen Selbstbehauptung und Anerkennung* (Schriften des Sorbischen Instituts 32). Bautzen: Domowina-Verlag.

Stalin, Joseph (1953), *Works* (vol. 5). Moscow: Foreign Languages Publishing House.

Ther, Philipp (2002), 'Expellee policy in the Soviet zone and the GDR', in David Rock and Stefan Wolff (eds), *Coming Home to Germany? The Integration of Ethnic Germans from Central and Eastern Europe in the Federal Republic*. New York and Oxford: Berghahn.

Tschernik, Ernst (1954), *Die Entwicklung der sorbischen Bevölkerung von 1832 bis 1945. Eine demographische Untersuchung*. Berlin: Akademie Verlag.

Conclusion

What light do these six cases shed on the role played by ethnic politics and ethnic nationalism in the Cold War? How should they be viewed in relation to the very different concerns which seemed to dominate those four decades: the geopolitical and military struggle between the two nuclear superpowers: the ideological and philosophical arguments between communism and parliamentary democracy, and the economic beauty contest between centralized planning and the market? Given the particularities of ethnic politics and the protean nature of ethnicity itself, there can be no single or straightforward answer, but these five concluding points, however tentative, may be made:

First, ethnic identities were more than just tools in the hands of Cold warriors; ethnic or ethno-national resentments and fears were not merely resources that could be turned on or off at will by policymakers. Even in communist regimes there was something like a semi-public sphere, where attitudes or mentalities were expressed, which might be at odds with the party line but which its leadership could not simply ignore. As Martin Mevius shows for Hungary, the party's rank-and-file, far from being just a transmission belt, was deeply enough embedded in society to share many popular prejudices. Similarly, the contempt for the Sorb minority culture displayed by some SED officials differed little from the broader attitudes in the rest of East German society, much of which was still marked by Nazi teachings of racial superiority. And Yugoslavia's claims towards Italy (and to a lesser extent southern Austria) at least in part came from a fear of being outflanked by the Slovene communists' liberal and conservative enemies who nurtured similar projects of territorial expansion.

Second, at the East–West border (Hungary/Austria, Trieste, Bulgaria/Turkey) the Cold War added an international and ideological twist to the dynamic of what Rogers Brubaker has labelled the 'nationalising triad.'[1] In its 'classic' form that developed as a minority on the 'wrong' side of the state, border became the object of deep suspicion by the power-holders and subject to increasingly coercive assimilationist ('nationalising') pressures. The repression often alienated and radicalized a section of the minority's elites, leading them to turn to the neighbouring 'kin-state' and often to irredentism; in a self-fulfilling prophecy the radicalization of the minority was then seen as confirmation of its treasonable intent and thus provided a further impetus for the state's repression. Where state border became the Cold War borders the stigma of national disloyalty was deepened by the perception that the minority was part of an overwhelmingly anti-national force, of international communism or capitalism. In the case of the communist rulers of Bulgaria, ethnic insecurity and collective memories reinforced an underlying sense of their own weak legitimacy.

Third, in contrast to these fears and the collective memory of the manipulation of ethnic identities by Nazi foreign policy, ethnic issues and grievances were used surprisingly rarely to subvert states. Yugoslavia may be the (partial) exception, which proves the rule, in the sense that its support for communist Macedonian guerillas was part of Tito's ambitious project for a Yugoslav-led Balkan federation. But its claims against Austria and Italy were more limited, reflecting as they did, the euphoria following victory over the Germans and their collaborators in the 'National Liberation War' rather than ambitions to transform the neighboring country. Where instrumentalization was perhaps most evident was in propaganda: in a positive sense, Communist governments sought to demonstrate the superior virtues of Leninist nationality policies, including the fostering of minority cultures; this resulted in the concession of what were – on paper – quite far-reaching autonomy regimes (for example, by Romania's Hungarians and Bulgaria's Turks). The negative side was the attacks on Western mistreatment of minorities, in which the attention was less on the ethnic minorities of Western Europe than the segregation of the U.S. South, as a symptom of Western racialism and imperialism. Molotov's use of the issue to counter American criticism of Soviet repression in Eastern Europe was described by the U.S. Secretary of State James Byrnes as 'a checkmate of the first order.'[2]

Fourth, for ethnic minorities and the 'ethnic entrepreneurs' seeking to mobilize them, the Cold War could be as much an opportunity as a constraint. South Tyrol experienced this early on when in 1946 it was treated by the West not, as might have been expected, as a German minority which had supported National Socialism but as an Austrian minority. The fear of the spread of communism (whether to Italy or Austria), made an agreement over its cultural identity a concern for Western governments. More broadly, the language of the Cold War could be adapted to the needs of ethnic politics. Part of the Italian-language press in Trieste transported its racialized understanding of Italian superiority and Italy's civilizing mission as a defense against 'Slavo-communist barbarism.' Some newspapers saw Slavs as innately lazy and passive and hence predisposed to accept communism. In a similar way, Hans Steinacher spoke in Austria of a 'Slavic–bolshevik' bloc threatening Southern Austria and the whole Western world. Steinacher, who had served the Third Reich from the Sudetenland to the Arctic, now saw an affinity between the attempts by Slovene leaders in Carinthia to resist Germanization and the way the Bolshevik minority exercised power in the Soviet Union: in both cases a minority was seeking to impose itself on a majority.[3] Consciously or not, this reduction of democracy to the will of the majority echoed President Truman doctrine's warning of the dangers of 'armed minorities' imposing themselves on freedom-loving societies.

Fifth, there were clear limits to the readiness of states on both sides of the Iron Curtain to exploit ethnic fissures. Even before the suppression of the Hungarian revolution, the West made surprisingly little attempt to exploit the plentiful ethnic grievances in communist societies. However, as Günther Pallaver shows for South Tyrol, Soviet foreign policy was not prepared to back ethnic nationalists where they were close to the extreme right. The wider Soviet concern was to get the post-war territorial *status quo* established at the end of the war, signed and sealed by the West. Whether this amounted to a kind of tacit agreement to keep ethnic genie in its bottle is debatable, but it does at least suggest that the Cold War was rather less than a total confrontation in which, as Tony Shaw puts it, 'virtually everything, from sport to ballet to comic books and space travel' was used as 'a weapon both to shape opinion at home and to subvert societies abroad.'[4]And it may even allow us to see at part of the Cold War more positively, not just as the statist straightjacket imposed on expressions of ethnic authenticity but as a stabilizing system which helped make Europe's post-war decades appear, in Ian Kershaw's words, 'unbelievably benign.'[5]

Notes

[1] Rogers Brubaker, *Nationalism reframed: Nationhood and the national question in the New Europe*. Cambridge: Cambridge University Press 1966.

[2] Walter L Hixson, *Parting the Curtain: Propaganda, Culture and the Cold War, 1945–1965*, New York: St Martin's Press, 1997, 129–33.

[3] See Robert Knight, 'Ethnicity and Identity in the Cold War: The Carinthian Border Dispute, 1945–1949', *International History Review*, 22 (2), (2000), 300.

[4] Tony Shaw, 'The Politics of Cold War Culture', *Journal of Cold War Studies*, 3 (3),(2001), 59–76.

[5] Ian Kershaw, 'War and Political Violence in Twentieth-Century Europe', in *Contemporary European History*, 14 (1), (2005), 123.

Bibliography

Brubaker, Rogers (1966), *Nationalism reframed: Nationhood and the national question in the New Europe*. Cambridge: Cambridge University Press.

Hixson, Walter L (1997), *Parting the Curtain: Propaganda, Culture and the Cold War, 1945–1965*. New York: St Martin's Press, 1997.

Knight, Robert (2000), 'Ethnicity and Identity in the Cold War: The Carinthian Border Dispute, 1945–1949', *International History Review*, 22 (2), 253–303.

Shaw, Tony (2001), 'The Politics of Cold War Culture', *Journal of Cold War Studies*, 3 (3), 59–76.

Kershaw, Ian (2005), 'War and Political Violence in Twentieth-Century Europe', in *Contemporary European History*, 14 (1), 107–23.

Index

CPSIA information can be obtained at www.ICGtesting.com
Printed in the USA
LVOW071125090912

297998LV00009B/39/P